First published May 2012 by Bunny Picnic

Editor: Elizabeth Smyth

Cover Design: Anna Willcox

Layout: Gez Smith

Gez Smith has asserted his right under the Copyright, Designs and Patents Act of 1988 to be identified as the author of this work.

ISBN: 978-0-9572754-0-9

Cover photograph of kitten by Tim Ebb's
(http://www.flickr.com/photos/ebbsphotography/)
and used under the CC BY 2.0 creative commons license
(http://creativecommons.org/licenses/by/2.0/deed.en_GB).

To find out why there's a picture of a kitten on the front cover, read chapter 7, section 7.

To contact the author, email gez@gezsmith.com

This book is dedicated to all the lovely people at those interesting little local councils across the UK, without whose puzzled expressions this book would not have been as comprehensive.

Chapters

Chapter 1. Introduction

When I was first formally working in the field of digital engagement back in 2003, my manager at the time, Stephen Hilton of Bristol City Council, said something that's stuck with me;

> *"There are people who understand public engagement, and there are people who understand the Internet, but what we need are people who understand them both."*

It's an idea that's been at the back of my mind over the last nine years, and it's a problem that this book is designed to solve.

I've been working in the field of digital engagement, connecting people with organisations and vice versa, for around ten years now, and have come across a huge range of different situations, from small companies starting to look at engaging people online whilst doubting that anyone will want to take part, to huge nationwide government engagement projects across the UK and USA.

Primarily, what I used to deal in was software, giving people tools to run online engagement and consultation exercises. After all, I needed to make money, and software was what the market wanted. Indeed, the National Project on Local e-Democracy[1], which gave me my first paid work in digital engagement, had been all about piloting software, and organisations like the Consultation Institute[2] here in the UK were, until recently, still running events called 'Technologies for Participation'.

Ever since the days of the National Project though, I'd had a nagging doubt in my head, that this whole digital engagement thing wasn't about software at all. Instead, I became increasingly convinced that it was about how you used the software, and that you would do better if you used the wrong software well than if you used the right software badly.

---

[1] I wish I could point you to a website containing all the information and reports the project generated, but the UK Government took it down a few years ago, and, to be honest, you're not missing much anyway. Times have long since moved on since those days now.

[2] http://www.consultationinstitute.org

Everything I've seen since has confirmed this view, so this book is an attempt to help people understand how to engage and consult people online, in part by looking at the principles behind it, rather than individual pieces of software in and of themselves.

Whilst the world seems to have mostly moved on from the view that software alone will fix problems like social exclusion and inequality of opportunity, there still seems to be an obsession with what software does rather than how to make best use of it. If you find yourself a social media trainer, chances are they will teach you the different functionalities contained within the social media platforms that happen to be currently in fashion. The sort of thing you could just as easily teach yourself by reading the help file of any given platform, to be honest.

On the other hand, for over 10 years now there has been a bunch of people huddling together at the other extreme in the world of academia. My mind boggles at the amount of funding academics seem to have gained access to in order to enable them to write theoretical studies on digital engagement and e-democracy. The problem with this though is that, well, they're all too theoretical and academic. I've tried to read some of these research papers from time to time, and despite having spent five years reading such things at university, I still struggle to make head or tail of them in places.

If I find them tricky to read, I can't see how they are of any use at all for the people actually out there doing digital engagement work on a daily basis. Indeed, this doesn't really seem to concern the world of academia in this area, as you occasionally see it announcing 'innovative new research ideas' that have already been piloted and abandoned as not workable by real life practitioners long ago. It's a shame in a way, as I suspect there may be some useful information hidden within the world of academia when it comes to digital engagement, but I doubt anyone's ever going to be able to find it, let alone make much use of it.

The private sector hasn't been much help in this area to date either. Driven to maximise profit in a market containing customers who don't know much, it has often spread confusion and disinformation left right and centre, in order to create an illusion of choice between competing software systems.

I remember once being phoned up by a prospective client and asked if our software had a specific piece of functionality that a competitor was promoting. It took me a while to understand what they were after, as what they had been told was 'functionality' was actually just an inherent property of the Internet, without which none of it would work. Still, this organisation had been told that it was unique to a particular supplier, and was completely unaware of the many skeins of wool being pulled over their eyes. I dread to think how often myths and half-truths have been propagated amongst keen yet innocent organisations in the name of 'maximising shareholder value'.

So, this book attempts to steer a middle course between the two extremes of academia and software. In places I will talk about the specific functionalities of certain software, but I will do so in order to draw out the wider principles behind an activity or concept. In this way, I hope I can leave you with enough practical knowledge to get going by yourself, but with a sufficient grounding in key principles to future proof yourself against the rapidly moving world of software capabilities and fashions.

I do hope you find it useful. The content has been very much shaped by the last ten years or so I have spent working with real clients on real digital engagement projects that have engaged real people, and to each and every one of them I am grateful for what they have both taught me and helped me learn. This is not an end though, rather much more of a beginning, so if you think I've got something wrong somewhere, or you know something important I have missed out altogether, do get in touch and let me know, so I can amend future editions accordingly.

In the meantime, good luck with whatever digital engagement work you do, and remember, the best way to learn how something works is to try it, so never be afraid to do just that.

Gez Smith
Bristol, April 2012

Chapter 2. The role of the Internet in a decision making process

Gosh, what a pompous chapter title, right?

Well, as I've said before, I think academia has contributed very little to the field of practical digital engagement over the last ten years or so, so I'm not about to write some great big academic essay on the nature of decision making, democracy and the role the Internet can or may play within it.

That said, there is something important to be considered here, for two reasons. First of all, getting people to participate in decision-making through the Internet is a very new phenomenon in the scheme of things, and one that is bound to have some impact upon the status quo. Second, and more prosaically, I think it's worth considering the Internet's role within a decision making process in order to allay some of the fears that those involved in the status quo may have.

I'll use the example of democracy as just one specific type of decision-making process in order to illustrate these points. However, the model holds for pretty much any sort of decision-making process you yourself might be involved in.

First then, what form of democracy do we have? How do our current decision making processes work?

Well, as an overarching view, we in the UK at least, and those in many other countries world wide, live in a representative democracy. One where nearly the entire populace is entitled to elect a number of representatives to make decisions on their behalf about how things are run. This is different to a direct democracy, where the people themselves make decisions en masse about issues, through processes such as referenda.

Immediately then, we see a potential tension, in that the Internet lends itself much more strongly to the idea of direct democracy than it does to representative democracy. Given you can now allow millions of people to state their preferences on issues quickly and (relatively) cheaply, won't encouraging decision making online undermine representative democracy, and move us towards the sort of populism that everyone seems to fear?

Well, I'd say that it doesn't do either of those things, but it does depend where you place digital engagement within the structure of the democracy. Obviously you can't place it at the decision making level itself, as that would be to replace representative democracy with its direct counterpart. But you can place it firmly at the level below decision making, feeding its outputs upwards into it, because this is what lots of other forms of representation are already doing anyway.

When a Member of Parliament or other elected official votes on a decision, how do they do it? Do they retire to the nearest library and study the political writings of Plato, Hobbes and Mill, in order to draw on the wisdom of the ages? No[3]. Most of the time they're told how to vote by party whips, and vote along party lines.

How are those party lines decided upon? Well, this could possibly be seen to be done by representative democracy, in that it is often government ministers, themselves elected[4], that guide and shape legislation through their departments. However, this legislation is also shaped to a great degree by other interests.

Whilst government in the UK is now better at ensuring no one special interest group dominates the making of policy[5], it is undeniable that there is a framework of lobby groups, think tanks and vested interests that all aim to shape government policy to meet their own ends, often at the expense of others. So how free is an elected member to be representative of the people that elect them, given they have to vote for what their party proposes, and that proposal itself risks having been shaped by the views of the few?

---

[3] Some may say sadly not.
[4] Although technically in the UK they don't have to be, as ministers can be drawn from those appointed to the House of Lords too.
[5] I have heard rumour that not so many years ago, entire policies were occasionally formed over lunches with 'key stakeholders' and plenty of wine. There's probably no truth in it, but it's an interesting rumour to have arisen.

When they do have a free vote on an issue, unconstrained by party affiliation, they often take soundings amongst their constituents, or are again lobbied by special interests to take a position.

There is, though, another quality of online consultation and engagement that stops it being seen as some direct democracy alternative to a representative democracy, or indeed any other form of government. That is that views gathered online might be representative of only one section of a society, or may not come from that society at all.

This situation arises because the Internet is largely an anonymous place. Sure, you can ask people to provide details about themselves, but who's to say that they will be truthful in providing this information? Similarly, who's to say that opinions coming in through the Internet will be representative of the populace as a whole? As a rule, people only have their say about issues that matter strongly to them; you very rarely see consultation responses that state 'neither support or oppose' all the way through for each question.

The Internet is just not as reliably representative as other research methodologies, and I doubt that it ever will be[6]. That's not to say it isn't representative at all, or shouldn't be used for representative work, but just to acknowledge a central fact about its character in comparison with, say, knocking on people's doors and asking them for their opinions.

So then, I propose that digital engagement be seen as another one of the interest groups that feeds into the decision-making processes of those elected to make such decisions. Indeed, if you see it this way, it takes on a new importance, one of balancing the weight and influence of the smaller vested interests of the few, with the weight of public opinion, collected in a process open to all.

---

[6] Indeed, I hope it never will be, for if you remove all shreds of anonymity from activity online, any gain in representativeness will be massively outweighed by the loss of privacy and risks to civil liberties that result.

The role of digital engagement in a representative democracy

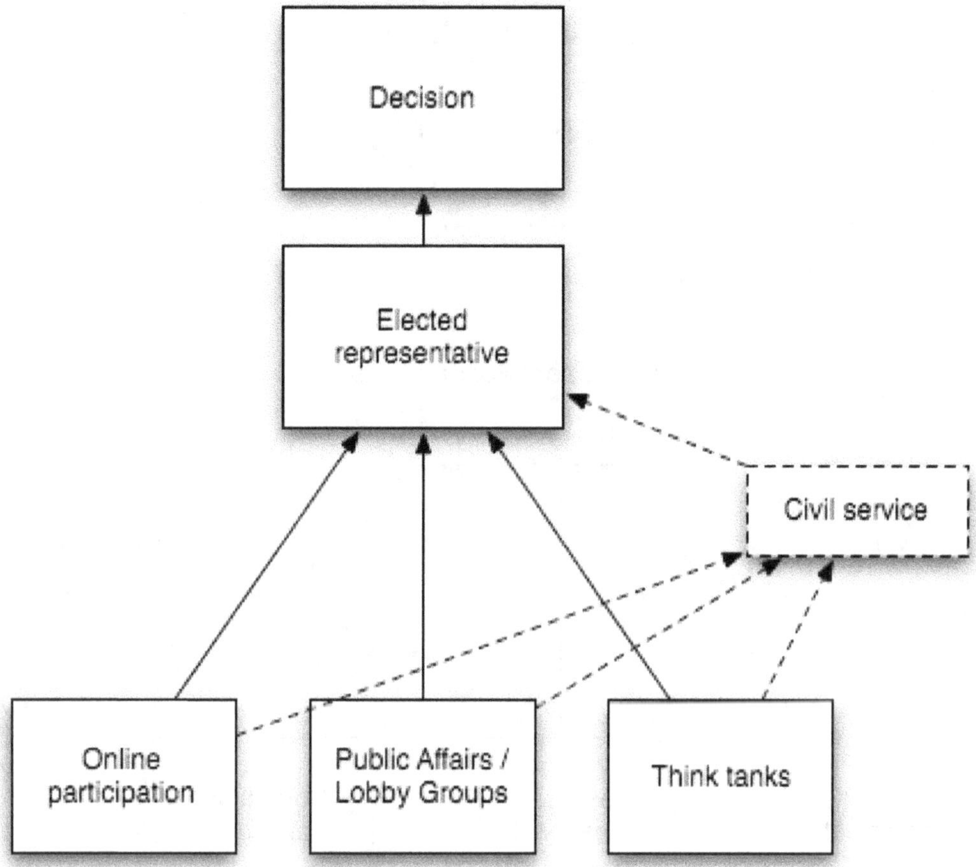

Alternatively, you could draw exactly the same diagram to represent the role of digital engagement in a commercial business.

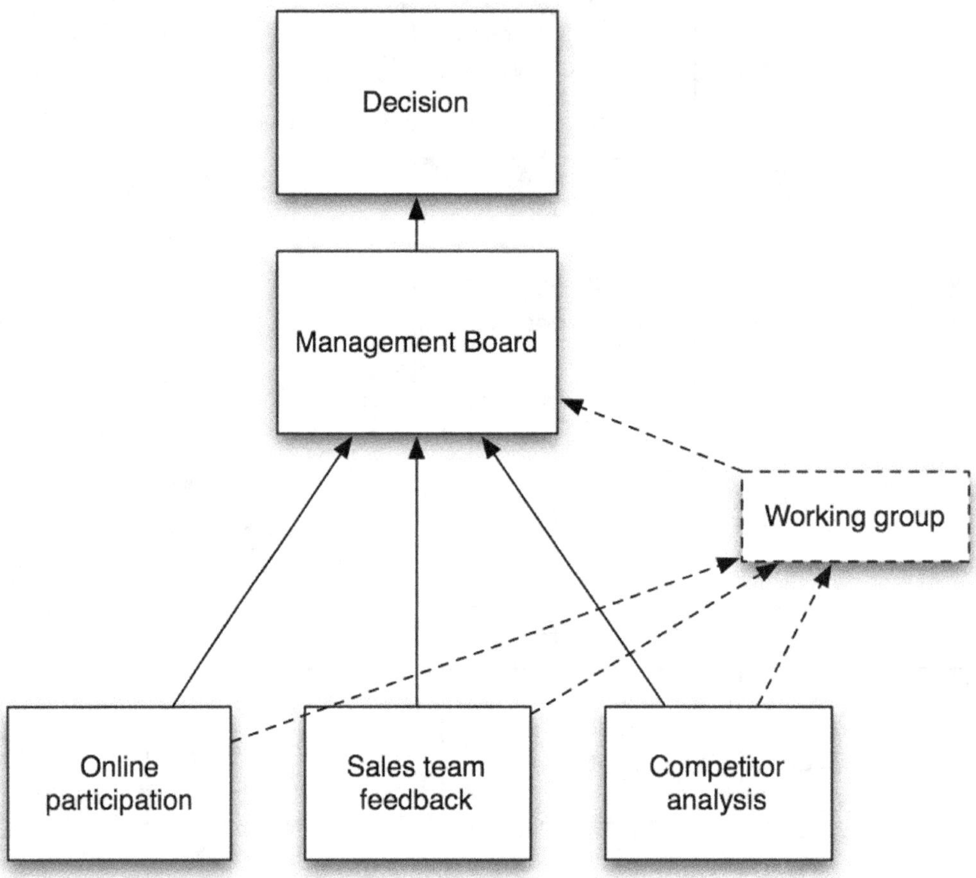

Now we know where digital engagement sits within a decision-making process, be it in a democracy or in a private business, we can start to develop ideas of when using digital engagement is the right thing to do, and how it should be used. We'll come back to this topic throughout the book, but there are three key ideas that flow from this conception of digital engagement which are worth covering now.

First of all, to a greater or lesser degree, it is generally part of making a decision to do something, and should be used as such. So, if you're running a digital engagement exercise, it should be about something, whether it's a small specific decision, a broad strategic issue or just an ongoing customer feedback exercise. The conclusions it arrives at have to go somewhere, and, if those to whom it goes wish to keep on getting elected or otherwise keep their jobs, something has to be done as the result of it.

Second, it's not limited in the form it can take. Just as there are myriad different influences that can go into making any decision, there are myriad different forms of digital engagement. It can be on any topic, involve any audience, be for any purpose and be as structured or unstructured as you like.

Third, it involves real people. It's often easy to forget this when online, but every word you see on the Internet has been written by a real person[7] with the same motives, emotions and reactions as anyone you may meet face to face. Indeed, as we will see in the next chapter, bearing this fact in mind at all times can help you make the right decision when faced with a query over what to do online.

For all this talk of democracy however, let us not be blind to the similarities between the public and private sectors in the field of digital engagement. Increasingly, companies these days are run along the lines of a democracy, with shareholders and corporate social responsibility programs, not to mention the democracy that is a free market. Indeed, you could say the only difference is that in one the voters vote at the ballot box, whilst in the other they vote at the checkout. The Internet has provided new possibilities for customers to share experiences with each other, and this has been known to cause very severe damage to company reputations and profits over time.

In some ways, the private sector is more at risk from digital engagement than the public sector, as at least the latter has long-term experience of the challenges democracy, public engagement and accountability can present. So, if you're lucky enough to find yourself reading this in the private sector, don't be put off by this book's occasional references to democracy and other such governmental notions. Change a few words around, and the model will fit you just as well.

---

[7] Apart from chat bots like Cleverbot I suppose - http://cleverbot.com/

So then, I hope we can conclude from this that digital engagement is actually an important part of a representative democracy, and indeed any other sector where people's opinions can make a difference, rather than being a threat to it. Given the fact that digital engagement will always contain inherent risks of being unrepresentative or swayed by minority interests, it should likely always form just one part of a decision-making process, rather than becoming a replacement to it.

However, it now seems fair to say that not involving yourself in it is to ignore a vital component of any interaction you may want to have with customers, voters or any other people with relevant opinions on your work.

Chapter 3. "It's like a participation party"

There's only one sentence you need to remember in this book. Not only remember it, but also bear it in mind when reading every chapter, and consider how this sentence relates to each point being made;

'Running a digital engagement project is like hosting a party'

There you are then, all pretty straight forward isn't it.

Seriously, if you bear this sentence in mind, any situation you encounter online usually is. Let's unpick this idea into its individual components, in order to get a better idea of how an entire field of work can be summed up in one sentence. As will become apparent, I'm using the term 'party' here in a pretty loose sense, to cover everything from a small dinner party to a massive illegal rave in a warehouse. Both of these types of party have their own analogous versions online.

First of all, if you're throwing a party, you need to set a date for it. It's often helpful to set and announce this date a month or two in advance of the party to make sure everyone can come. Now of course, the nature of digital engagement is often slightly different to a party with regards to time, as a party tends to happen for just a few hours, whilst digital engagement projects are open to visitors for longer than that. That said, there's no reason why a digital engagement project needn't be a one off and relatively short lived. Perhaps you want to hold an online discussion around an offline event such as a public meeting, in which case the digital engagement will last as long as the event itself.

There is also another factor to consider when looking at the date for your project, and that is ensuring it's not held on a date when a large number of those you intend to invite cannot make it. If you run an online consultation during July and August, you will almost always get a lower response rate than if you hold it from September onwards, due to everyone going on holiday. You see this same effect very clearly if you look at how sparse your local nightclub listings become during the summer months, as promoters just don't bother putting on big nights whilst everyone is away on holiday or festivals.

So, you've got the date set, next you want to choose the venue. Perhaps you want to invite people round to your house, giving you more control over the set and setting in which your party takes place. Alternatively, maybe the party will be too big for your house, or you think you'll get a better turnout if you hold it somewhere else.

All of these situations have direct comparisons in digital engagement, where your house could be considered to be your organisation's website, and alternative venues could be the websites of other organisations, perhaps Facebook or a dedicated digital engagement software supplier.

You can make an analogy with cost here too. For it's generally not worth building an extension to your house to throw a large party when you could just hire in a temporary marquee. The same is true of digital engagement, where trying to build a new part of your own website to run the process will generally be far more expensive than making use of software someone else has already built. Especially if you can hire, buy or borrow that software for a short time.

You've got the date, you've chosen the venue, but what's the party about? What sort of party will it be? Well, just as with digital engagement, the range of party types you can hold is practically limitless. Perhaps you want a small dinner party for a few selected people, or alternatively you might want to throw the mother of all raves, open to anyone and everyone. You've not just to decide the scale of the party either, you need to decide on a theme for it. With real parties, themes can be set through elements such as the sort of music you want to play, asking people to dress up, or even whether or not food and or alcohol will be provided.

This idea of theme setting is one of the most important elements of a digital engagement 'party', as very often the theme will be the main reason why the party is being held in the first place. It would perhaps be nice if more organisations held online gatherings with no set purpose, just to see what new ideas and connections come out of them, but in times of limited budget, digital engagement projects usually have to have a clear purpose. This purpose may be to gather people's views on a specific subject, or to get to know a specific audience better, but it is nearly always there. Just as with the offline world, unless you are an accomplished host of some experience, it may be best to stick to a theme or set purpose from the start.

Of course, very closely linked to the idea of a theme is who to invite to your party. After all, you can invite who you like, but unless those you invite like the look of your party, then they're reasonably likely to send their apologies. I know I wouldn't have wanted to invite my mother to the sort of parties I threw at university, and nor was she likely to have come along even if I did. It sometimes pays not to be too prescriptive here however, as a housemate's mother once turned up to one of our parties and drank us all under the table.

So it is with digital engagement, in that you're more likely to have people turn up if you invite them to take part, and you never know just who might surprise you with their presence. This seems to be one of the most frequently overlooked elements of digital engagement projects at the moment. Despite the fact that it would never work in the real world, organisations often seem to think that if they put some digital engagement software online, then participants will just turn up out of nowhere. Of course, sometimes this does happen, but it happens a lot less often than you might think.

This last point hints at a slightly different quality to a digital engagement party than one in the offline world. In the offline world, most parties have invitations that are sent directly or spread via word of mouth, whilst with digital engagement, you have tools such as search engines indexing your website and allowing people to find out about your party by themselves. You can of course stop this happening, by setting your site not to be indexed by search engines, but unless you have good reason, it's generally best not to do so.

If you do want to restrict who can take part though, you can do this just as easily with digital engagement as you can at a real party. For where a real party generally has a lockable front door preventing the uninvited from gaining access, any website can easily be set to have its access restricted to those possessing the approved username and password. Alternatively, you could control access by requiring people to register their details with the site before they can take part, although I tend to recommend against this approach for a whole host of different reasons. The fact remains though, that you have just as much control over who attends your digital engagement party as you do over a party you may hold in real life. We'll come back to this idea shortly.

Once the party is all set up and all of your guests have been invited, the next step is to make sure people feel welcome when they arrive. There are lots of different ways to do this, depending on what sort of party you want to hold. Perhaps you want to be there at the door, greeting people as they arrive. Alternatively, you could just make sure the venue is as pleasant and welcoming as you can make it, with clear signs for the bar and toilets.

Points such as these are almost directly comparable with any digital engagement process you care to mention. If you're running a process involving ongoing discussion between individuals, there is very often something to be said for being an active host for the gathering, directly messaging new registrants to welcome them to the website and seeing if they have any questions or concerns you can deal with. Alternatively, you can focus on the first impressions people gain when visiting your site. The content or subject of a digital engagement project has to be pretty compelling in order to have people stick with it when the website it sits on looks ugly or is difficult to use.

Whilst first impressions are important, very often the difference between a successful party and a failure is the quality of the hosting throughout the evening. As a host, it's your job to keep people happy, keep the place tidy and perhaps introduce people to one another in order to spark interesting conversations for all concerned. Now of course this role is sometimes much reduced in large public gatherings, as much out of necessity as anything, given the impossibility of playing an active hosting role towards thousands of people, but it is still a role that is worth considering. Might you want to make changes to your website or process once people start arriving and problems become apparent?

As touched on above, there is of course a less pleasant hosting task that has to be undertaken from time to time, that of removing troublemakers. Unless there really is no way for those you have invited to interact with one another, such as with a simple online survey, you're almost guaranteed to have to step in to deal with trouble by or between participants at some point. Sadly, this need often seems greater in the online world than in the offline, as the anonymity provided by a screen and keyboard seems to bring out the worst in people.

How you deal with these problems is up to you, but I've often found that thinking of your project as a party can again help here. After all, it is your party, you're providing the facilities, inviting the guests and presumably covering the cost, so if you want to throw someone out, then you're more than entitled to do so.

Having put all of this work in, the time will almost always arrive when you have to close everything down again. Now unless you want to run an ongoing project, open to all for all time, then remembering to close things down at the end is often a task as important as it is overlooked. There's nothing worse than turning up to a party only to find that's it's pretty much over already. On the Internet, this can be doubly important, as with no physical crowds of people to observe by their presence or absence, it can sometimes be hard to tell whether the project is still running. People feel foolish when they attempt to take part in the process that has ended, and will consequently become less likely to take part in your processes in the future should this happen.

That's not to say you wouldn't want to throw another digital engagement party at some point in the future though, and you can very much use one party to help another you may wish to hold. If someone's been especially good to have in one party, be sure to invite them to your next one. Collect people's names and email addresses in each party you hold, so you can invite them back again. Perhaps ask people to invite their friends next time too. The more you do this sort of work, the easier you will find it to run larger and more successful parties in the future.

So then, I hope I haven't stretched any analogies too far in my attempt to demonstrate to you that running a successful digital engagement project is just like running a successful party in the real world. Behind all of these analogies though is one essential truth, that is all too easy to forget when working on the Internet.

This is the fact that the Internet is used by real people. Just because a virtual network is being used, rather than a solid tangible face-to-face event, doesn't mean the people involved are any less 'people-y'. They still behave in a very similar way online and offline.

I haven't seen this point articulated like this anywhere before really, and I suspect that's not because it's too obvious, but because people's focus, in the UK for the last 8 years at least, has been on the technology rather than the people using it.

The media helps maintain this impression too, making us believe for example that 'hackers' are mysterious faceless villains using super advanced computing methods, when very often they're just bored teenagers guessing peoples' passwords from their bedroom. Similarly, the media tends to portray a social network like Twitter as interesting because it's 'Social Media', rather than because it contains interesting thoughts written by of lots of interesting people.

The only difference between people on the Internet and people in the real world is the fact that the former communicate with each other remotely rather than face to face. They're still real people at the end of the day, and if you think of them like this, then I've found that you'll not go far wrong.

Chapter 4. Basic Internet principles

Before we start to look at the different forms digital engagement can take, it is worth giving ourselves a good grounding in some basic principles of the Internet.

Of course, this is a huge area, encompassing web design, web usability and a whole host of other specialisms that many people make a living in, even when the specialism is rather niche indeed. However, I've often felt that the basics of making good use of the Internet are actually pretty simple when you boil them down, and the reason many people can make a living from them is that there are those out there who don't yet realise this. So let's have a look at them now.

4.1 Content is king

As I said in the introduction to this book, digital engagement is not about software, and you will often do better by using the wrong software well than the right software badly. Nine times out of 10 though, what makes the difference between a successful digital engagement project and a failed one is the content it contains.

On the web, content can take many forms. Of course, plain text makes up a large proportion of web content, so it makes sense to know a little about how to write for a web audience. However, content can also include images, videos, sound files and pretty much anything else you can imagine. Often it is through using the right piece of content in the right way that you will find success.

Why is content so important though? Well, ultimately, it's the content that your audience is going to interact with. If we think of a website like a human body, then the website software is the skeleton, the design and colour scheme you apply to it is like the skin[8], whilst the content it contains is like the organs, muscles and, in some cases, fat. A website with no content is like a body of just skin and bone, not much use for anything, and very often pretty dead.

---

[8] Indeed, the term used in the trade for applying a design to a website is 'skinning'.

Time and again, I have seen poor content be the downfall of digital engagement websites. Now, no-one intentionally puts poor content on their site, but it often ends up there because people don't realise how damaging it can be, or because people assume that what is interesting within their organisation will be interesting to those outside it. Especially if you're looking to get people actively engaging and interacting with your content, you need to make sure that what you're providing is actually interesting and relevant to them.

Which would you be more likely to take part in, a consultation about an organisation's five year strategic vision, or a consultation about bulldozing your house?

Now, this may seem like an extreme, but consider these two titles. Which one would you choose to click on first if you saw them both on a web page?

"BBC Trust Strategy Review - May 2010"

"Consultation - Save BBC 6 Music!"

If you chose the latter, you're amongst tens of thousands of others in the UK and across the globe who made exactly the same choice, even though they're both titles for exactly the same consultation.

In May 2010 I was working as a consultant to the BBC Trust, helping them from time to time with the online consultation website I'd designed for them. One day, after about 6 months of them using the system, the servers on which the consultation part of their website was running suddenly went offline. We looked into it, and found there had been a massive spike in the number of people going to the site, far more than it had ever been thought it would need to be able to handle. So, the server did what servers sometimes do to protect themselves, and went offline[9].

Immediately we set about getting it back online with more capacity, and at the same time, one of the people I was working with noticed that the

---

[9] See Chapter 10 of this book for more on this problem from a security perspective.

hashtag[10] '#savebbc6music' was trending on Twitter, that is, being used by lots of people all at the same time. Tweets with that hashtag all contained links to our consultation, along with messages telling people to click on the link and fill in the consultation.

I phoned the client to let them know about the server and the trending hashtag, and they were really surprised. The consultation was simply a strategy review, and they weren't expecting any more or less interest in it than any of the other consultations they'd run using the system up until now.

As it turned out, the consultation ended up breaking the UK record for number of responses received; nearly 48,000 valid completed responses in three months[11].

The reason for the surprise was in how the consultation was presented and the content it contained. From the client's point of view, it was a review of the strategy of the BBC, which happened to contain some proposals on closing BBC 6 Music. From the public's point of view, it was practically just a vote on whether or not to close a station with a passionate fanbase.

It was the fans that spotted this interesting content, not the client or I, and thanks to the Internet, it was the fans who told each other about it in a more interesting way than the BBC Trust normally would have done, making the consultation, in participation terms at least, a big success.

So then, how do you make your content interesting?

First of all, it's important to remember that everybody is different, and so everybody will find different things interesting. Think about the sites you visit regularly. Would they be of interest to everyone you know, or would some people probably find them boring and prefer to go somewhere else online?

---

[10] See the section on Twitter in Chapter 7 for more.
[11] http://www.bbc.co.uk/bbctrust/our_work/strategy/supporting_evidence.shtml

So, before we can decide whether or not content is interesting, we have to decide who it should be interesting *for*.

4.2 Choosing and knowing your target audiences

First, let's clear something up. The Internet is not just for young people. Neither are young people the only people who use the Internet. Time and again I've seen well meaning people state that they want to start exploring digital engagement 'as it's a great way of getting more young people involved'. It's really not you know, and if you think like this you're going to end up sorely disappointed sooner or later.

Of course, young people do use the Internet, and more of them use it than older people. But if you look at the latest figures in the UK, some interesting patterns emerge.

First of all, it only takes a brief look at Internet usage by age to discern that it's not just young people who are there to be engaged with online. After all, 83.5% of people in the UK have now used the Internet, and it's not as if 83.5% of people in the UK are in a category that could be described as 'young'.

The figures below give a clearer picture of what percentage of each age group has now used the Internet[12].

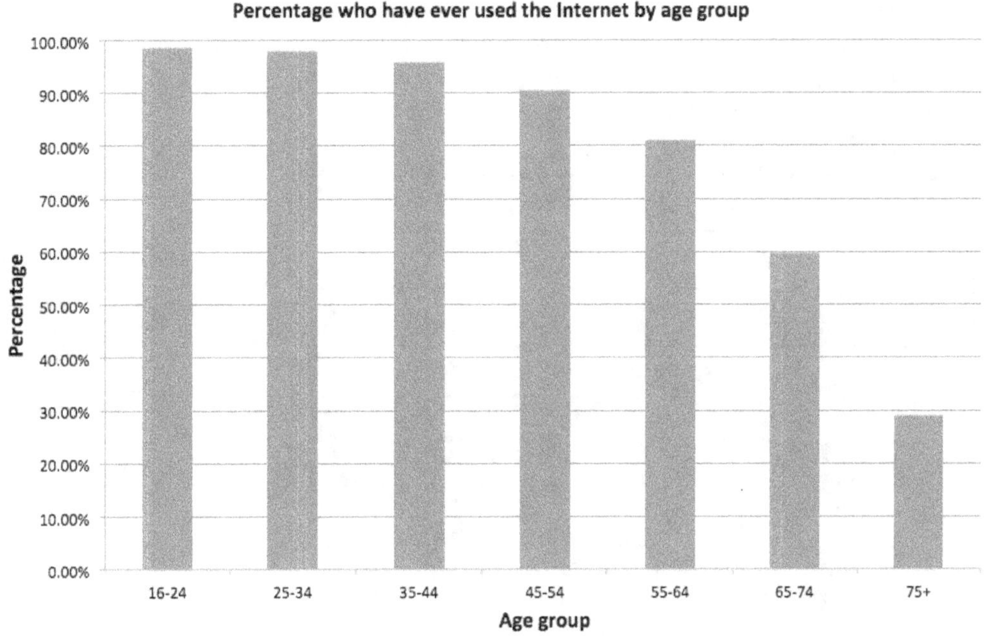

From the above, you can first of all see that it is true that young people do use the Internet, 98.7% of those aged 16 to 24 stating that they have done so in the past. But there isn't a lot of difference in the amount of people who have used it when you move up the age groups. Even when you get to the 45 to 54 age group, you see 90.5% of people have used it, less than a 10% difference with the age category for 16 to 24 year old 'young people'. There is a bigger drop off once you get to those aged 65 to 74, but even then, 59.8% of that group having used the Internet still represents a majority of them who have.

Even more interestingly, if you're looking to carry out some online engagement from a policy or political viewpoint, then saying the Internet will engage young people is missing the point somewhat [13.]

---

[12] Data for Q4 of 2011, taken from http://www.ons.gov.uk/ons/publications/re-reference-tables.html?edition=tcm%3A77-226794

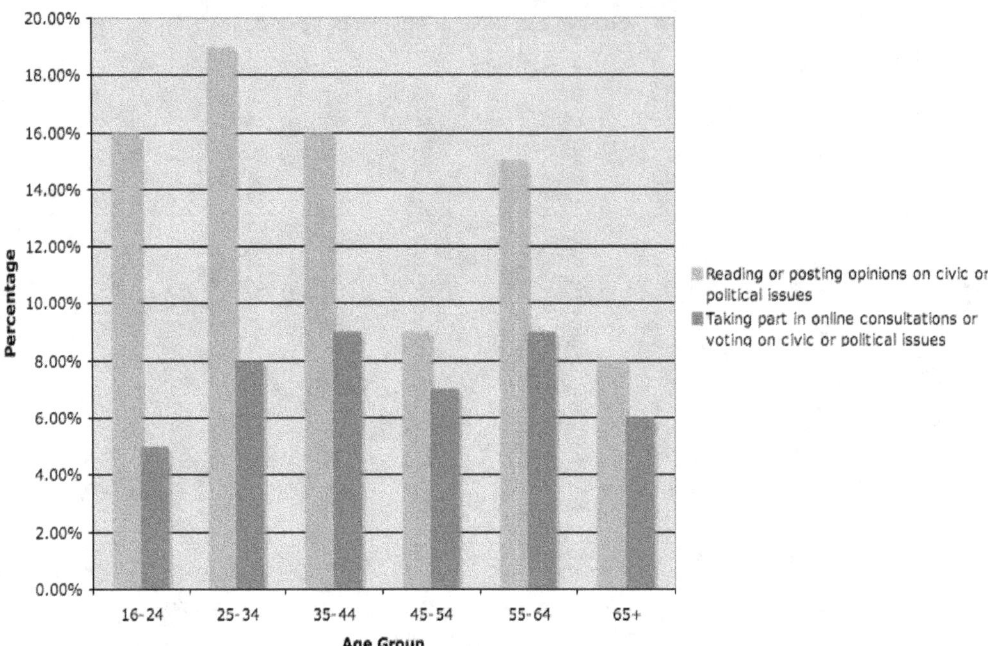

If you look at the above chart, you can see that the percentage of people using the Internet to take part in online consultations or post opinions on civic issues is admittedly small, rising no higher than 19% in any category. However, when it comes to reading or posting opinions on civic or political issues, it is those aged 25 to 34 who are the most likely to do this (19%), followed closely by those aged 16 to 24 and 35 to 44, both on 16%. So, you can say that those aged 35 to 44 are just as likely as 'young people' to get involved in political or civic discussions online. Those aged 55 to 64 aren't far off this group of young people either with 15%.

When it comes to more structured processes such as consultations or voting, it is in fact those aged 35 to 44 and 55 to 64 that are most likely to

---

[13] Data for 2011 taken from http://www.ons.gov.uk/ons/publications/re-reference-tables.html?edition=tcm%3A77-226727 . 2012 data not yet available at time of publishing.

take part in them online, both with 9%. This is followed by those aged 25 to 34 (8%), then those aged 45 to 54 (7%). In fact, 'young people', those aged 16 to 24, are the least likely of any category to take part in online consultations or voting processes, with only 5% of them reporting that they do so.

Now, there is of course a big caveat here. It may be that these figures are being caused by the fact that the standard of online engagement and consultation in the UK is currently pretty low, so it is not likely to be engaging to young people in and of itself, compared with an older age category who have more of a vested interest in taking part in such online processes, for example for work or due to a stronger sense of civic responsibility which comes with age. If the standard of digital engagement projects in the UK were to rise, it is possible these figures would level out to match more closely the overall Internet usage figures by age that we looked at in the first chart.

Intuitively however, I doubt this. I suspect that the degree to which young people are interested in taking part in engagement processes online is entirely dependent on the content of those processes, rather than the fact that they are online or any other similar factor. If my feeling on this is true, then it would be final confirmation that the Internet is not just about engaging young people, and possibly never will be. It is not the technology that matters to young people, or any other age group for that matter, it is the degree to which the content of any given process is relevant and engaging to them. Putting the process online merely makes it easier for some to access, rather than acting as an engaging factor in and of itself.

It is not just age categories that confound people's common expectations of the Internet. In a 2008 study carried out by Leonard Cheshire Disability, a UK based charity campaigning to provide more opportunity for disabled people, it was found that 90% of disabled people in the UK had access to the Internet, a higher percentage in 2008 than the UK average three years later in 2011.

I have it on good authority from a friend of mine, badly physically disabled in a car crash many years ago, that using the Internet can be a crucial means of communication for disabled people. As my friend sees it, when he has to meet someone face to face, they see and treat him as a disabled person, but when he talks to people online, his disability is completely hidden, and he is treated just like anybody else. As such, he much prefers to communicate online than face to face, and tells me that the same is true for many other disabled people that he has met.

I hope these two examples have shown you how important it is not to second guess or make assumptions about who you can engage through the Internet, and that almost no matter who you want to engage, you'll probably find them somewhere online.

Given this, it is important to remember that, as a rule, you want your content to be interesting to as many people as possible. After all, you're not looking to exclude people from looking at your website are you? If you are looking to exclude certain groups or individuals from looking at your content, then you're probably better off not putting it online in the first place, or at least protecting it with a password.

Of course, you could be one of those awful people who like to make information available whilst simultaneously making it as inaccessible as possible, in order to get away with something people might object to. However, if you are doing this, then you'd better be aware of the Streisand Effect[14], as it will get you one day.

But of course, there are likely to be some types of people you're more interested in making sure visit your site than others. If you're publishing proposals aimed at a specific audience, then you want your content to be as appealing and interesting to them as possible. So first of all, know your audience. There are lots of different ways of doing this of course, and the field of 'consumer insight' in market research is far larger than the scope of this book, but here are some initial ideas of how to get this important first step ticked off.

---

14 "The Streisand effect is a primarily online phenomenon in which an attempt to hide or remove a piece of information has the unintended consequence of publicizing the information more widely. It is named after American entertainer Barbra Streisand, whose attempt in 2003 to suppress photographs of her residence inadvertently generated further publicity." from http://en.wikipedia.org/wiki/Streisand_effect retrieved on 08/08/11.

- Write down who your intended audiences are.

- Share this list along with some information on your project amongst your friends or work colleagues, and ask them if they can think of any more groups or types of people who might be interested in knowing about your project.

- Get in touch with some people in those intended audiences, and ask them if they'd mind taking a look at your content and saying what they do and don't find interesting about it.

- Write up their feedback and use it to inform what information you present and how you present it.

Now, that all sounds rather simple and obvious, but it's amazing how many times you don't see it happen. When people are working on a project, they get all caught up in its details and their day to day work, and forget about the people they're wanting to target. This is especially easy to do on the Internet, as the people there aren't 'real'. You may never see or hear from them, and you often don't know who they are. They are real people though, and as we saw with the concept of the 'participation party' above, you can treat them in largely the same way as would work in the offline world.

Once you've used the information you gained above to put some content for your website together, run it past those same people from your target audiences again and see what they think of it.

- Are there parts they don't understand?

- Are there parts they're really interested in that you've not made very visible?

- Do they think the content looks interesting overall?

- Would they tell their friends about it?

Use questions like these to refine the content for your site and the messages it contains in as many rounds (or 'iterations') as you can, or as many as you feel to be useful, before your site ever goes live. Work you put in at this stage will generally save you work further down the line. A site with content so good that it effectively markets itself can save you a fortune in the long term. Or indeed make you a fortune, depending what line of work you're in.

4.3 Basic principles of writing for the web

Having said that the people who look at your site will be similar to your audience in real life for the purposes of testing your content, there are some important differences between online and offline communication methods. I won't list them all here; I doubt all of them have been discovered yet anyway, but some of the easiest and important to remember are;

- Keep all your text short - People read text 25% more slowly on a screen than they do on a printed page[15]. So people will get bored of reading your text 25% sooner on a web page than on a printed page. When people get bored, they move on and look at something else instead.

- Nvr try 2 wrte in txt spk tho. U wil alwys lk stpd.

- Images are good, but only when they look good, and are relevant to the content they are next to.

- A stretched, pixelated or slightly random image will make things worse than if there had been no image at all.

---

[15] http://en.wikipedia.org/wiki/Screen_reading

- I always tend to think images of real people are generally best avoided too, as they're too easy to get wrong in all sorts of ways. Just look at this screen shot taken from a page on Wikipedia for a doubtless unintended example[16].

- Be very careful with time-limited content or content that makes reference to time, as if you don't update or remove it, it can make the site look out of date and so less interesting.

- If you're particularly interested in the differences between online and offline communication methods, then read work by Jacob Neilsen[17]

- Actually, even if you're not that interested, Neilsen presents information so interestingly that you should still go and read some of his work. Whichever bits you find interesting of course.

It is also at this point worth picking out two rules of online communication which come from the important world of accessibility, the practice of making websites usable by all, even those with impairment, which will be covered in more detail later in this chapter.

---

[16] Scopophobia is the fear of people staring at you, and this screen shot was taken from the page about it on Wikipedia (http://en.wikipedia.org/wiki/Scopophobia), at a time when a 'personal appeal from founder Jimmy Wales' was running across the top of each page of the site, featuring his picture. Image taken from Wikipedia and released under the CC-BY-SA license - http://creativecommons.org/licenses/by-sa/3.0/

17 http://www.useit.com/jakob/

- Make all links descriptive. For example, 'click here to see the author's website' is much better than 'click here if you want to see the author's website.'

- Make sure all images have descriptive Alt text. If this sounds like Greek to you, don't worry, it's explained below in more detail.

Images are good

Images are one of the great benefits of communicating online, and it always really confuses me when I see huge pages of plain text but no images on a website, because online communication has one major benefit over offline. Namely that the cost of publishing images is a whole lot less online that it is offline.

Think about it for a minute. If you put an image into a written communication and print it, you risk using a lot more expensive ink than if you just printed plain text, especially if you're printing a colour image. On the Internet though, there's no printing involved, so the additional cost of displaying an image is these days negligible. What costs there are for using images online, such as data storage and bandwidth, are nearly always outweighed by the benefits created by using images.

I say 'these days', because it hasn't always been the case. Up until relatively recently, if website visitor was on a very slow Internet connection, then it could take a long time for the image to load on a page when they viewed it, costing them time and losing the site viewers. If the user was paying for their Internet access in a 'dial up' manner through their telephone line, then the additional time was translated into a very real additional monetary cost on their phone bill as well.

Nowadays, with a majority (68%) of UK Internet users accessing the web through a broadband connection[18], images download quickly, and users are generally charged a fixed cost rather than for each minute of time

---

[18] Figure taken from 'UK broadband speed report 2011' published by Ofcom and available at http://maps.ofcom.org.uk/broadband/

they spend online, meaning using images presents little problem to the majority of users.

The only exception to this is mobile phones, where images can be costly and time-consuming for the end user to download. Although this too is decreasingly the case, just as with home Internet connections, it's an issue worth bearing in mind, given around 30% of UK Internet users use a mobile phone to access the web[19]. We will look at this in more detail later in the book.

So, you've little excuse for publishing pages and pages of plain text online any more[20]. But what images should you put in and when?

4.4 How and when to use images

This is one of those sections of this book that could easily be its own library, let alone its own section, as the use of images online is something lots of people are paid lots of money to work out. However, after a few years of working with them, I began to realise that they were all using more or less the same principles, and that anyone can get a reasonable grasp of how to do it by following these simple rules.

- **Your logo does not need to be big**

  Seriously, unless the main message you want to communicate through a site is your company logo itself, the logo should just be there to identify who owns/runs the site if people care to know. It certainly shouldn't distract visitors from the actual content you're trying to communicate

---

[19] from http://www.statistics.gov.uk/pdfdir/iahi0810.pdf
[20] I should of course note that early e-democracy pioneer, the late great Chris Lightfoot, thought otherwise - http://ex-parrot.com/~chris/html.html

- **Images you use must be relevant to their context**

  This may seem obvious, but it's forgotten more often than you'd think. If a picture paints a thousand words, make sure the picture you use is painting the words that surround it, and vice versa.

- **Images should be as big as they need to be and no bigger**

  If you need to be able to see the contents of the image clearly, then it normally needs to be at least 600x800 pixels in size. However, if it's just for illustration purposes or to break up the layout of the text, then it could be much smaller.

- **Images must look as good as you can make them**

  Think about how you feel when you see a brochure with a photo in it that's been taken by an amateur. A shoddy looking image on a website can be worse than no image at all.

- **You must have permission to use the image online and on your site**

  See below

- **Don't make your logo too big**

  Really, please don't.

How to add an image to a page

There are two primary ways of adding an image to a page on the Internet, using HTML code, or using a piece of software called an editor.

When you use code to display an image, you're writing the code that the computer uses to display the image on that page. Don't worry though, it's dead easy. Basically, you need to write the following into the page when you're editing it;

<img>THE URL OF THE IMAGE ONLINE</img>

So, for example, to display a picture of the author in a web page, you would type;

<img>http://www.worthyfm.com/wp-content/uploads/2010/12/Gez-Smith-150x150.jpg</img>

and see this as a result

It can be easier than that though, as many websites now provide what is called a 'Visual Editor' in the site's administration panel, that lets you upload and manipulate images just as you might in a word processing document or similar.

You often see these visual editors in the row of buttons that run along the top of the box in which you're typing text. If you do, it typically appears as a button with an image on, in this case an image of a tree.

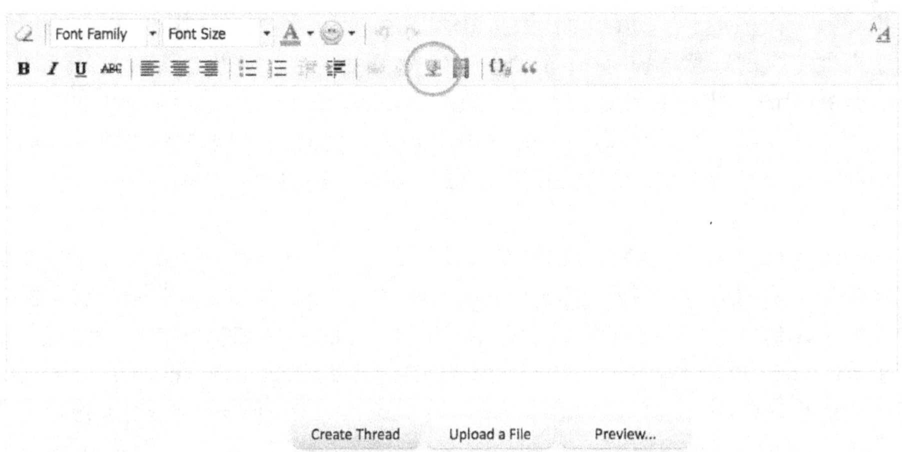

When you click on this button, it pops up a box, into which you type the URL of the image and click 'insert'[21].

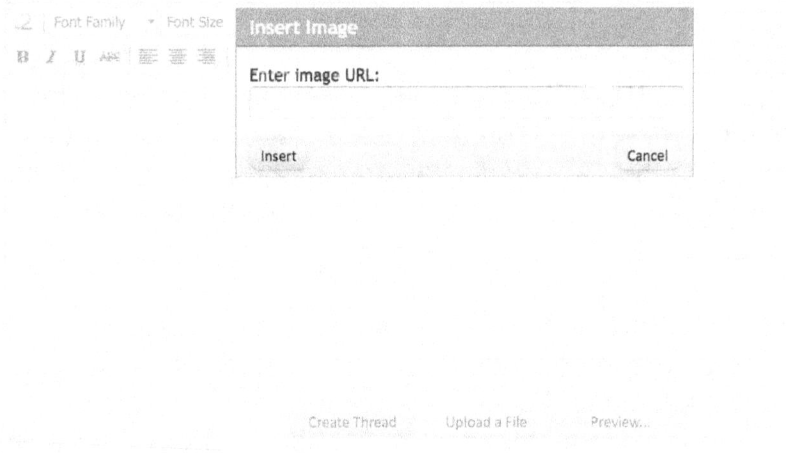

This inserts the image into your post or page, and lets you see it as it will appear once published as well.

---

[21] Images taken from the XenForo Discussion Forum Software (http://xenforo.com) and used by kind permission

How to use images safely and legally

If you want to use an image on the web, you either have to own the copyright for it, or seek the permission of the person who does. This is an area that's ignored so often online, that it's only through the sheer number of people all doing the wrong thing that courts across the world aren't busier than they already are. However, the fact remains, an image online is just as subject to copyright as an image offline, and people can and do sue other people for using their images without permission.

I once saw this first hand in an old job, where an intern had found an image online through a Google image search[22] and used it to illustrate part of our monthly newsletter, not realising that the copyright on it belonged to a large corporation. A few months later, we received a legal notice informing us that the corporation had noticed that we'd used it, and demanding many hundreds of pounds in settlement rather than taking us to court. We had no choice but to pay, and never do it again.

There is though, another risk in using other people's images online without permission, and it comes through a feature of the Internet called hotlinking.

When an image is displayed on a website, it has to be live on an Internet-connected server somewhere. You then use a piece of HTML code to tell the computer loading the page to display that image. Most of the time, websites are displaying images that are hosted on the same server as the site itself, and no problem arises.

However, it's just as possible to use the same HTML code to display an image that's stored on someone else's server, as after all, all the code is doing is displaying an image that's online somewhere, it doesn't matter where. The thing is, doing this means that the other person's server has to transmit that image to the user's computer when it loads it, rather than your server doing this. Each piece of information a server transfers uses what is called bandwidth, and bandwidth costs money.

---

[22] http://www.google.co.uk/imghp?

Linking to an image on someone else's server like this, or hotlinking, is a practice frowned upon, quite apart from any copyright issues, as you're using bandwidth that someone else is having to pay for.

So what though, someone else pays some of your server costs, it's not going to cost them a lot of money is it? Well, whether it does or not, it's illegal unless you have the permission of the site to which you are hotlinking to do so, and it's a significant risk for yourself too, given these two examples.

First of all, if your page, forum post or blog contains an image that's hosted on someone else's site, if that person's site goes down or they delete the image, then the image will disappear from where you've used it as well. Worse though, is something I've seen happen more than once, where the person who's being hotlinked from notices, and replaces the image you've hotlinked with something else.

Some websites have the ability to detect if content on them is being hotlinked, and automatically replace the image with one telling the world that the person posting it has hotlinked it, often in a rather offensive way. The best ones though come when real people notice hotlinking and change the image in a subtle way that the original hotlinker may not notice for some time. I haven't got permission to print the image here, but here's a link to what happened as it happened;
http://www.b3ta.com/board/archive/32027

So how do you know if you've got permission to use the image or not? Wouldn't gaining permission for every image you want to use be a slow and laborious process as well? Well, not necessarily, if you use something called the Creative Commons licence.

4.5 The Creative Commons Licence

The Creative Commons licence is a legal licence that has sprung up to deal with the issue of copyright on the web, acknowledging that sometimes you just want to grab an image and stick it in a site, and that many people will do so regardless of the law anyway.

If a piece of content online, be it image, video, sound file or text is published under a Creative Commons licence, then that generally means the original owner is happy for anyone to use it, so long as they follow a few rules that the original owner has set out.

One of the most common rules is giving credit to the original owner alongside the image where you use it. So, for example, you may put an image in a page and put a note next to it saying 'Image by xxx on Flickr', as well as making that text a link to the page where the original owner originally published it. There are other restrictions content owners can put on images too, such as stating that they can only be used for non-commercial purposes. Creative Commons licensing is very simple and clear to read, so it's worth spending a few minutes reading up about for yourself too at http://creativecommons.org/licenses/.

Once you've got to grips with Creative Commons licensing, you can use it to find images and content to use all over the web, often very simply. For example, if you search Flickr, the world's biggest image sharing site, for an image, you can set the search just to display images that are issued under a Creative Commons licence, meaning you can use everything you find when you search[23].

4.6 Using video

Having a video in a site can do wonders for bringing it to life, although it has to be used in the right manner. One only has to look at the usage figures of a video sharing site like YouTube to see how common it is now for people to watch videos online, mostly I suspect due to the increasing dominance of broadband as a means of connecting to the Internet.

It's very easy to be put off using video if you can't find the right one to go with your other content, and you think making one is only a job for the professionals. Whilst the former is sometimes a problem, the latter is most certainly not true. I've known it not to be so for a long time, but I finally got the opportunity to prove it once and for all in the summer of 2011, an experience I will share with you to show how easy it is.

---

[23] See the bottom search option at http://www.flickr.com/search/advanced/?

In June that summer I was working for Worthy FM, the onsite radio station of Glastonbury Festival in the UK. As part of the work, I ended up camping on site for over a week before the festival opened its gates to punters, and as I was working on social media for the station, I used the opportunity to try out a few different things.

First of all, I noticed that a lot of people in a variety of places online were growing increasingly concerned about how muddy the festival would be, given the inclement weather in the weeks running up to it. I tried to tell people in forums and on blogs that it wasn't yet muddy at all on site, but it didn't really seem to get noticed.

So one day, on my way back to our compound from lunch, I decided to make a short video of the lack of mud on site at the moment, to prove to people that all was well. To make it, I just took my digital camera out of my pocket, set it to record video, pressed record and filmed a couple of minutes of my walk back, narrating what I was seeing at the same time.

When I got back, I stuck it on the free YouTube channel I had created for the station, embedded this YouTube video in a blog post on the Worthy FM website and published the blog, which in turn then automatically placed notifications about it on our Facebook and Twitter pages.

When I checked back on it a few hours later, I was amazed to see it had already received hundreds of views and was being discussed on various different forums, as people were taking the initiative to share it with their friends. In a very small way, my video was going viral.

I made a few more videos in this way in the run up to and during Glastonbury that year, and they all ended up getting viewed thousands of times. One even hit over 50,000 views in the first week it was up, having been picked up and reported on by BBC Radio 6 Music, ironically enough.

So, if I can do it, anyone can. All I needed was a video recording device, which most cameras and many mobile phones contain as standard these days, and a computer to upload my video to the web. I didn't bother with lighting, editing, sound levels or anything like that, and it turned out just fine. Indeed, some of the feedback I got on them was that people liked the informal and honest style that this low budget approach created. If

you want to see these videos for yourself by the way, just go to
www.youtube.com/worthyfm.

I'm no expert on what makes a good video or not, but I think it would
actually be best to leave my comments on using video online there
anyway. As the more I tell you, the more you will be influenced by how I
do things, rather than coming up with your own style. It's up to your target
audiences to tell you what they like and don't like in the videos you
create, so why not make a quick video, stick it online, and let them teach
you what works?

I will make one final point about using videos online though, and that is
that the rule about minimising the number of steps needed to participate
(see below) applies to video just as much as it does elsewhere. Happily,
in the last few years I've seen two pilots that have summed this up really
well.

The first was by Mansfield District Council in the UK, where the authority
set up a large tent in the town centre with a video camera in it. They then
invited young people to come in and record a short piece to camera about
the best and worst things about their local area. Once they'd spent a day
recording different young people, they edited the pieces together and
made a really interesting and engaging short video about the views of
young people to be shown to elected members and anyone else with an
interest. It cost them very little in terms of equipment and staff time, and
produced a great piece of content for use elsewhere.

On the other hand, another council, which I shall call 'Whochester',
decided to commission an entire website to be built, to allow the public to
record their responses to various prompt questions, and then upload
them to the site. Unsurprisingly the site saw very little participation take
place, and despite the authority giving it lots of promotion, it was
eventually quietly taken offline and abandoned.

To see why one video project worked and another didn't, let's look at the
different steps each required the participant to take.

Mansfield District Council

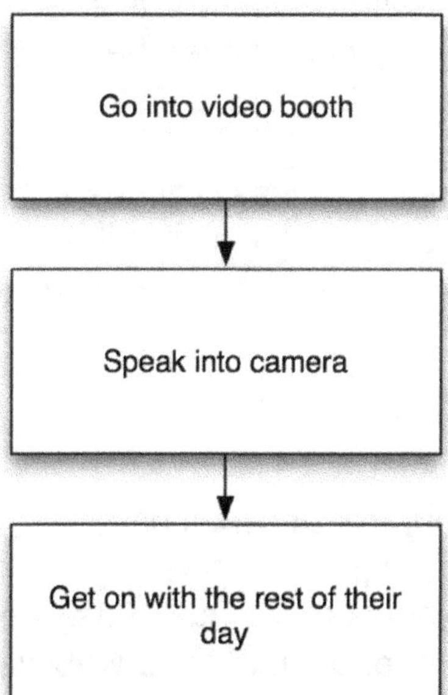

Whochester Council

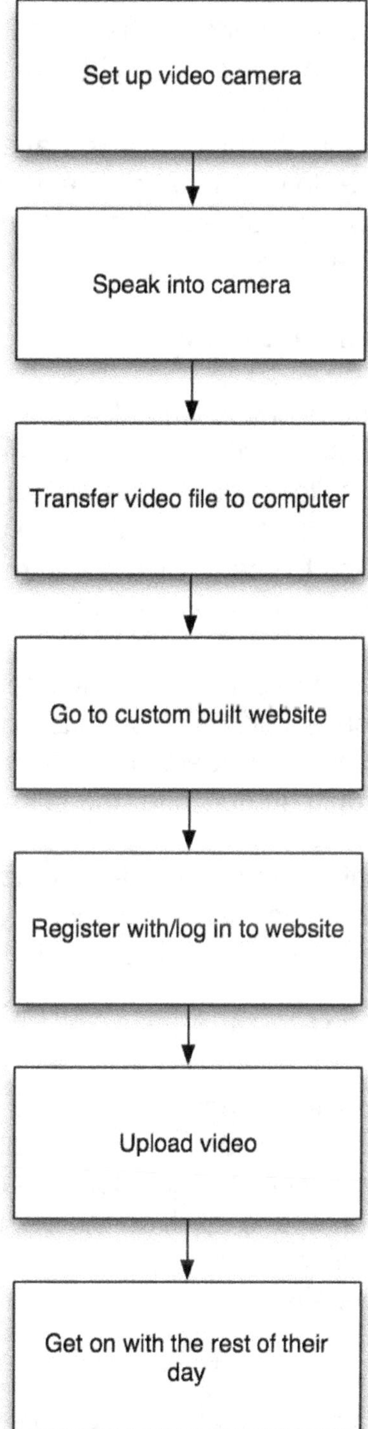

The difference between the participation steps the user had to take with each of the different approaches is pretty stark really. It doesn't take much to work out the advantage the Mansfield project had over the 'Whochester Council' example.

Mapping out the steps that any digital engagement process requires a user to take can be an extremely effective way of judging whether it will work or not, and that leads us nicely on to our next basic principle of the Internet.

Don't make me think

Those of you who already know something about this area will have spotted that I've taken the heading of this principle from the title of the excellent book by Steve Krug[24]. I make no apologies for doing so, as with this title, Krug has absolutely nailed the key point about making a website easy to use. The less you make people think about how to do things online, the more likely they are to do them.

Of course, if you've any interest in this area I really would recommend you read Krug's book, as perhaps unsurprisingly, it's really clear and simple to understand. However, to help you get started in this area, I would humbly offer the following approach.

There are many different facets to removing the need for people to think about how to do something on a website, but the one I generally run through with clients is called 'User journeys'.

4.7 User journeys

A user journey is the path a user follows in doing a specific task or action on your website. For example, someone getting in touch with you through your website might follow a user journey that saw them start at your homepage, click on the link that says 'Contact us', type their details and message into some text boxes, click 'submit' and then go to a new website.

---

[24] http://www.amazon.co.uk/Dont-Make-Me-Think-Usability/dp/0321344758

Very often it's nice to set user journeys out as a flow chart. In which case the above example would look like this.

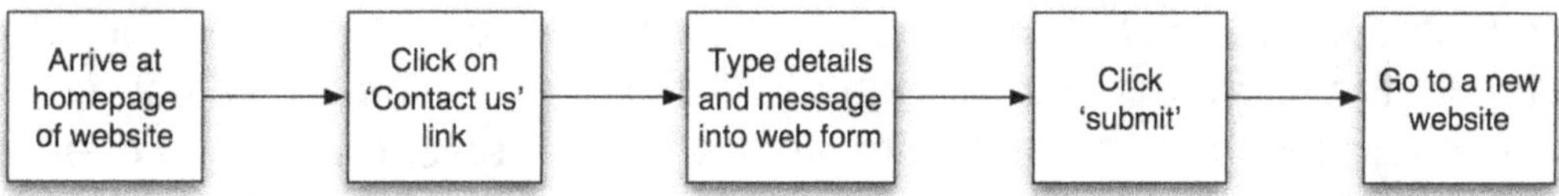

Of course, a user journey isn't just the same thing as a list of the pages on your site a viewer visits and in what order they do so. It's more a way of describing the steps or actions a user takes, even if that action is as simple as reading a piece of text. Very often the end goal of any specific user journey will be one you have identified as relevant and worthwhile during the website design process. At least, that's what it generally should be, which points to one way of going about writing user journeys.

Once you've identified all your user stories (see below), you can start to go through them and pull out the actions they contain and any end goals that relate to them. So, the above example user journey might have been formed from such user stories as;

As a member of the public

I want to get in touch with the organisation

So I can ask them a question

Or

As a potential customer

I want to be able to contact the sales department

So I can find out how much the software costs

Now, both of those are valid user stories, but one of them is a bit of a red herring. You see, you could turn the second user story there into a user journey and put it in the specification of the website, but you may well be better off realising that a common user story will be people looking for your costs, and so give them the information up front and online, to help them meet the needs within their user story even more quickly.

This hints at one of the most useful elements of user journeys, at least when it comes to digital engagement. You see, I always think that the primary use of user stories should be to check that the vast majority of the needs of your website's visitors can be met as quickly as possible. As a result, the shorter the user journey to each goal, the better. Of course you can go too far with this and make the journey so short that the overall experience becomes confusing, ironically leading to it taking longer to complete. As a rule though, if you can cut out a step on the user journey, or merge it with another one, then so much the better.

We'll come back to this aspect of user journeys later in the book, as they're a useful way of analysing why some web projects work and others don't, even when they might initially look quite similar.

If you're going to get serious about user journeys, then you shouldn't neglect the ways in which different user journeys can be combined with one another, or where they might cause problems by overlapping. For example, it's one thing to have someone come to your site and successfully complete a user journey, but it's a lot better to keep them on your site by leading them straight into another user journey. Clever sites will keep you on them for a good while, at least until you've completed all the journeys that they want you to.

A slightly more simple approach to this sort of work can be achieved by altering the setting of certain links to other webpages that you put on your site. Some links you can set to open in the same Internet browser window as the one you are currently looking at, in essence taking you from one page to another. Other links can be set to open in a new window or tab, leaving the original page still open in your browser.

This way, even though the viewer has moved to look at a new website, they still have your site open and may return to your site to complete more user journeys once they have finished with the one in the link.

As I say, we'll keep coming back to user journeys at various stages throughout this book. You don't have to use them for everything you do, but used in the right place at the right time, they can be extremely effective.

4.8 User stories

Whilst they form part of a much bigger software development methodology that it's probably not worth you learning, user stories are one of the most useful tools I've come across for building successful digital engagement websites, so I want to share them with you here.

A user story is a sentence or couple of sentences that set out in plain english three pieces of linked information, these being a type of website user, a task they will want to perform using a website, and the reason they want to perform this task. I generally try to write user stories in just one sentence, using the following template format;

"As a.....I want to....so I can...."

For example, when I first developed my website www.gezsmith.com, I came up with user stories such as;

"As a potential client, I want to be able to find Gez's email address, so I can contact him about his day rates"

"As a recipient of Gez's training, I want to be able to find his training resources, so I can download them to refresh my memory"

Of course, both of these are quite business oriented, but a user story can cover anything you can think of online. For example, you could plausibly write a user story for Google's search engine that went;

"As a complete lunatic, I want to be able to search for the name of the current Prime Minister, so I can reassure myself that I have not time travelled during the night"

Whenever you are looking to develop or buy a piece of digital engagement software, or even if you are using a free third party system like Twitter, writing down all of the user stories that cover what you want to achieve can help to make things so much clearer. Not only in terms of what you need to include in your project or website, but also in terms of the things you thought you would need but can actually leave out.

When writing user stories, I generally work through the following simple process.

1. Write down all of the user stories I can.

2. Go around anyone else involved in the project on my side, and ideally some of the potential project users/participants as well, and ask them to write any user stories they can think of.

3. Gather together all of the user stories created so far into one document, and merge together any very similar or duplicate ones.

4. Go through each of the user stories in turn and have a more detailed think about whether they are likely, valid, or otherwise worth including, deleting any that I think are not.

5. Share these final user stories with others for their second opinion before considering them done.

A document of user stories should always be saved with a version number in the filename though, as often you discover new ones or want to remove old ones as your project goes along. A user stories file should always be a living document, but if people start to work from different versions you can easily get in a right mess, so be careful how you save it!

To help you get started with writing user stories, I've included a template user stories document in the appendices to this book, as well as on my website[25].

---

[25] See www.gezsmith.com/resources

4.9 Accessibility

Accessibility, or 'the inclusive practice of making websites usable by people of all abilities and disabilities'[26], is another of those elements of the Internet that has massive importance and yet not many people really worry about too much.

To be fair, I didn't used to either, until about 5 years ago when the marvellous Mr Anthony George made me realise it's not just a niche concern for certain disability charities, but something that, when done right, makes the web better for everyone. I really am indebted to Ant for developing my interest and knowledge in the area of accessibility, as it's helped in so many other areas of my work.

So in this section I'd like to do for you what Ant did for me, and help you realise that web accessibility is an important and satisfying area to work on and get right, without fetishising it into something it's not, as some advocates have been known to.

First of all, when we talk about accessibility in these terms, it's important to understand that it isn't some stand alone area of software development, or just another Quality Assurance process a website has to go through before it can go live. It's much bigger than that, and can be seen in every single component of website development, from the building of the software to the writing of the content.

This way of thinking about accessibility has a number of practical advantages. First of all, it stops accessibility seeming like some big, monolithic and specialist topic that's best left to the experts. Instead, it breaks it into small parts that over time just blend automatically into the rest of your work. Second, it makes accessibility something that feeds into all of your work, which is a highly underrated skill at the moment.

You see, at its heart, accessibility is just what it says it is, a way of making things accessible to people, so they are able to use them. As a result, writing good content for a website that is clear and written in

---

[26] Taken from http://en.wikipedia.org/wiki/Web_accessibility 04/11/11.

everyday language can be seen as an important part of accessibility. There's not a million miles between the concepts of accessibility and usability when you look at it in this way too, and indeed the Swedish Government's regulations around accessibility also include requirements around usability too. Sadly this approach is all too rare at the moment, and much accessibility legislation is framed in a legalistic and intimidatory tone. Perhaps it's no wonder people don't want to think about it too much as a result.

When you look at things like colours on a website, accessibility states that you should have sufficient contrast between the colour used for some text and the colour of that text's background. This is to make the text readable by the partially sighted and colour blind. However, well contrasted text is also easier to read for the non visually impaired, and it generally makes your website look better overall as well. So whilst it's an accessibility requirement, it's a requirement that benefits areas such as usability, engagement and branding at the same time.

There are lots of situations like this in accessibility, but whilst I want to encourage you to think of it as something useful and beneficial to get right, I should probably remind you that there are various laws, regulations and organisational policies out there with which you often have to comply. So this section can't be seen as saying 'Here's how to get accessibility right', because 'right' means lots of different things to different people.

Thankfully though, there are some international guidelines that have been developed around web accessibility, and to which a great many organisations now subscribe. They've been drawn together by an international body that rules on many of the standards necessary to make the web work across the world, and appropriately enough, they're called the World Wide Web Consortium, or W3C for short.

W3C has produced many sets of guidelines, but the relevant ones here are the 'Web Content Accessibility Guidelines' or WCAG for short. These guidelines are split into three different levels of compliance, the first being requirements you must meet, the second being requirements you should meet and the third being requirements you may meet. Accordingly, they're referred to as A, AA or AAA compliance respectively.

Now, as you can see, these three levels aren't like some computer game, where each level gets progressively harder and has to be completed in full in order for you to win. Instead, they're guidance and best practice examples in many ways, set out into three very different forms.

- For level A, you must meet all of the requirements, and so the requirements here are correspondingly the most important.

- For level AA, you should meet all of these requirements, and they are still for the most part reasonably independently measurable and provable.

- For AAA though, WCAG states that you may meet these requirements, and they're typically on things that are harder to control or measure, as well as having a lesser or less widespread impact.

Accordingly, it's pretty tricky to prove that you're AAA, and all organisations I've come across have taken AA as the acceptable standard[27]. Indeed, the WCAG guidelines state;

'It is not recommended that Level AAA conformance be required as a general policy for entire sites because it is not possible to satisfy all Level AAA Success Criteria for some content.' [28]

As a result, if you're going to worry about the legal or policy based approach to accessibility, and you probably should a bit, then get to grips with A and AA standards first, then have a read through of AAA too and see if there's anything in there that might be of use.

Also, don't forget to use this new found knowledge in your shopping for software too. If a supplier says that their software meets AAA standards

---

[27] Apart from one which said they wanted AAA, but when I phoned and asked why, they said they didn't know, it just sounded like the best one.
[28] From http://www.w3.org/TR/2008/REC-WCAG20-20081211/#conformance-reqs, Note 2, taken on 04/11/11.

without a *very* detailed explanation of how it does so, you can either laugh at them then run a mile, or laugh whilst running, it's up to you.

So as I said above, this section can't really be one on how to do accessibility perfectly, as there are lots of different elements to it based on your own particular circumstances. I do strongly suggest you have a read around the topic yourself.

The page at http://www.w3.org/WAI/intro/wcag is a good place to start, and there's a handy guide at http://www.w3.org/WAI/WCAG20/quickref/ which gives you an overview too.

I know you're going to find something else to do other than read those pages though, so to prove to you that learning about accessibility is the same as learning how to 'make good Internets' generally, here are the overview headings from the current WCAG overview guide [29].

- *Text Alternatives: Provide text alternatives for any non-text content so that it can be changed into other forms people need, such as large print, braille, speech, symbols or simpler language*

- *Time-based Media: Provide alternatives for time-based media.*

- *Adaptable: Create content that can be presented in different ways (for example simpler layout) without losing information or structure.*

- *Distinguishable: Make it easier for users to see and hear content including separating foreground from background.*

- *Keyboard Accessible: Make all functionality available from a keyboard.*

- *Enough Time: Provide users enough time to read and use content.*

- *Seizures: Do not design content in a way that is known to cause seizures.*

---

[29] Taken from http://www.w3.org/WAI/WCAG20/quickref/. Copyright © 1994-2007 W3C® (MIT, ERCIM, Keio), All Rights Reserved.

- *Navigable: Provide ways to help users navigate, find content, and determine where they are.*

- *Readable: Make text content readable and understandable.*

- *Predictable: Make Web pages appear and operate in predictable ways.*

- *Input Assistance: Help users avoid and correct mistakes.*

- *Compatible: Maximize compatibility with current and future user agents, including assistive technologies.*

There, now don't those all sound like perfectly sensible things that will just make your website a whole lot better? Told you.

4.10 Multiple language websites

Strictly speaking, providing content in more than one language on a website is a separate issue from that of accessibility, but it's very much in the same ballpark. If you need to make text content readable and understandable, then for some audiences you may well need to make it available in a different language to your own.

On the face of it, this may seem fairly straight forward, but unfortunately it usually isn't. This part of the book is very much coloured by my experiences of working with the UK public sector here, which is governed by all sorts of rules when it comes to languages. Not just rules of local policy guidance either; in Wales, the provision of all web content in both English and Welsh is mandatory for all public sector bodies[30].

Now there's nothing in any way wrong with this requirement in principle[31], but I am keen to challenge the attitude that it shouldn't generate a whole lot more work and cost. You see, there are a number of ways dual language content can affect websites, each of which brings with it its own

---

[30] The fact that I've never seen a client specify whether the dual language site had to be in North Welsh or South Welsh makes me suspect few clients are actually that concerned about the details of their dual language requirements.
[31] Cymru am Byth.

range of problems. Let's look at it in the context of the Welsh language requirement.

On the one level, there's the content the client puts into the website. Here, the client covers the cost of translation to ensure it is in both English and Welsh. But then they need to have two different websites to enter the content into. This will invariably mean the web company at the start having to deploy and test two versions of the site, incurring twice the cost.

On the next level though, there is all of the text that is in the website already when it is launched; text like 'next', 'previous' and 'submit' on buttons within the site, the text in the sidebars, etc. All of this text is often auto-generated, to save you the job of having to create a new button for every new page you add.

So to provide a dual language site to this level, you then have to go back through the software you have already built, and swop over each piece of inbuilt text with its dual language alternative, a mammoth task. Indeed, it's such a big task, that you sometimes see websites where buttons just have both languages on, to cut out some of the development time.

Of course, you could build all of these capabilities into your software or website from the start, and I know some companies do indeed do this. But even then, the companies will need to recoup this higher initial development cost somehow, and nine times out of ten it will be from its customers.

If you start to add up the costs of this work they can sometimes be astronomical, to the point that the whole project has to be abandoned. An unintended consequence of dual language legislation I am sure, but a consequence none the less.

Now all of this would be fine, and I probably wouldn't be making such a big issue of it, if you saw a return on investment for your dual language work, but the fact is that you pretty much never do. I'm sure other fields are different, but in every dual language Welsh/English public consultation or engagement project I've seen, the ratio of responses submitted through the English site compared with the Welsh site is just nuts.

I don't think it's an exaggeration to say that I've not seen more than a handful of responses submitted in Welsh in all my years in this field. One organisation ran a series of UK wide consultations using both Welsh and English sites, and received hundreds of thousands of responses in English, and only two in welsh. That puts the cost per response of those two welsh submissions in the tens of thousands of pounds. Given what else you could do with that money, I'm just not convinced dual language Welsh/English websites are always worth it.

This is not to say though that you should just ignore provision of information in other languages through your website, far from it, for there is a way that can meet most guidelines whilst still remaining quick and cost effective.

The method I've come to use over the years is to provide the main website and all of its content in the primary language of the client, typically English in my case. Then, for each of the minority languages spoken by around 2% to 5% of the target audience (the exact percentage tends to vary per client), you write the name of that language in the website's footer, written in that language. You then make this language name a link to a page on your site containing further information on the consultation and how to respond to it, along with key dates, further contact information and so forth, again all written in the relevant language.

This way, each additional language only requires one additional page of static text and a link, neither of which should cost much at all. Anyone wanting to access the consultation or engagement exercise then has the ability to do so as well as the ability to get in touch and ask for further documents to be translated and sent over to them should they need them.

It's this model that's allowed clients to comply with their regulations whilst saving thousands of pounds over the years. It's also a model that I've never seen a member of the public complain about, which is not something I can say about websites that have cost an arm and a leg.

Chapter 5. Formal/structured consultation online

By a formal or structured consultation, I mean one which is required to be conducted for legal purposes, or which relates to a specific document or set of information, inviting the respondent to give their opinion on it in a variety of ways. Typically it not only provides all of the content that can be considered by a respondent, but also a pre-determined format for how responses should be supplied. As a result, this chapter is likely to be very relevant for people in a government setting, but is just as relevant for anyone who ever wants to run an online survey on any topic.

In theory, a formal consultation should be the easiest digital engagement process to run online. After all, you usually have a pretty firm idea of the content, and a format for the responses that you want to receive. You may also have an organisational consultation policy to follow, and of course any best practice guidelines as well, for example from the government or an industry regulatory body such as the Market Research Society. Indeed, some formal consultations are so prescribed that they can be subject to judicial review and legal challenge if not conducted correctly.

So, if everything's pretty much set in stone before you even think about the Internet, then putting such a consultation online should be easy, shouldn't it?

Well, yes and no. Sadly, this line of thinking over the last 10 years has led to a really unfortunate phenomena, the downloadable document consultation. This is where a consultation document is prepared for offline response, putting all of the consultation content and questions into one printable document, before uploading this document onto a website. If people want to take part, they have to download the document, fill it in and post or email it back to the consulting organisation. Alternatively, organisations sometimes don't leave any space within the document for responses to be completed, and instead ask people to send emails or post letters separately containing their comments.

This is an unfortunate phenomenon for two reasons. First of all, it's really off putting for any potential respondents. To take part they have to download a document, read all of its contents, type their responses into it and send it back. This is a process then that contains 4 different steps as a minimum. Since the more steps you ask people to take online, the more likely they are to abandon the process, providing a downloadable document as a form of consultation is pretty exclusionary to a great many people.

Second though, it represents a missed opportunity for the consulting organisation, who then have to read through all of the information sent back, be it in questionnaire forms, letters, emails and many other possible formats, then collate it accurately, before they can even think about analysing it. Wouldn't it make more sense if respondents could just type their responses straight into a system that collates responses, identifies possible duplicates and even starts to analyse the data without the organisation having to do anything?

Well, if a formal consultation is run properly online, the respondent should find making their response quick and simple, and the organisation shouldn't have to do any work to collate all of the responses, identify duplicates or even view the top-line results, whether in numerical or free text formats.

The biggest barrier to this happening however is convention. Often practices have developed around formal consultation processes that meet people's needs in the offline world. Indeed, where software has had any influence on the structure and content of the consultation, it has often only done so by requiring the data to be collected in a specific manner to fit the needs of a software based data analysis package.

So, running a formal consultation online is often like trying to fit a square peg into a round hole. At the risk of stretching an analogy too far, let's see what corners we can shave off the peg to match the online and offline processes up.

5.1 The typical formal consultation process

As can be seen from the diagram below, most formal consultations follow a standard process.

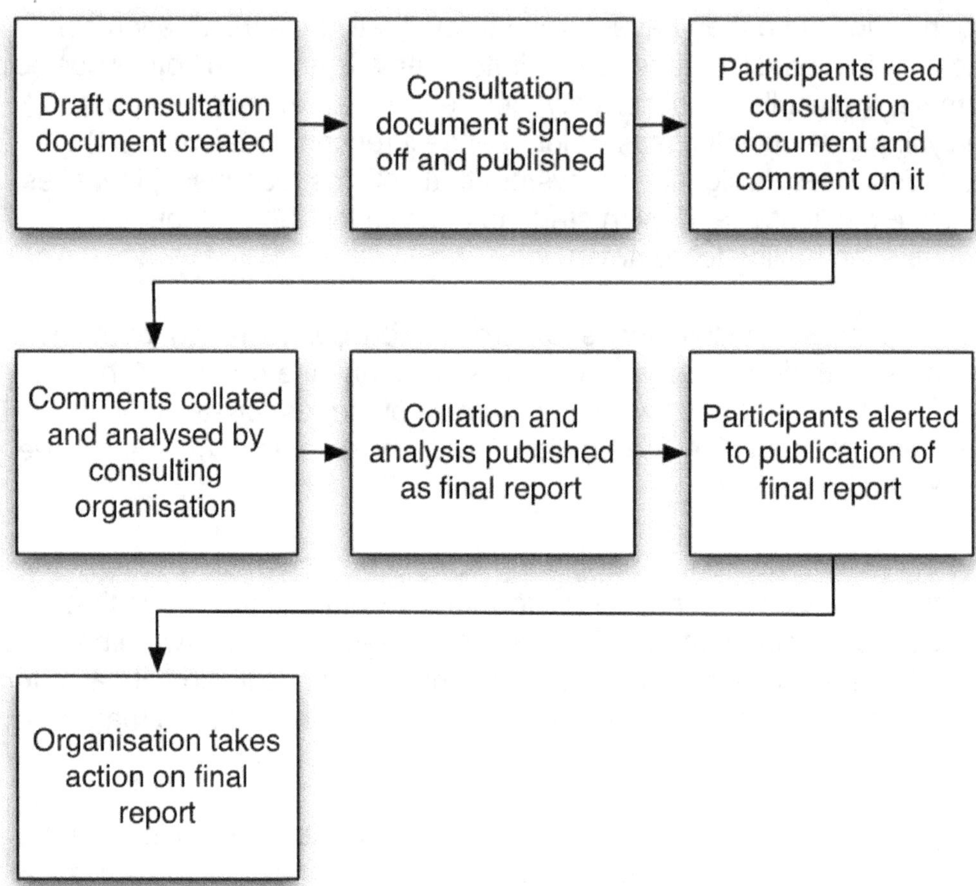

The policy or proposals being consulted upon are broken up into sections, often called chapters, and respondents are invited to comment on these chapters, or comment on the contents of the chapters broken down into smaller sections. These comments are more commonly requested in a free text format, allowing the respondent to write as much or as little as they like, as opposed to more simply asking them closed questions, such as 'do you agree, yes or no?'

Once the respondent has written their comments, they are often asked for some information about themselves, for example whether they are responding as an individual or on behalf of an organisation, before they submit their response.

The good thing is, the Internet is great at accommodating broadly this approach. Indeed, on more than one occasion I was surprised to hear a prospective client phone up and ask if I had any software that would break information into smaller sections and allow people to comment on each section, as if it was some special piece of functionality, when in actual fact it is just what any web page can do.

There are different ways of managing each section of a formal consultation online though, so let's look at each one individually, and then put them all back together then to create a framework for the ideal online formal consultation.

5.2 Introducing your consultation

All consultations should have a clear introduction provided with them. There are two aims to this; making the participant aware of what is going on, and making them feel encouraged to take part. Often this may be written in the form of an introductory statement by the figure responsible for the consultation, a government minister or similar, and whilst this is good, in as much as it gives a personal face to the process, it can be difficult to integrate online, given people read text more slowly on a screen than on a page as mentioned above.

How you structure your introduction is of course up to you, but I would recommend making sure that the following are included in the introduction to all formal consultations run online.

- **Welcome message**

  For example 'welcome to our consultation on X'. It's a small point, but starting with a positive and welcoming tone gives a good impression and encourages the visitor to take part.

- **Consultation overview**

  For example, 'this consultation covers topics such as x, y and z'.

- **Statement on what will be done with the information once collected**

  This is in part good practice and a demonstration of openness on the part of the consulting organisation, but is also aimed at complying with principle 2 of the Data Protection Act 1998[32].

- **Statement of how long it will take to complete**

  There's nothing worse than entering into an online process that you think may be brief, only to find yourself still ploughing through it half an hour later. If responding to the consultation is likely to take some time, then be clear about this. After all, respondents can always choose to return later when they have the time to complete it.

- **Information on who to get in touch with and how to get in touch with them if the respondent has any queries**

  It is often best to give more than one contact method here, and to keep them simple. So, for example, include an email address and a telephone number, rather than a postal address.

- **Thanks message**

  Whilst you want to thank people once they have submitted their response of course, it's also good to make public your gratitude to people for responding at the start of the process.

---

[32] For more on the UK Data Protection Act and what it might mean for you, see Chapter 10.

So, for example, here's a good standard introduction to a formal online consultation.

> *"Hello, and welcome to <organisation name>'s consultation on <topic>*
>
> *This consultation is being carried out to look at <x,y and z>, and the results from it will be used to <purpose>*
>
> *The consultation should take no more than <time> to complete, and you can save your response at any time in order to complete later if you require.*
>
> *If you have any questions about this consultation process please email <address> or call <telephone number>.*
>
> *Thanks in advance for taking the time to share your thoughts with us"*

5.3 How to structure your information

Presenting information clearly and simply online can be an art in and of itself, and there are doubtless people who make a living purely from this area of work alone.

However, over time I've noticed that there are some simple approaches to follow which will do wonders to turn a large amount of complex information into something simple and usable for the majority of respondents.

Use three levels, no more

For any given section of information, be it a chapter of a policy document, or just one particular topic within the consultation, the three levels rule is great.

In essence, it refers to providing the same information in three different forms of increasing detail or complexity.

So, for the first level, you provide a simple statement of the information, summating it into a sentence or two. This is presented on the webpage in full to every user visiting that page.

Next, provide the information in a more detailed form, perhaps in a few paragraphs or thereabouts. This level of information should present everything that the vast majority of users would want or need to know about the particular topic. It need not be presented immediately to someone viewing the page, and indeed it is probably better if it is not. Instead, it can be hidden away in a section of the page that expands when clicked upon, or linked to from the page, as long as that link opens in a new window.

Finally, if the previous two levels haven't presented all of the information available on this particular section of the consultation, then provide access to all the information that remains. It is likely that only the most specialist or ardent respondent will want to read this information, but by providing it, you demonstrate openness and reduce the risk that people may accuse you of trying to hide anything.

How you implement this on the page is up to you, and there are a number of different ways of doing it. As a visual example, here's how we implemented this rule on the open source online engagement platform I designed to run various UK Central Government consultations[33].

In this example, at the top of a page of questions, there is some brief top-line information, representing the first level of information aimed at everyone.

Example Page

Progress   Page 2 of 3

This is some introductory text to chapter one of the consultation.

If you're pressed for time or interest, you can just read this before responding.

Related information

---

[33] www.citizenspace.com

When you click on this 'Related Information' text, the space below it expands to reveal some more text, representing the second level of information, aimed at people likely to have more of an interest in the topic or topics at hand.

Example Page

Progress ▓▓▓▓▓▓▓▓▓▓▓▓▓▓▓▓▓▓▓▓▓▓▓   Page 2 of 3

This is some introductory text to chapter one of the consultation.

If you're pressed for time or interest, you can just read this before responding.

Related information

This is some supporting information on the consultation. You could read more background information here to inform your response.

If you want to read all of the background information, click here to download it as a pdf document

Within this text is a link to a complete document, representing the third level of information, which can be downloaded and read by anyone wanting to have access to all of the available information.

As can be seen, using this three level rule you present the same sort of information in three different ways for three different types of respondent; the casually interested, the quite interested and the hugely interested, all through the same page, without allowing the requirements of any one user to impede the requirements of any other.

Divide your content in a way that works for the end user

If you've got lots of content in a consultation, then it's likely you will instinctively start to divide it up in some way. Perhaps different parts of the policy overall fall naturally into different projects your organisation is working on, or perhaps it impacts on different departments. Perhaps even the analysis of different parts of the responses received will be the responsibility of different individuals.

All of these factors could lead you to structure the consultation document in different ways, and the likelihood is that each of the approaches they lead to will be bad for the respondent. Why? Because you're structuring it in ways that fit how you work, which are not necessarily ways external people will understand, nor should they have to really.

I saw this most starkly once in a consultation run in the USA, where the initial topics for discussion were grouped on the site in terms of which government department they affected. This made sense from the point of view of the consulting organisation, but from a respondent point of view, the only way this made sense was if a respondent had a particular interest in the work of a specific department, a somewhat unlikely scenario.

Instead, the respondents wanted to see the information presented in a way that made sense to them, so the information was rearranged to put information and questions on similar subject areas together, regardless of the department they affected, and the participation rate suddenly rocketed upwards.

Of course, it made analysis a bit more difficult, as the information collected then had to be rearranged back into departments again, but this small additional time investment after the process closed paid dividends in terms of the quantity and quality of the responses received.

Similarly, more than one consultation I have worked on has ended up running for a long time, often involving more than one phase of consultation or engagement. In this scenario, it has made sense to split the presentation of the content by time, so participants are clear which bits of information relate to which phase of the consultation and, most important, which content they should be looking at to take part in the most current phase.

Ultimately, there's no right or wrong answer as to how you divide up and present your content, but which ever way you choose, make sure it makes sense for the end user, rather than just for yourself internally. It's better to receive lots of data and rearrange it yourself later than it is to receive no data in the first place.

Images are your friend

People like and understand images, often more than they do with text. So, if you've got the opportunity to present some parts of the information in the form of an image, then make sure you do so.

The specifics of using images in websites are covered in the previous chapter. However, if you think an image might help convey some information, then do use it. For example, some planning consultations I've seen have embedded maps and street views from Google to illustrate the areas likely to be affected by the consultation's outcomes. This really brought the consultation to life in a way that words never could, and really made things easier for respondents to understand.

5.4 Different methods of allowing people to respond

So, you've got the information that you want to collect people's views about, all presented in an orderly and clear manner, but how do you get them to respond?

Well, there is a surprising number of different ways to do this, so perhaps it's best broken down in terms of different question types, and the responses they allow.

Free text - small and large

This is the most common form of question type provided for individuals to respond to formal consultations, and in essence allows them to type a text based response into a box provided on the web page, as per the image below[34].

Please explain below why you chose that option.

---

[34] All illustrative images of question types are taken, with permission, from the Citizen Space system, unless otherwise noted. See www.citizenspace.com.

All very straight forward, but there are a few points to note here.

First of all, word limits. Whilst it is tempting, and eminently feasible, to place a limit on how many words can be typed into a free text box, experience tends to show that it is best not to. As whilst you may not want to read pages and pages of text from each respondent, if you try to stop them, they will just send it to you in a different way, for example by email. This then leaves you both reading all of that text, as well as tracking and collating together responses submitted online and via email by the same person. This invariably creates more work than you would have had if you'd just let them type everything they wanted to in one place.

If you do want to make sure you don't receive the equivalent of 'War and Peace' from each respondent, there are two better ways of doing this. First, look at how you word the question. 'What are your priorities for this area?' and 'What are your top three priorities for this area?' will both fundamentally receive the same responses, but the answers will likely be markedly shorter for the latter question when compared with the former.

The other method lies in the size of the text box provided. If you fix the text box to be just one line long on the page, with the first words written disappearing from the page as more words are added, you're likely to receive a much smaller response than if you provide a text box multiple lines deep. After all, it's hard to keep track of what you've written if it starts to disappear the more you write. The image below is an example of such a 'single line text box'.

What is your name?

Name

Using this single line text box approach is also best practice for free text responses you can reasonably expect to be shorter as well, for example people's names and email addresses.

One thing to be aware of though, is that whilst you may not have put a character limit on what people can type in response, other programs might. This is a common issue I've found with programs like Microsoft

Excel, which, probably because it's a package designed for dealing with numbers, seems to cut off text after around 255 characters in each cell. This is a pity, as .csv format is an excellent way of exporting data from survey systems for import into analysis systems, and the most common way to open a .csv file is with Excel. So, if you're looking at a data set gathered online and start noticing that respondent's answers are getting cut off before the end, check it's not an issue being caused by Excel first.

Inline commenting

With the text box options above, the process is very much designed around a comment being written in response to some information, and then being submitted to an organisation for consideration and analysis.

However, there is another method of doing this which has been popularised, in the UK at least, by Steph Gray, a former UK Civil Servant, now running a company called Helpful Technology[35].

With this 'Commentpress' approach, users can add comments to text on a webpage at any point in the text. These comments can be seen by other respondents, who can then comment either on the text or the comments already submitted.

This approach allows a much more flexible and fine-grained alternative to respondents only writing comments in the spaces you provide. Of course, as options for respondents get more and more flexible, the work involved in analysing and summating these comments likely gets greater, so only undertake this approach if you actually have the time and resources available to deal with what comes in.

Wiki editing/collaborative writing

This approach is the most flexible of all, but as a result is also in many ways the hardest to keep on top of. In essence, it involves placing text based information on a page or series of pages, and allowing people to edit it, delete parts of it and perhaps add in new parts of their own. Others

---

[35] www.helpfultechnology.com

can then read the information, review changes made to it and add their own.

Through this process, what you end up with is less a series of responses to information and more a collaboratively written final document, that represents the thoughts of participants, or at least those participants with the most time and/or motivation to make sure the final edit of the document contains their thoughts.

It's an interesting approach, and there are a number of free pieces of software available that allow you to do collaborative document writing in this way. However it is, by its very nature, unlikely ever to be suitable for formal or legally challengeable consultation, as it would be perfectly possible for an individual to go in and change the original content in its entirety, potentially unduly influencing the responses of others. It is perhaps best as an exercise undertaken amongst a smaller group of known individuals, to whom editing access is restricted.

Radio button

Let's move on now to look at answer types that provide numerical or statistical data, as opposed to free text. A radio button is perhaps the most common of quantitative answer types, and is encountered all across the Internet these days. By convention, it is represented by one or more circles with options written next to them, with one of the circles having another smaller circle appear within it when selected.

Please select one of the following options.

⦿ Yes

◯ No

◯ Don't know

The unique thing about radio buttons is that, wherever they appear in groups, you should only ever be able to select one of them. So, if you click on one of them, it should change appearance to indicate it has been selected. Then, if you click on a different radio button in the same group, the one you first clicked on should become unselected and the new one appear as selected in its place.

Radio buttons are best for questions where you have a range of options from which respondents may choose, but where you only ever want them to be able to select one option as their answer. It naturally follows that the options presented using radio buttons are usually mutually exclusive as well, for example 'yes/no/don't know', or 'male/female/rather not say'.

Presenting too many radio buttons in one long list though can be difficult for people to use. If you do find you've got more than around 5 options for radio buttons, consider using a drop down list instead (see below).

Check box

A check box is like a radio button, but instead allows respondents to select as many options as they wish to from a list. A check box is by convention presented as one or more squares with options written next to them, and when selected it traditionally displays a tick within each square that has been selected.

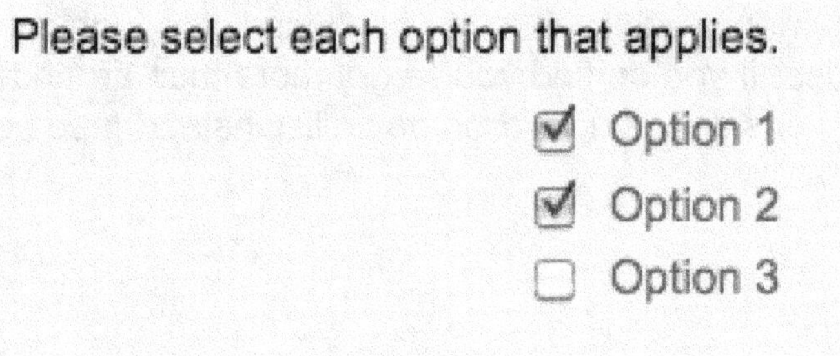

Each check box operates independently from every other one, so it may be that multiple check boxes are selected by the respondent within one question.

Check boxes are best for questions where you're asking respondents to select more than one item from a list, for example 'Which of these activities have you done in the last 6 months?'.

Check boxes can be harder for people to use if there are too many of them in one place though. If you have more than around 5 options for people to choose from, consider splitting the options into different sections, or using a different type of question to gain the same information.

Quick polls

Having looked at radio buttons and check boxes, it is worth briefly considering one of the uses to which they are sometimes put. Called a 'quick poll', this type of functionality generally presents the respondent with one question and asks them to select one or more answers in response. Once the respondent has submitted their response, they are presented with a top-line view of the results so far, normally in form of a horizontal bar chart with percentages next to each bar.

A quick poll ready to be answered

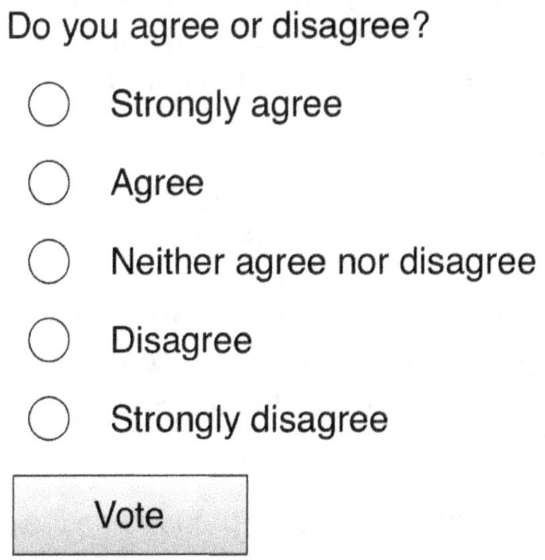

Do you agree or disagree?

- ○ Strongly agree
- ○ Agree
- ○ Neither agree nor disagree
- ○ Disagree
- ○ Strongly disagree

[Vote]

A quick poll having been answered

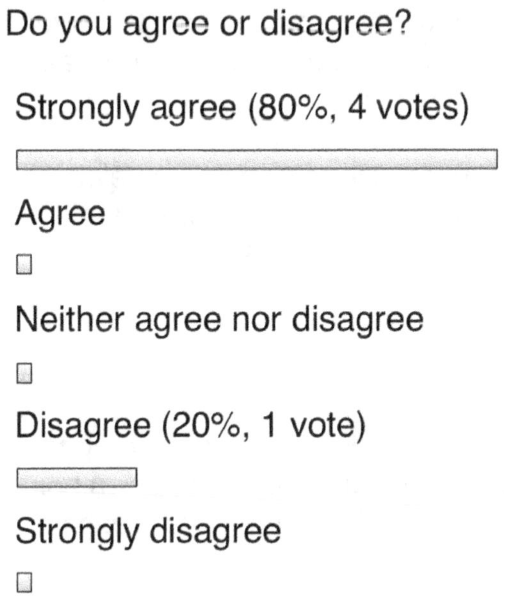

Do you agree or disagree?

Strongly agree (80%, 4 votes)

Agree

Neither agree nor disagree

Disagree (20%, 1 vote)

Strongly disagree

You tend to see these quick polls on the homepage of a website or within an individual blog post, although they can also be used in discussion forums, allowing the person creating a new discussion thread to add a poll, in order to bring the discussion to life some more.

Quick polls are often a fun and engaging form of surveying people, but they have turned out not to be all they are cracked up to be. However, back in the early days of digital engagement, many people, myself included, used to believe that they were an important part of building online engagement.

The idea behind this was that people were inherently nervous, confused or otherwise reticent about participating through a website, and by presenting them with a quick poll on the home page, you would encourage them to start taking part in a simple manner with immediate feedback, giving them confidence to go and take part in more complex participation processes. I even once heard this theory needlessly dressed up as being part of 'the virtuous circle of participation'.

I'm not sure who started this oft repeated idea, but I'd be proud to be the person to put an end to it. In all of the projects I have worked on, and all of the websites I have used, I have never seen the slightest bit of evidence for this theory about quick polls being true. People nowadays are often far more technologically adept than the organisations trying to engage them online, and the presence or otherwise of a quick poll makes absolutely no difference to their likelihood of taking part.

Use them if you want, as they can be fun (though statistically unreliable) methods of gauging opinion on specific topics. However, please don't believe they hold any greater significance to the process of digital engagement than that.

Dropdown

A dropdown question type is one where respondents click on a 'dropdown box' in order to give their response. Once clicked on, this dropdown box expands down the screen to reveal a number of options, one on each line.

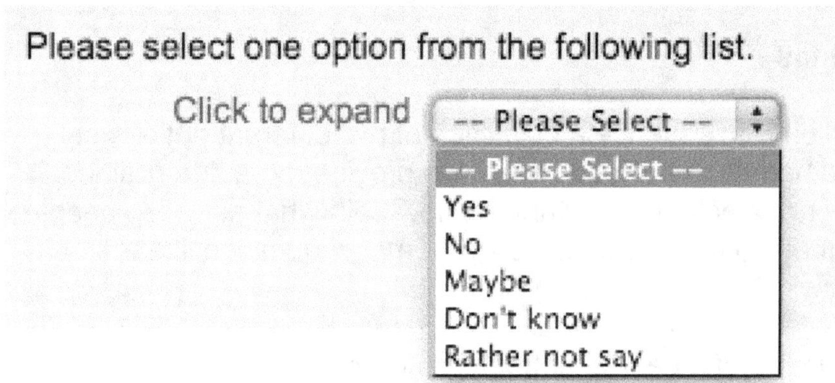

Normally respondents can only select one option from a dropdown list, and whilst it would technically be possible to allow them to select more than one, this would have usability problems, so a check box question type is better where more than one option can be chosen.

When using a dropdown, always make sure that the first option in this list is 'Please select', rather than one of the possible answers. Otherwise, people skipping over the question risk providing the first answer on the list as their response by mistake.

Matrix questions

A matrix question is in essence a collection of two different options set against each other, allowing respondents to provide more fine-grained information. For example, if you want to know both what activities people do and when they do them, you could use a matrix question like the examples below.

There are a number of different matrix types of question.

Matrix of radio buttons

A matrix of radio buttons is, as its title suggests, an arrangement of radio buttons going both down and across the screen.

Please select one option for each statement.

	Option 1	Option 2	Option 3	Option 4	Option 5
Statement 1	●	○	○	○	○
Statement 2	○	●	○	○	○
Statement 3	○	●	○	○	○

This presents a new problem though, because radio buttons have an element of mutual exclusion in them, meaning more than one cannot be selected at the same time. This means that in a matrix, there are number of different ways radio buttons within the same question can interact with each other.

There are three ways this can happen;

- **Horizontal excluding**

  This is where only one radio button per line going across the page can be selected.

- **Vertical excluding**

  This is where only one radio button per column going across the page can be selected.

- **Two direction excluding**

  This is only one radio button per column AND per row can be selected at one time, for example in the question 'Please select which of the following three options are your first, second and third preferences'.

Matrix of check boxes

A matrix of check boxes is more straightforward than a matrix of radio buttons, in that two options are compared against each other, but any possible combination of responses can be selected.

Please select from as many of the following options as you wish.

	Option 1	Option 2	Option 3	Option 4	Option 5
Statement 1	☑	☑	☐	☐	☐
Statement 2	☐	☑	☐	☐	☑
Statement 3	☐	☑	☑	☐	☐

Matrix of drop downs

A matrix of drop downs almost isn't a matrix question at all, or at least it doesn't necessarily look like one.

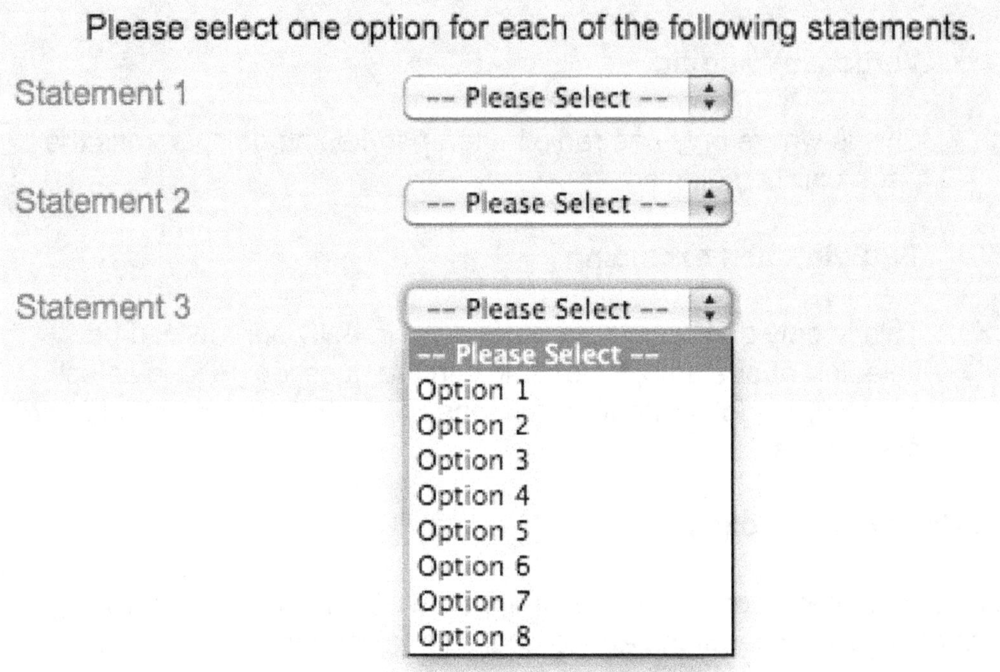

This type of question presents a number of different dropdown menus from which users can select their choices, typically one choice per option presented. The only reason this is technically a different type of question is because the alternative would otherwise require presenting the dropdowns individually, one per question, which may appear to be unusual to the end user.

File upload

This is a question type that doesn't exist on many online survey or consultation systems currently, but when it does it can be extremely useful.

This type of question allows the respondent to upload a file in response to the question, be it a word processed document, an image, a sound file or even a video, and generally looks something like the below.

Please use this section to upload a supporting file along with your response.

Browse...

There are a number of key benefits to using a question like this;

Collating responses

In previous consultations I have worked on, respondents have been so eager to ensure that their views are heard that they have filled in the online survey, sent comments by email, printed the same comments and posted them in, and sometimes even faxed the same comments in as well. This has generated 4 different responses, but all from the same user, a situation that creates a real headache in ensuring that each respondent's view are counted at least once but no more than once

If you provide a document upload question somewhere within the survey or consultation, you can ask respondents to upload any additional information they wish to provide into the system. This will then store this information alongside the respondents details, keeping all of the data in one place and removing problems with keeping track of responses

Providing flexibility to respondents

This type of question also provides additional flexibility for respondents. No matter how well written you believe your consultation to be, some respondents will always wish to provide additional information that you have not specifically asked for. Others may wish to provide it in a visual format, such as a picture or a map. Providing this type of question gives respondents the additional flexibility they require, whilst minimising the additional workload this can create for the consulting organisation.

Promoting accessibility

It should not be forgotten than many people with disabilities actually find it easier to participate in consultation and engagement exercises through the Internet compared with public meetings or handwritten questionnaires. Allowing respondents to upload files with their response enables them to upload a spoken word response, recorded as an audio file, or even a message recorded as a digital video.

Sound / video recording

As far as I know, this is a hypothetical type of online question at this stage, but I have no doubt it could be built technically should someone wish to fund its development.

With this type of question, a respondent would be able to click a button to start and stop recording a message through their computer's webcam or inbuilt microphone. This recorded message could then be automatically stored in the system for analysis by the receiving organisation.

5.5 When to make questions required

With all questions asked online, it should be possible to set them so that they have to be answered before the respondent can move on to the next page of questions or submit their response.

This may initially seem useful, as you want as many people as possible to answer your questions, don't you? However, it can have its downfalls, so setting questions as required is somewhat of a fine art.

The problem with it arises in the tension between providing good usability and ensuring good responses. If you set no questions in a survey or consultation as 'required to be answered', then you make it very easy for someone to skip past every single question and submit a blank or barely completed response. This will not cause any long-term harm, but can make a mess of any top-line results data being automatically generated by the system. After all, a percentage calculated using 10 valid responses will look very different from a percentage calculated from 10 valid responses and 90 blank ones.

However, if you set too many questions as 'required', you can quickly drive the user away from your site through frustration. It may be that they do not feel able or willing to answer every question you ask, but by forcing them to, you leave them no choice but to either give an untruthful answer, damaging your results, or just to abandon their response altogether.

So then, how do you achieve this balance between maximising the response rate whilst ensuring valid data is submitted? There is no hard and fast rule for this, but generally I find it best to make only those questions that you absolutely have to have answered as required, leaving all of the rest as 'non-required'.

For example, if you were consulting on new planning schemes across a town, it might be vital to know in which area the respondent lives in order to put their comments in context. However, whilst perhaps useful for general monitoring purposes, it appears much less essential to know the sexuality or ethnicity of that respondent when considering their comments. Thus you would set a question asking for their postcode[36] as mandatory, and leave the other questions as optional.

---

[36] Although most people can't be exactly located by their postcode, some respondents feel wary of providing this information, so it is usually best just to ask for the first three or four digits of their postcode, rather than their code in full.

5.6 Saving a response in order to complete it later

It would seem sensible at this juncture to consider how a respondent might save their response in order to return to it later on, rather than having to fill it in all in one go. However, there are a number of quite large considerations to be made within what seems like a relatively simple area, so we should break these down in turn first.

The issues to consider centre around how the user identifies themselves to the system, and how this identity is kept secure whilst remaining simple and usable. The traditional way for a user to return to a survey or consultation after saving it lies in user registration, so let's have a look at that first.

User registration

If I'm known for anything these days, it's for my vehement opposition to user registration in websites, the process that requires users to fill in and register details about themselves before they can take part.

On the face of it, user registration seems like an excellent idea. The user gets to create their own profile within the site, potentially saving them from filling in their demographic details on each activity they take part in. They can also use their registration for other purposes, such as to return to a partially completed consultation response at a later date.

From the point of view of the consulting organisation, it can track which users have responded to which consultations and when, perhaps in order to make sure key stakeholders have responded, or to maintain an active and participative panel of regular respondents such as a citizens' or residents' panel.

However, to my mind, all of these benefits are vastly outweighed by the one key problem with user registration, in that's it's massively off putting to anyone wishing to take part.

This is for a fairly simple reason, illustrated in the following two hypothetical participation workflows for user registration and non user registration.

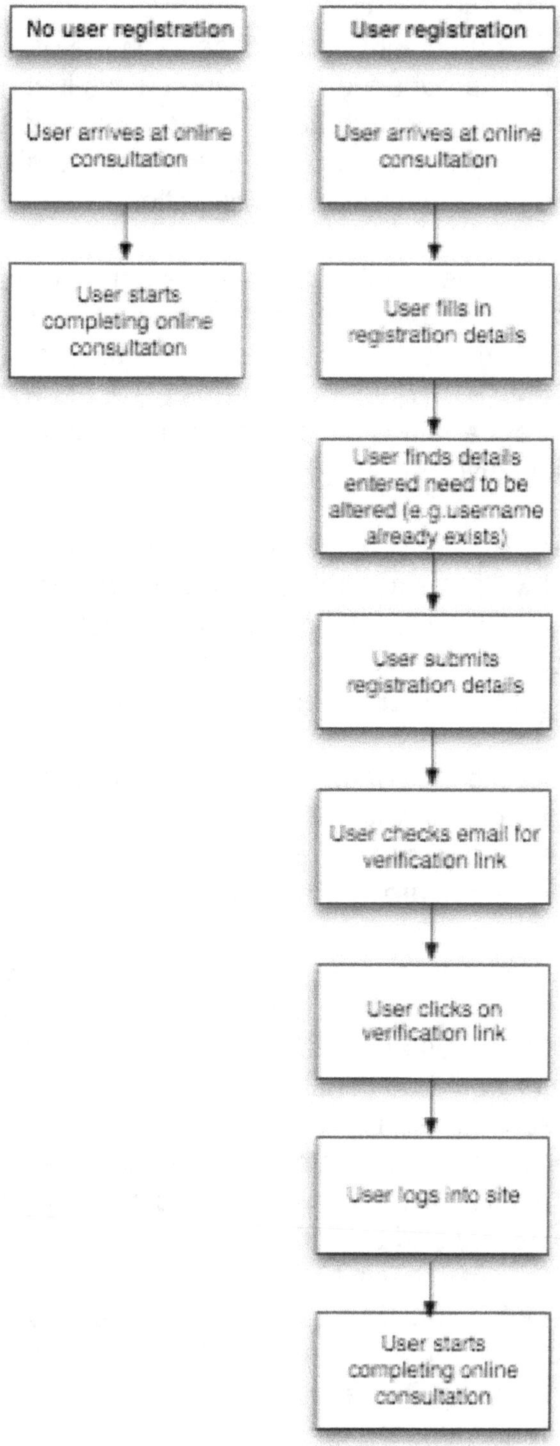

Which of the above two consultation workflows would you rather take part in? Yep, me too.

Whilst the above is a particularly worst case example of a user registration process, it is not uncommon, and shows just how many steps you are making a user go through before they can take part. As each step is an opportunity for the user to become frustrated and give up, user registration provides a real barrier to participation.

This is just to consider the initial act of registration as well. If a user wants to return to the site to take part in another consultation, they have to remember the username and password they initially registered with. If they cannot, then they either have to re-register, or search around for their login details, both again large barriers to participation that will see a majority of users just give up.

Of course, they may have just used the username and password they use for most sites, and will have no problem logging back in to your site. But if they have done this, then your system has just required them to share what should be confidential information in yet another location, reducing the security of their common username and password.

Couldn't you just set the system to issue people with reminders of their login details if they have forgotten them though? Well, you could, but then you've just exposed everyone to a risk, as you've created another channel through which private information can be accessed by others.

Indeed, the worst example I've ever seen of this is a system that sent me my username and password in the same email, both in plain text. If I'd used one of the usernames and passwords I use for important sites (and you'd hope your site would be considered important wouldn't you?) then this would have been exposed to anyone with access to my email, or anyone with access to the server storing my email, or anyone who wants to undertake the relatively simple task of intercepting my email too. Needless to say I never used that site again.

But what of the benefits of user registration? As we've come across above, user registration provides a convenient way for people to return to their response to complete it later on, and for organisations to track who's responding to what and when.

Well, there are arguments made in favour of user registration along these lines, although I do know that sometimes these arguments in support of user registration in consultation software are made because it's the easiest way for the software to be built and sold for profit, rather than because it's of use[37].

As the benefits are largely indisputable, the question though should be 'are there other ways of creating the same benefits without having a user registration system in place?'. Thankfully, there are, and these are explored in the table below.

Benefit of user registration	Alternative way of creating the benefit
Ensuring that demographic information about the user is collected	Creating an engaging and usable demographics page. Making key demographic questions compulsory before submission.
Allowing users to be tracked across multiple consultations	Match users automatically in the administration side of the system, using email address or other rarely varying variable
Allowing users to save their response and return to complete it later	Ask users to enter an email address to which a unique link to their partially completed response will be sent
Preventing multiple responses from the same individual	User registration cannot be used as a reliable method for preventing this. See section on identifying respondents below

---

[37] I've seen quite a few instances over the years of software functionality existing purely because it's the easiest (and thus cheapest) way for the software to be built. Businesses then make a virtue out of necessity, and make up all sorts of reasons why this functionality is important and should be left in the system. Buyer beware.

Benefit of user registration	Alternative way of creating the benefit
Save user from completing demographic information on each consultation	Use user email address to autofill demographic fields. This also allows users to review their demographic information, making and saving amendments over time

5.7 Identifying respondents

I've yet to see a formal consultation that has not asked respondents to enter some information about themselves, from simple location information (where do you live) to full blown demographic information (sexuality, gender, religion, ethnicity, etc.).

The thing is though, I've not seen many formal consultation reports that have made much real use of the demographic data collected. Often when I've asked if all of those demographic questions have to be asked, I've been told they do 'for monitoring purposes'. But when I've asked what those monitoring purposes are, no one really seems to know. Indeed, I was once told I can't understand how local government works if I think asking myriad demographic questions can be avoided. I replied that I did understand how local government works, I just disagreed with the way it does.

So then, what demographic information to collect? Well, the golden rule is

"only collect demographic information that you are actually going to use"

This rule has many benefits. You save respondents from having to type more than they need to. You keep your datasets more simple and clean, and, if you're in the UK, you also comply with Principle 3 of the Data Protection Act 1998[38].

---

[38] See Chapter 10 for more.

It's not worth going through each possible demographic category here, as the principles behind using them are the same as for any consultation, online or offline. However, there are two pieces of identifying information that need to be considered with specific reference to online consultation.

Firstly, the respondent's postcode, zip code or other information that identifies their approximate location. In offline consultation, this can be useful for seeing if people in different areas have different views, and of course this still holds true for online consultation. However, online it also has another benefit, that of checking where in the world the respondent is based.

It is, after all, unlikely that you're consulting on a policy that will have global implications[39]. But being online, your consultation could well receive responses from across the globe. There are three ways to deal with these responses really.

The first is just to ignore them. After all, if the person doesn't live or work in the area affected by the contents of the consultation, then why should they be allowed to have a say on it? It's an appealing view at first, but I actually tend to think these people's views shouldn't be excluded from consideration.

I first arrived at this position whilst working in the consultation team at Bristol City Council in the UK. We had a response to an online consultation from someone who lived in Australia, but included a message with their response, stating that they had recently emigrated there after 20 years of living in Bristol. So, whilst they may not have been affected by the proposals we were consulting on, they had a better grasp of the city and how it worked than many of the people more recently arrived who would have been affected. After a bit of thought, we included their response in the analysis process.

Over time, I came to realise it shouldn't just be people in this sort of situation who should have their views heard from afar. After all, the

---

[39] Apart, maybe, from environmental policies, whose impacts cross borders with ease.

quality of opinions or ideas you have aren't affected by where you happen to be when you have them. Indeed, it may well be that being removed from a situation by distance gives you an insight that those caught up in it may not be able to perceive. If you truly think everyone has an equal right to express their opinion, and I believe you should, then a person's location shouldn't exclude them from taking part.

Of course, that doesn't mean you have to just merge the views of 'outsiders' into your final report without taking any notice of location. Why not use the fact that people can respond from across the world to bring your reports to life, by producing an overall report with separate sections for the views of those within and those without your area? That way you turn a unique oddity of online consultation into a positive benefit for your understanding.

Where to put the demographic questions

So, once you've decided what demographic questions you're going to ask respondents, the question remains whether to place these questions at the start of the consultation or at the end. This isn't just a stylistic thing, as it can have real effects on how a user responds.

If you put the questions at the start, you're more sure that they will be seen and responded to by each respondent. However, respondents only have so much time they're willing to spend filling in a consultation online, and since they're online, they have millions of other sites to act as potential distractions to them taking part as well. So, if you hit people with too many questions not related to the consultation itself at the start, you risk them dropping out before they've even read the first real question.

However, if you put the information at the end, your demographic questions might be the last straw to a bored respondent, causing them to give up and not submit all of the responses they have filled in, leaving you with no data in this instance as well [40].

---

[40] You should never analyse response data that has not been formally submitted, see Chapter 10 for more on this.

On balance, I generally find it preferable to ask the demographic questions at the end of a consultation process, rather than the beginning. As long as the demographic questions you're asking aren't too onerous (and they shouldn't be if you've followed the previous steps correctly), then filling in a little information about themselves provides a nice closure to the process, almost akin to signing a letter before sealing it up and posting it off.

How do you know they are who they say they are?

If you've followed all of the above, then you should be sure of receiving the right amount of information about each respondent who takes part in your consultation. There's only one problem remaining however; how do you know that what they say is true, and that they are who they say they are?

This is a problem that people seem to worry about with specific reference to online consultation oddly enough, when actually it extends to every type of consultation to a greater or lesser degree. After all, it's not exactly impossible to take piles of survey forms left in a local library and while away a long winter's evening by the fireside filling them in under a range of different names and addresses.

All consultation and participation activity relies on trust to some degree; trusting that the respondents are who they say they are. The fact remains though, there is a certain anonymity about the Internet, and one that sometimes causes people to adopt different or multiple identities for certain purposes[41].

So, how do you prevent that? Well, user registration is often seen as a way of doing this, but in truth it provides little protection, as people can just register multiple times with multiple email addresses. Attempts to stop this happening, no matter what form they take, will inevitably put off potential real respondents as well.

For example, if your survey puts what's called a cookie on a computer to identify it as already having submitted a response, that same cookie will stop anyone else responding from that computer, an untenable situation where households share one computer, or for computers in public libraries for instance.

The truth is, there isn't any great way of preventing people responding to online consultations multiple times. There is though a great way of identifying multiple response and filtering them out of your dataset before you run any analysis.

When a computer visits a website, the website nearly always records the IP address[42] of that computer, as well as the date and time of the visit, and the web browser/platform the viewer was using to view the site.

---

[41] I remember sitting with a group of local government elected members once as they were having their authority's new e-petition system demonstrated to them. The session went downhill somewhat when the demonstrator clicked on a petition asking a councillor who was in the room at the time in no uncertain terms to reverse a decision he had made. It went downhill further as the demonstrator scrolled through a publicly visible list of signatories, each with less plausibly genuine names than the last. The session reached rock bottom when the councillor saw that, according to the e-petition website, he had apparently signed the petition opposing his own decision as well.

[42] The numerical address of a computer or network that uses the Internet.

So, if you set your system to record this data for each respondent alongside their response, then you can look for duplicates within it. The easiest way to do this is to export your dataset as a .csv file, and open it in Microsoft Excel. Having done this, select the entire sheet and sort it by the column containing the IP addresses. Add a blank column next to this column, select the first cell in the column and enter into it the formula '=<first cell in IP address column>=<second cell in IP address column>'. So, for example, if my IP addresses were in column A, I would make column B a new blank column and enter into cell B1 the formula '=A1=A2'. Copy and paste this formula down column B, and look for any cell in column B that now displays the word 'Yes'.

In essence, what this formula is doing is comparing the contents of one cell with the contents of the cell below it, and where the contents match, it displays the word 'yes'.

So you can now go and look at the cells next to each 'yes' and see that the IP addresses match.

This isn't yet enough to treat the responses with matching IP addresses as from the same person, as IP addresses are not linked to individual people or even necessarily individual computers. It does flag up that these responses are worthy of further investigation however, so have a look at the browser and platform that were used to submit the responses with the same IP address. If they too match, then have a look at the date and time the response was received.

Generally, if people are looking to manipulate the results of a consultation, they will do so for about half an hour in one go, so you would expect to see the dates and times of submission to be very similar as well. If all of these bits of information match, have a look at the actual responses that have been given. If these too are very similar or matching, you could well be looking at one person submitting multiple responses.

One final check worth doing is looking up who the IP address of the matching responses belongs to. You can often, but not always, look up who uses which IP address by searching for it on websites like https://apps.db.ripe.net/search/query.html. This is an important step, as I found when I ran a controversial consultation about hospital closure.

When looking at the responses, I noticed about 30 of them all came from the same IP address using the same browser and platform, and were all submitted within about half an hour of each other. Suspicious data then, I thought. But when I looked up the IP address, it turned out to be that of a school local to the area of the consultation, so I gave them a call. When I explained why I was calling and they looked into it, they found that a teacher had asked their class to respond to the consultation online during one of their lessons.

So understandably, the responses the children submitted looked to all intents and purposes like they had been submitted by one person using one computer. Once I had confirmation of the class filling in the consultation though, I put the data back into the final analysis.

What you do when you find multiple responses that you suspect to be from the same person is ultimately up to you. You could remove them, although unless you're absolutely certain they're false responses then doing so would be morally and ethically risky. You could identify in your final report that X amount of them were found. You could even separate them out and run an analysis on them alone, before comparing it with the results from the non suspect data, to see if it varies wildly. It's your call, but at least now you can be aware of how to check for multiple responses, in a way that, to some degree, is more reliable than you could achieve with many forms of offline consultation.

Incidentally, if you think this method of looking for multiple responses is somehow an invasion of privacy, be aware that your IP address and other information is likely being logged by every website you visit online. You may feel anonymous when you're browsing, but you're very much not.

5.8 Presentation and branding

Oddly enough, often one of the hardest parts to match up between offline and online consultations is the branding and design.

Obviously, you want your online consultation to match your corporate branding. Not just out of pride, but also because matching branding gives the respondent more confidence that the site they're entering information into is legitimate and run by who it purports to be. However, there is a large amount of the law of diminishing returns[43] operating in this area, so I'd personally say it's rarely worth the cost to get your online consultation looking exactly like your offline one.

However, this is not to say that this part of the work should be quick and simple. I've heard tales of people offering software where you just copy and paste in your stylesheet[44] and the consultation will look just like the rest of your site. To my mind this is as dangerous as it is nonsense. The presentation and visual appearance of your consultation matters, as does its accessibility, so a copy and paste job risks introducing errors, as well as leaving these errors unnoticed.

There are three main elements I would recommend worrying about when it comes to the visual design of your online consultation; the URL, the logo and the colour scheme.

The URL is perhaps the most important, as it is often used online to verify that the site collecting data is genuine. It is a trivial matter these days, pretty much no matter what software you're using, to make the URL for your consultation match that of your organisational website. However, it does involve a level of technical know how that is beyond what is worth explaining here, so ask an IT professional to do this for you. Just be assured that if they say it isn't possible or is too difficult, they're wrong.

As your consultation URL should match your organisational URL, it is worth making sure that the consultation URL is short and memorable as well. You organisation may have a rubbish website that produces URLs that are tens of characters long, but that's no excuse for not making sure your consultation has a bespoke URL that works well, for example

---

[43] http://en.wikipedia.org/wiki/Diminishing_returns
[44] A stylesheet is a file that contains code controlling the visual style and appearance of your site, allowing it to be separated from the content of the site itself and so control the visual aspects of each page on the site through a single file.

www.organisationname.com/consultationname. If people tell you that can't be done either, tell them that you know it can and you need them to do it.

Alternatively of course, if your consultation is of sufficient longevity or importance, it may be worth buying a whole new URL just for the consultation itself. This should only cost a few pounds, and can be well worth it in terms of providing strong identity and reassurance of security through the site.

Second, your logo, or indeed the logos of all of the partners involved in the consultation process if applicable. The role this logo plays in an online consultation is primarily again to provide reassurance that the site collecting the information is run by who it says it is. It doesn't need to be large, and could sit nicely in the top right or top left corners of the screen, appearing on each page. If more than one logo is required, it often looks nicer to lay them out across the bottom of the page, rather than at the top.

Finally, the colour scheme. It's important to match this to your existing site, or organisational colour scheme more generally, but don't spend too much time worrying about this. Picking out two colours, perhaps three, and matching these up throughout the consultation usually just works fine. Be aware though, that some colours and colour combinations don't work very well online, for example there may not be enough contrast between them to be clearly visible for accessibility purposes.

5.9 Publishing the report, publicising the next steps and giving feedback

So then, the consultation's closed, the final report on the findings is written and sent to those who need to decide what to do, and that's that isn't it? Well, whilst you'd be forgiven for thinking this is the case given the way many organisations work these days, it really isn't, and nor should it be.

One of the most important elements of any consultation activity is to feedback to those who took part about what was said, what your organisation thinks about what was said, and what's going to happen now. There are of course lots of different ways of doing this, some of which will fit some situations better than others.

Report publication

One thing every formal consultation should feature is a final report, collating the findings and drawing some conclusions from them, as well as perhaps offering some thoughts on the next steps to be taken. Since this report nearly always gets written, and is almost certainly in an electronic format already, it makes sense to ensure that this is uploaded to the Internet for others to view as standard.

Publishing the final report online not only provides information for those interested and demonstrates openness, it also holds a number of hidden benefits for yourself and your organisation.

First, consider what might happen if your computer crashed or the data on it became corrupted. You might well lose the final reports you have already written. However, if you have published them online, then you can easily retrieve them once your computer issues have been resolved. Following on from this, publishing a final report online means you can easily direct others to the web when they ask for a copy of it, rather than having to dig it out and send it over each time.

The most important benefit of publishing final reports online though was demonstrated to me when I worked as a Scrutiny Officer, working on a Select Committee for Older People.

As part of its work, the committee was obliged to produce a consultation report considering the views of older people themselves on the issues being considered. However, there was no time or budget for running a new consultation. Thankfully, as the authority was scrupulous in ensuring all consultation reports from the last 5 years had been published online, I was able to search through these reports, pulling out relevant sections and collating them together into a new report specific to the requirements of the committee. This saved weeks of additional work and cost, and took all of half a day to complete.

'We asked, you said, we did'

A final report is all well and good for demonstrating the detail of the consultation responses and the next steps to be taken as a result of them. However, a majority of people aren't going to invest the time needed in downloading the full report and reading it to find the information they want. So, as a complementary approach to publishing the final report, why not use a 'we asked, you said, we did' model?

With this model, you summate the contents of the final report even further into three sections; one summating what the consultation asked, one summating what the respondents said and a final one summating what will be done as a result of what the respondents said. For example;

"We asked what you thought of our opening hours at certain locations. You said they were broadly fine, but that late night opening would be useful in some areas. We will now be piloting late night opening in the city centre and other locations to see if it proves useful"

There you go then, a nice and simple summation of a consultation process and its outcomes. It doesn't have to be long, one short sentence per section is fine, as you are trying to engage and inform those with a passing interest or limited time here, leaving the finer details to those who wish to download and read the full report.

Twitter has provided a good guideline here with its 140 character limit on postings. So try to keep each of the three sections to 140 characters, or even try to make all three fit into 140 characters overall. If you find you're writing more than this, you're probably writing too much, and should instead direct people to the final report for that kind of detail.

One thing worth noting however is that not all consultations can or should fit this 'we asked, you said, we did' model. All consultations should allow the first two sections to be filled in. However, demonstrating specific and tangible outcomes of a consultation process can be extremely tricky, and sometimes trying to write about them in a succinct manner can look worse than not writing about them at all.

In my experience, around 20% of an organisation's consultations are fit to have all three pieces of information written about them, with the remaining 80% not doing so. So don't feel bad if you can't provide this sort of information every time, just focus on doing it as often as you can.

Responses publication

Another method people use for feeding back on consultations is to publish the contents of every response received, as long as it has not been marked as confidential.

There are a number of reasons for doing this. First, most clearly of all, it demonstrates openness. Second, it allows individual respondents to recheck their response, to ensure that what was considered for the final report was what they actually submitted, and that it was not altered or corrupted in any way during submission or analysis. Third, at least in theory, it allows anyone so minded to take all of the raw data and attempt to reproduce the final report and its findings themselves. If they cannot, then they might have grounds to challenge the consultation and even force it to be re run.

However, in practice, I remain pretty unconvinced by any of these explanations and the process of publishing all of the responses in this manner. For example, respondents generally contact the consulting organisation itself if they want a copy of their final response, and the likelihood of anyone attempting to rerun the entire analysis and recreate the final report themselves seems slim in the extreme.

Certainly this approach demonstrates openness, but given the risk of publishing confidential data by accident, especially in consultations that receive a large number of responses, I personally tend towards avoiding recommending this method of feedback wherever possible.

Respondent data interrogation

There is though a method of providing the above results publication approach that works much better, although it is sadly yet to receive the attention that it deserves, at least in the UK.

This method involves presenting all of the consultation response data in an aggregated form through some manner of analysis interface. In essence, it allows users to interrogate the data received in exactly the same way as the consulting organisation, producing tables, charts and cross-tabulated comparisons of the data in as many ways as possible.

As mentioned though, not enough work has been done in this area to my mind, and it remains a largely unwritten field waiting for someone to explore. So here are just some ways in which it has been explored already, which, I hope, will give you inspiration to push the boundaries of this area yourself.

Simple data interrogation tools

I've not yet seen an online example of this, but I have seen an offline example. In this example, an Excel spreadsheet was used, with one sheet within it containing the raw data, and another containing a series of dropdown options from which the user could select. For example, they could select a question asking about satisfaction and a question asking about the respondent's gender. Once these has been selected, a section of the spreadsheet automatically presented a table of data on the same page, allowing the user to see at a glance the satisfaction levels of respondents by gender, and notice any differences in satisfaction between the genders.

It always surprises me that this approach has not been tried out more regularly online, as such simple data interrogation tools are readily available to administrators within many consultation software packages, and making them available to the public as well should be a relatively simple task.

Visual data interrogation tools

One more interesting method of allowing respondents and interested parties to interrogate and report on the data received in a consultation lies in doing so visually. With this method, rather than being presented with tables of data, the interested party is presented with the information in a visual format, for example a chart or a graph.

It may sound odd, but there are believed to be certain sorts of people who understand information more easily in a visual format than in a written or numerical format. So always be sure to include data in visual formats when appropriate. This need not be complicated; bar or pie charts alongside tables of data, all appropriately labeled, can be all that is needed to allow people to understand information at a glance.

There are other sorts of information that lend themselves more obviously to being represented in visual formats. For example, if you collect postcode or zip-code information from respondents, then you can create a map of where your responses came from quickly and easily using a free tool such as Google Maps[45]. With slightly more sophisticated (and sometimes expensive) software, you can map responses to certain questions by location, for example to gain an understanding of people's satisfaction with a service based on where they live. In effect, you are producing a visual form of a cross-tabulated table.

There are of course many other forms of visualising data, plenty of which I suspect are yet to be discovered. A few years ago I worked on a pilot of visual data interrogation in collaboration with a number of UK local authorities, which produced some interesting results. The pilot was called Picture Poll[46] and featured a series of 'quick poll' style consultations, each allowing the respondent to give a response to two different variables using a sliding scale. Once they had given these responses, their response was presented to them on a 'Cartesian plane' or a graph with four sections.

---

[45] http://maps.google.co.uk/

[46] See www.picturepoll.org

However, not only was their response presented, but so were the responses of all of the other respondents so far. In this way, the user could see where they sat in comparison with other respondents, as well as clicking around the responses to read any comments other users may have submitted on the topic in hand. The image below gives an example of one of these sorts of polls.

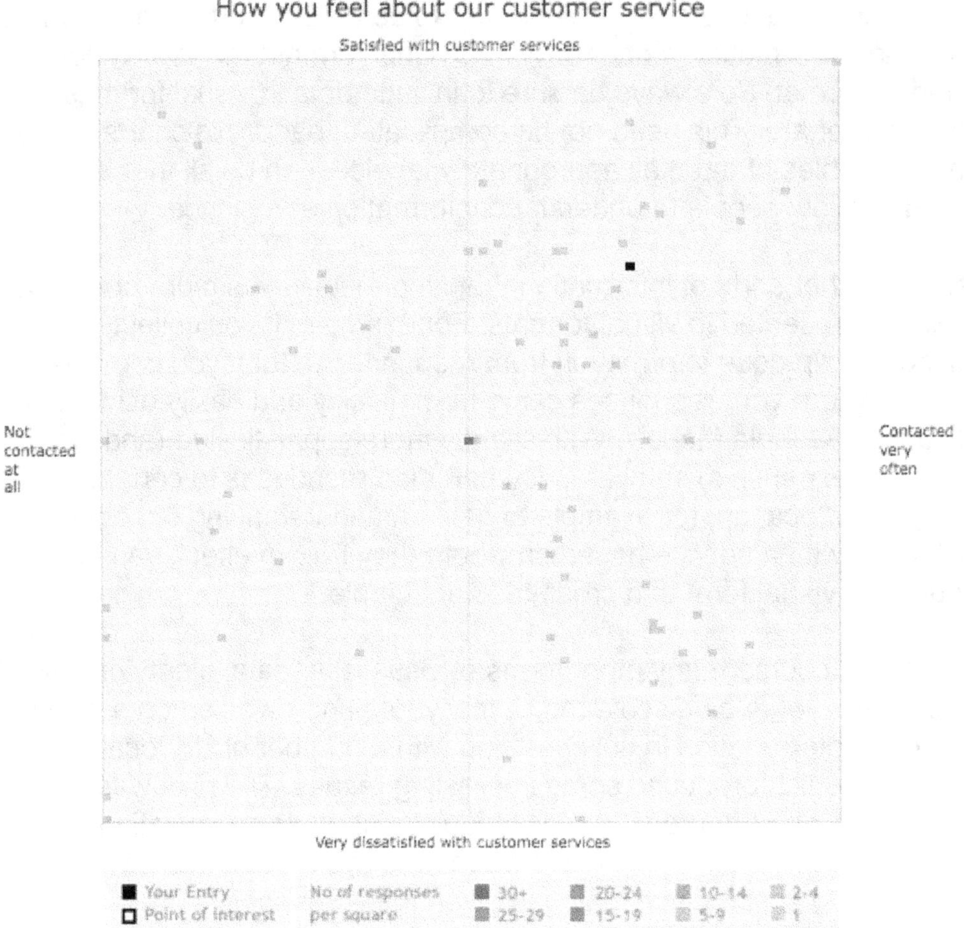

The pilot went well, and it produced some interesting consultation responses to my mind, but was never really carried forward after that, perhaps having come to life at a time in which online consultation work was little prioritised or recognised.

In a similar vein, I once proposed to pilot a system that plotted more questions against each other and presented the user's response in the form of a 'spider's web' graph, before overlaying it with other types of response, perhaps averages of the responses from different types of respondent.

The pilot never received funding in the end, so it remains just an idea. However, if anyone is interested in trying it out, get in touch and I'll let you have the rest of the information required for it to work.

5.10 Notifying interested parties

Finally then, once you've decided how you're going to publish the feedback on the consultation you have run, you have to let people know about it.

Of course, just through the act of publishing the information it is likely people will find it. However, it is good practice to inform those who may be interested as well. Methods of promoting information online are covered elsewhere in Chapters 6 and 9.

However, it is worth noting that for promoting feedback on formal consultations, the two methods I have found to be most effective to date are email and RSS functionalities, with all other methods lacking impact, almost to the point of not being worth attempting.

Chapter 6. Unstructured online consultation

In this chapter, we'll look at unstructured online consultation. This isn't the same sort of well-defined area as structured or formal consultation, covered in the previous chapter, but when carried out, it can be even more effective and useful.

The primary differentiation between structured and unstructured online consultation lies in the tasks the respondent can perform. With structured consultation, the respondent has to work through a structure set by the consulting organisation, for example reading pieces of text and commenting on them, or even just clicking buttons to indicate agreement or otherwise. In unstructured consultation, there are fewer, if any, structures for the respondent to work through, leaving them more free, both to give their response and potentially to interact with other respondents as they do so.

To give an example of this, it is worth looking at how it might be used in practice. If an organisation were consulting on a policy document online, that consultation would in all probability be a structured consultation. The consulting organisation wants respondents to read through the policy document itself, add their comments at predefined points and answer pre-written demographic questions about themselves. Thus in this consultation there are three points of structure being provided by the organisation for the respondent.

However, if the organisation had wanted to consult on the initial writing of that policy document as well, then it might have used an unstructured format, allowing respondents to suggest ideas for inclusion, perhaps letting them edit and refine ideas submitted by others, before voting on the best ideas submitted. In this way, you allow the users to shape the very structure of the final result, rather than just shape the content that goes into the policy document's structure.

Let us not forget though, that time itself is a form of structure, and so another defining characteristic of unstructured consultation can be the lack of time limit given to an unstructured online consultation process. In this way, users can engage in constant interaction with any content generated on an ongoing basis.

So what might be real life examples of this form of unstructured consultation? Well, very often unstructured consultation comes in the form of ideas generation, asking respondents to submit ideas that might be included into a later and more formal process. Some manner of discussion mechanism might be included, to allow respondents to discuss ideas with each other in an unstructured way before arriving at conclusions. As touched upon above, a voting mechanism might also be included alongside any content generated by respondents, although respondents would not necessarily be required to vote for any or all of the content if they did not wish to.

So then, whilst it might seem easier to run a less structured process, given there are fewer specific requirements to meet for legal purposes or to match up with offline activities, running an unstructured consultation well can be a difficult task. To pick out some of the pitfalls and understand the aims more clearly, let's look at a few different forms of unstructured online consultation.

6.1 An ideas generation process

Of all the areas of digital engagement projects I've worked on, and of all of the online consultation and engagement projects I've run, it's unstructured ideas generation projects that I've found to be both the most enjoyable and the most rewarding. It's enjoyable because there's flexibility for everyone involved to come up with something interesting, and it's rewarding because it's often in these processes that you can see actual change take place as a result of people's input.

With an ideas generation process, you set people a broad proposition to consider, and let them suggest ideas around it. Generally, you add another layer of ideas generation to that, in as much as you allow others to read the ideas submitted and either suggest their own ideas inspired by them, or suggest ideas to refine the original idea some more.

So then, there are two main elements to an ideas generation process, one being the proposition for people to consider, and the other being the method in which the ideas can be suggested.

Of all of these, the proposition is far and away the most crucial, so let's consider that first.

6.2 Choosing your proposition

First of all, it's worth noting that whilst I use the term 'proposition' here for the sake of simplicity, what you suggest to people needn't be a proposition at all, but could be a question or any other form of wording. The key facets to it are that it has to be;

- **Simple**

  The more people that can understand your proposition, the more will take part and so the more ideas and refinements you will receive to choose from.

- **Specific**

  If your topic is too broad, people will either not be inspired to take part, or will take part in so many different ways that you get little of use out of the process for yourself.

- **Short**

  The more you write about your topic, the more you constrain people to work within your parameters rather than creating their own.

So, to give some examples, "Tell us what you think we should do as an organisation in the future" is probably too broad a proposition to be of use. Conversely, "Tell us what you think we should do with regards to sub section B of work stream Z over the next three months" is almost certainly too specific to see many people take part, as well as not being particularly simple.

However, a proposition such as "How do you think we could save money over the next year?" is about right. It's simple, it's specific, given it's about a specific year, and it's nice and short too.

Getting the proposition right for an ideas generation process is an art in and of itself, and often one that benefits from bringing in experience to help with its creation.

6.3 Ideas suggestion methods

So then, you've got the proposition sorted; now how do you want people to be able to interact with it? Generally there are four main elements to this, each with their own merits.

Ideas suggestion

First of all, you need people to be able to suggest an idea. This is best done using a free text question, allowing the respondent to enter their idea and submit it. So, at its most simple, this part of the process could look like this.

That said, you could if you wished provide more of a structure, to allow different respondents to shape their ideas consistently with each other. So you could have an ideas submission element that looks like this

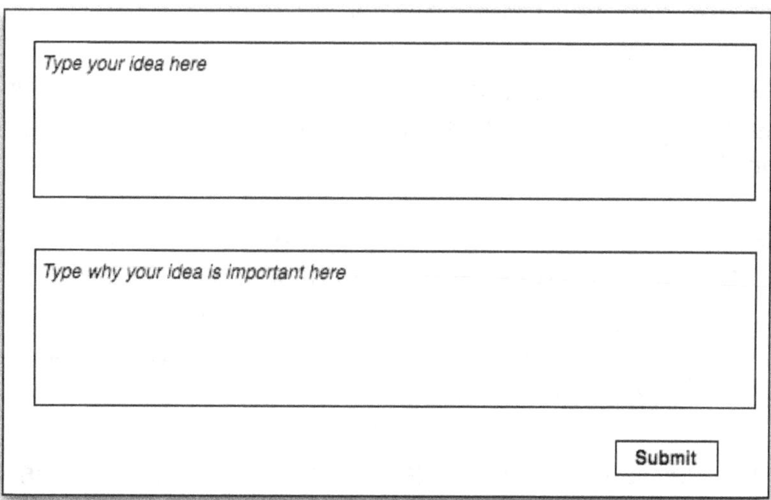

6.4 Ideas publication

Once a user has submitted their idea, you then want it to appear on your site for others to read and comment on or rate. The thing is, do you trust a whole load of anonymous users to post content onto your site for others to see? Probably not. So this is where the idea of content moderation comes into play.

We'll look more at content moderation in Chapter 7 of this book, but for an ideas generation process you only really need to have the following in place;

- A moderation policy, which should state clearly what sort of content is allowed to be published on the site, and what sort of content is not. As standard, you should not allow content to be published that is offensive, legally risky (e.g. libelous) or that personally identifies an individual or group of individuals. There's a generic moderation policy you can modify for your own use in the appendices to this book.

- An ability to set each idea submitted as live on the site or hidden from view. You should never delete a comment altogether, or even be able to do so, in case it is needed for legal purposes.

- The time and inclination to read each idea and check that it complies with the moderation policy.

We'll cover these sorts of points some more later in the book, but it is worth considering here the difference between pre-moderation and post-moderation too.

In pre-moderation, each idea submitted to the site is hidden from public view until it is approved and published by a site moderator or administrator. Post-moderation therefore is the opposite of this, with each idea appearing in public view automatically, and only being removed if a moderator or administrator removes it.

Instinctively, every organisation opts for pre-moderation of ideas. After all, letting people post anything they want on your website seems risky at the very least. However, legally speaking, at least in the UK, post-moderation is far less risky an approach than pre-moderation.

When you pre-moderate each idea that appears on the site, you legally become the publisher of that idea. If an idea you publish is then challenged legally, you are the one responsible for its publication and thus are the one who is legally liable for any harm it may cause.

However, if you post-moderate, then the legal publisher remains the person who submitted the idea, and as long as you can demonstrate best efforts in making sure the site remains free of legally liable content, then the liability remains with the person submitting the idea, not yourself.

There is also a more prosaic motive for preferring post-moderation to pre-moderation, in that if an idea is pre-moderated, the person submitting it has to wait until it is approved before they see it on the site. Often, users think this means that the idea has not been successfully submitted, and so submit it again and again, leading to a moderation headache working out which ideas to approve and which ideas to leave unapproved as duplicates.

6.5 Ideas discussion

Once an individual has submitted an idea, it can be extremely useful to allow others to comment on that idea and discuss it with one another. It may be that their comment just adds weight and support to the idea already submitted, or it may be that they can see a flaw in the original idea and wish to submit an amendment to it.

Allowing discussion of an idea is relatively simple, requiring little more than a free text box and a submit button. The discussion may also flow more easily if the participants have some sort of consistent identity within the site, allowing them to identify one another during the debate.

6.6 Methods for rating ideas

The rating of ideas, allowing users to indicate support for their most favoured ideas, can be a really useful tool when it comes to the final analysis of the ideas submitted. For not only do you receive qualitative data in the form of the ideas themselves, you also receive quantitative data in the form of ratings.

However, there are a number of different ways of allowing users to rate ideas submitted, each with their own benefits and drawbacks.

- **Simple 'support' rating**

  This rating is the most simple of all the methods of rating ideas, allowing users to click a button next to the ideas they support to indicate this fact. However, it only provides an account of how far ideas are supported, and allows no measure to be taken of how many people oppose the idea.

  This rating method is of little use for research purposes, but is of use for more general engagement purposes, specifically during unstructured discussion. As users are only allowed to support something, you remove the potential offense that may be caused by an idea being unsupported, and the additional moderation work that inevitably goes with it.

The most famous example of this principle at the moment is Facebook, where users can click to indicate that they 'like' content posted by someone else, but have no ability to click to 'dislike' it.

- **Simple 'support/oppose' rating**

This rating is similar to the one above, but gives participants the ability to click a button to either support or oppose each idea submitted just once, leaving you with an indication of the level of support for each idea, although bringing with it the possibility of offense mentioned above.

The problem with this rating method is that it can mask vast differences in feeling between ideas if all that is examined is the final 'score'. For example, two ideas, one with one vote in support and another with 1000 votes in support and 999 votes against, will both have a positive support rating of one, masking the differing strengths of feeling between the two.

- **Finer grained support rating**

An alternative method is to allow participants to select from a rating of one to five for each idea, with, say, five being the most support and one being the least. The problems with this approach are that users can only vote in support of an idea, note vote to oppose it. In addition, an idea with one rating of five will, at first glance, look to have been more supported than an idea with 100 ratings of five and one rating of four.

- **Likert scale rating**

  By working through the above examples, we come back to one of
  the most common question types in market research, the Likert
  Scale[47]. This system presents five options, two in support, two in
  opposition and one lying neutrally in the middle, typically in the
  following order

  Strongly agree
  Agree
  Neither agree nor disagree
  Disagree
  Strongly disagree

  By using this scale for a rating system, the user is able to indicate
  their feeling about an idea more accurately, and on the analysis
  side, you can calculate top-line figures such as net support
  (percentage support minus percentage opposition). Given they can
  be presented as either positive or negative values, these top-line
  figures can give you an excellent and accurate means of ranking
  ideas in terms of their popular support or otherwise.

Ideas tagging and tag clouds

If your ideas site is a success, you will pretty quickly run into a problem.
For a user visiting the site will want to look at the ideas most of interest to
themselves, but will find it increasingly difficult to find them as the site fills
up with content. After all, there are only so many ideas you can display on
a page, and only so many ideas a user can read before getting bored and
moving on.

One simple solution to this is to summate the contents of each idea in the
form of a few tags. Tags are single words or short groups of words that
highlight the basic contents of the idea, the key points of what it is about.

For example, consider the following idea;

------

[47] See http://en.wikipedia.org/wiki/Likert_scale for more.

"I think we could save a lot of money by sending our monthly newsletter to all of our members by email, instead of posting it to them"

So, what tags would you use to describe that idea in a way that others could find it more easily? Personally, I'd go for;

"Saving money", "Communications", "Membership" and "Internet"

You can also tag content in other ways, for example by the quality of the idea rather than its content. Since the above idea is something that could be implemented relatively quickly, it might be interesting to tag the idea with "Quick win" as well. This way, you create an easy method of searching for those ideas you can act on most quickly in order to demonstrate that the ideas are being listened to.

But once you've got these ideas tagged up, how should the tags be used? Well, in the past, one way might have been to have the tags searched by a search engine. However, search engines are now sufficiently powerful as standard that you can have them search the contents of a whole site easlly, rather than just searching through tags. Instead, the best way to use tags is with what's called a tag cloud.

A tag cloud is a collection of words that have been used as tags, all appearing within one small space. Crucially, the words in the cloud vary in size, dependent on how many times they have been used as a tag, with the largest ones being the most used. When a user clicks on one of the words in the tag cloud, they are taken to a page that displays only those ideas that have been given that word as a tag. So, for example, if lots of ideas had been tagged with the words 'money saving', if I clicked on those words in the tag cloud, I would be taken to a page that displayed all of those ideas.

So tagging and tag clouds really can be a useful way to allow users to find content in the site that is of greatest interest to them quickly and simply. But the one issue we haven't looked at yet is who does the tagging?

Now, from a software perspective, it is sometimes easiest to allow only administrators to do things like tagging, as the fewer people you have able to edit data on a site, the more secure it generally is. However, if we only allowed administrators to tag ideas, then not only would they have a lot more work to do, but we would be forgetting the point of this sort of consultation. After all, it's an unstructured consultation, so why not let the users themselves create the structure surrounding their ideas by tagging them themselves?

This is exactly what we did on two large projects I worked on with the UK Government called 'Your Freedom' and 'Spending Challenge'. Both projects asked people to submit ideas, the former asking for ideas on which laws could be abolished, and the latter asking for ideas on how the government could save money.

In these projects, anyone who went through a simple registration process was able to tag ideas, either tagging their own idea when they first wrote it, or tagging other people's ideas once they had read them. This tagging process led to some really interesting results, people tagging ideas not just in terms of their content, but also in terms of what they thought of them. For example, there was some pretty vehement strength of feeling against some of the ideas suggested, so people started tagging them with the word 'oppose'. This then allowed others to find all of these controversial ideas, and then use the rating system to vote them down.

6.7 Flagging up objectionable content

As mentioned above, it is generally preferable to use a system of post-moderation rather than pre-moderation in any site where users can submit content for publication. However, as this is an unstructured consultation, why not let the users themselves act as moderators for the content that has been submitted?

To do this, all that is required is a simple button on each published idea that, when clicked, alerts a site administrator or moderator to look at that idea, usually both by email and by visual alert when they log into the site. This way, users can flag up ideas that might break the site's terms and conditions, allowing them to be reviewed and removed from view if necessary.

There is only one problem I've come across with this relatively simple flagging process, and that's what words to use on the button which users click to flag an idea. They have to be short and snappy after all, but also have to signify to the reporter that the button is only to be clicked if the idea breaks the site's terms and conditions. Otherwise, you can end up with users alerting moderators about ideas they themselves find objectionable, rather than just those ideas that should be removed from view.

eBay goes with the words 'Report item' for this purpose; some discussion forums go with just 'Report'. I quite like 'Alert a moderator' as a form of wording myself, as it describes most clearly what will happen if the button is pressed. Ultimately though, there is more testing and research needed in this somewhat niche area to find the best form of words to use.

Other forms of unstructured consultation

So then, if we've looked at ideas generation, then we've pretty much covered everything haven't we? After all, all unstructured consultation can involve ideas generation can't it? If it doesn't, then it's not a massively different process from the one outlined above. Well, that may very well be true, and at the end of the day there's only so much you can say about unstructured consultation, because it's, well, unstructured.

But that said, there is another form of unstructured consultation, from the respondent perspective at least, even if it does contain elements of structure here and there as well, which is known as e-petitioning.

6.8 e-Petitions

e-Petitions are an electronic form of an age old process, that of getting people to add their signature to a statement or request for action, the hope being that the more signatures are gathered, the more likely this strength of feeling is to lead to action on the part of the organisation or individual being petitioned. Being an online mechanism, a signature as such is not required for an e-petition, and more often people are asked to provide a name and email address. However, the act of adding your name to an e-petition is still referred to as 'signing' it, just as it is with its offline counterpart.

First of all, let me be up front about my opinions in this area. Over the last 8 years or so, I've ranged from merely annoyed by to actively hostile towards e-petitioning. There have been a few different reasons for this.

The first is the slightly cynical practices e-petitioning can bring about, on both the sides of those petitioning and those being petitioned. I first saw e-petitioning up close when I was a project manager on the ODPM sponsored National Project for Local e-Democracy, working at Bristol City Council. As part of the council's work on this project, it piloted an e-petitioning system.

All well and good, but what shocked me was that the person who wrote the original e-petition got given the email addresses[48] of those who signed it once it had closed, in order to keep the signatories up to date with how things progress from there. The site of course got the signatories' permission to do this, as part of the terms and conditions of signing the petition.

This may all sound perfectly sensible, but as a councillor at Bristol pointed out to me, they could create petitions on their election campaign issues, wait for people to sign them, then add all of those email addresses to their election mailing lists. Thus what happened to the petition once it had closed, which is what mattered to the signatories, became of lesser importance to the person who originally wrote it, leaving them little incentive to actually make sure what was in the petition was one day implemented.

There is another form of cynicism that can arise through e-petitions, that of submitting petitions knowing full well that the organisation being petitioned cannot comply with its requests, but actively promoting the petition in order to make the organisation or those running it look bad. Again, this is a common tactic in UK local politics using paper petitions and campaigns, but e-petitioning just makes this unconstructive and petty sort of politics quicker, cheaper and simpler than it has ever been.

---

[48] You needed to provide an email address in order to sign the petition.

That is not to say petitions in and of themselves are a bad thing, or are always used for cynical and ineffectual purposes. Just look at the Road Pricing Petition that appeared on the 10 Downing Street website back in February 2007. It gathered 1.8 million signatures and, despite protestations to the contrary, led to alterations in government policy where none had previously been expected[49].

Finally, the thing that really drove me mad was that the government created a bizarre software market around e-petitioning, by making it compulsory for every UK local authority to have an e-petitioning system as part of their website by April 2010.

The thing was, an e-petition system is hardly the most difficult piece of software to build. In fact, out of all of the different types of digital engagement software available, e-petitioning may well be the simplest. Second though, at least one e-petitioning system had been developed and made available to all to use for free as open source software[50]. There was thus no need to have local authorities each spend money on an e-petition system, and the government could have promoted this fact nice and clearly to every local authority, generating savings in the hundreds of thousands of pounds.

Instead, a bizarre range of often hastily cobbled together systems were sold by different suppliers to their existing clients. Even if the same amount of money had been spent by UK local authorities overall, imagine how much that money could have paid to develop if pooled collectively[51].

Quite apart from the waste of money this government law brought about, it also introduced another problem, and one that threatened digital engagement as a whole. The law said that all UK local authorities had to have an e-petitioning system live online. It didn't say they had to have any process in place for doing anything with those petitions when they were submitted.

---

[49] See http://news.bbc.co.uk/1/hi/uk/6349027.stm for more.

[50] See https://secure.mysociety.org/cvstrac/dir?d=mysociety/pet for more.

[51] If you can't imagine, let me imagine for you. It would probably be the most usable, secure and polished piece of e-participation software the world has yet seen.

It may seem crazy, but there certainly were, and may still well be, local authorities who, when a petition closes, just send the signatories an automatically generated thank you email, and perhaps forward the petition to the relevant elected member to do with as they see fit. No form of accountability, no process to run the petition through, no requirement to do anything at all once the petition had closed.

To be fair, this fact has been noticed by more than one person now, and it's one of the reasons why the UK government's move into e-petitioning has incorporated a commitment to hold a parliamentary debate on any petition reaching over 100,000 signatures. However, even this seemed to have run into problems at the start, as whilst this commitment was made, no actual process seemed to be put in place to ensure that it was honoured in reality[52].

But how then is e-partitioning a form of unstructured consultation? Well, whilst there may sometimes be an organisational process involved in considering it, the acts of creating a petition, deciding on its content and promoting it to others are all the responsibility of participants themselves, rather than the organisation doing so.

I would also argue that e-petitioning is a form of consultation, as each e-petition is essentially a one question online survey, asking the participant if they agree with the contents of the petition and/or want to see them happen. Of course, there's only one answer from which the participant can select, that of 'yes' by adding their signature.

This though is another drawback of e-petitioning, that whilst you can see how many people are in favour of a proposition, you can't see how many are against it. Now, the same could be said of parliamentary democracy as a whole of course, which asks you to vote for one person or shut up. However, at least with parliamentary democracy, whilst the only answer you can ever give is 'yes', you do get a range of questions in the form of different candidates to say yes to.

---

[52] See http://order-order.com/2011/09/07/backbench-business-committee-bites-back/

So there is a real risk then that e-petitioning becomes the sort of democracy that Plato feared, the one that forms the last step on the way to tyranny[53].

Can you tell I'm not a fan of e-petitioning yet?

There is one good purpose behind e-petitioning though, one that is shared by an ideas generation process, but is made simpler through the simplicity of the e-petitioning process. That is the way in which it can act as a safety valve or early warning system for an organisation, to let it know that there are people annoyed about a certain issue, and just how many people are prepared to visit a website and click a few buttons to say so. If the number is great, it would be a foolish organisation that carried on regardless without looking into it further.

Personally, I think an interesting addition or adaptation of an e-petitioning process would be to base it around the idea of research. After all, how many ideas get submitted as part of petitions that are fully researched, costed and impact assessed? Few to none I'd wager. Once received, how many petitions have the recipient thinking "Ooh, I don't know about that, sounds like it might be tricky, can't see it working myself, let's forget that was mentioned'? I suspect a fair few.

So, what if a petitioning system was slightly rebranded as a 'feasibility study' tool, where the public could request the target organisation to conduct and publish a feasibility study on any issues they raise? Like with the UK parliament's system, you could implement a signatures threshold as well, with only those feasibility petitions that have received sufficient signatures having the study carried out.

The outcomes from this tool could also then feed into other areas of consultation and research, letting the participants set the research agenda, allowing them to tell the organisation what matters to them and see action taken upon it.

---

[53] See http://en.wikipedia.org/wiki/The_Republic_(Plato)#The_dialectical_forms_of_government

Chapter 7. Online engagement

Let's start this chapter by defining some terms, as more than any other type of activity online, 'engagement' is possibly the most vaguely defined. Indeed, you sometimes see it used when people just don't know what other word to use to mean 'let's do something online'.

In this book, when I talk about online engagement, I'm referring to anything that isn't a structured or unstructured consultation. This might seem like a bit of a wooly definition, defining it by what it is not, rather than by what it is, but there's no point in trying to define a term to mean something other than how it is commonly used. The term 'online engagement' really can mean a whole range of things.

Here's how I see its relationship with structured and unstructured online consultation presented for you visual types.

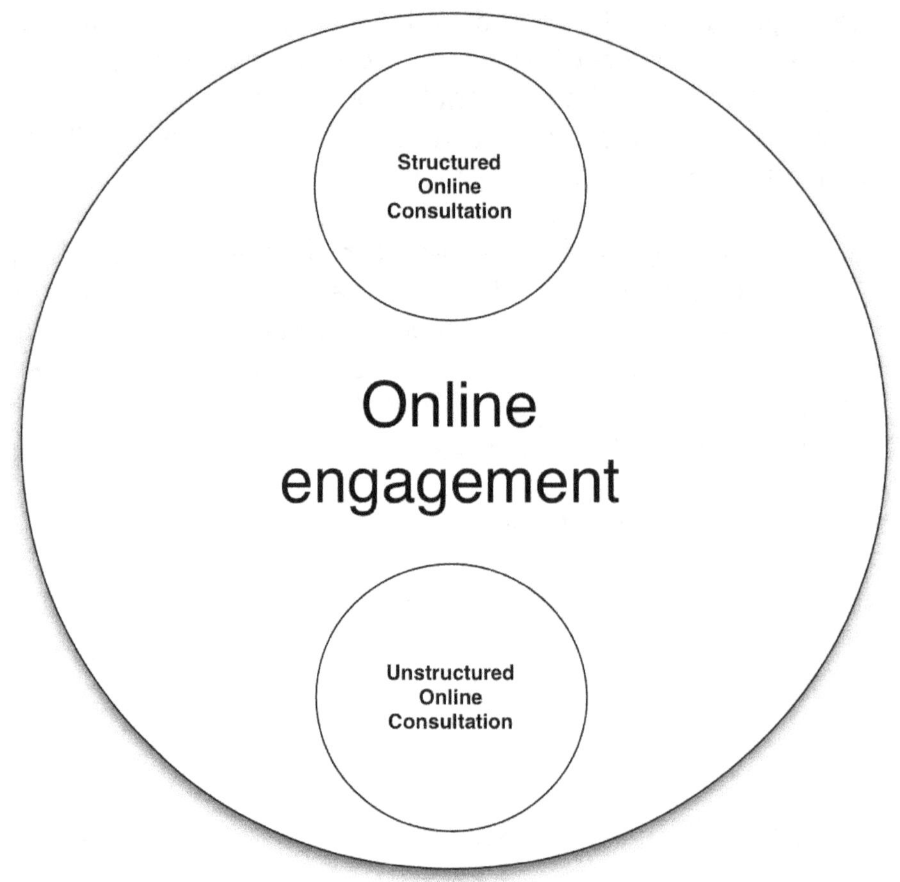

So, as we can see, structured and unstructured online consultations are both forms of online engagement, but the latter term encompasses so much more as well.

Sometimes, an online engagement project can be relatively narrow in scope or end goal, for example a marketing campaign to get people to visit a certain website, or take part in a defined process. It can also be short lived, although you can of course have multiple simultaneous engagement campaigns running at the same time, or run one after the other for as long as you want.

However, you could also theoretically have an online engagement process that runs indefinitely, and is very broad in scope. For example, running a Twitter account for an organisation to communicate with anyone interested in their work.

In a way, thinking of online engagement in this way, as well as matching the reality of how the words are currently used, also matches how the word engagement itself is more generally understood. After all, to say you 'engage someone in conversation' is to say nothing about how that conversation lasts. Engagement doesn't have to mean a two way conversation either, as you could listen to a very engaging presentation given by someone to a group, or watch a very engaging video on YouTube.

So, it's fair to say the term 'online engagement' is a very loose one, and this is fitting really, as what happens in online engagement activities can be very loose too, in as much as organisations are very often not in control of what takes place. Indeed, and I suspect this is why some public sector organisations struggle with it, the less control you try to have, the more you are likely to be successful.

This is because this lessening of control, whilst a higher risk perhaps, carries with it much greater rewards for less work. If you've ever heard of people wanting their work to 'go viral', then they're seeking to have as little control as possible over where their content goes and who interacts with it, whilst reaping the rewards of huge amounts of global attention, often within just a few hours.

If you think about it, the more you attempt to control every part of an online project, the more work you are creating for yourself to do. If you try to control where your content goes online, then you're doing work that could easily be done for you by the people you're trying to engage. Work that, if it's done by others, also appears all the more authentic and thus has all the greater impact.

The more you try to control what content people can or cannot post on your website, the more people you will put off engaging with you and the less sincere your engagement project will appear. Finally, the more work you try to do in an online engagement project, the less likely you are to do it all, or do any of it to the highest standard.

So then, if less is generally more, how do you go about running an online engagement activity?

7.1 5 top tips for online engagement

Before we consider some of the specific elements of online engagement, there are five key points which you should bear in mind throughout every aspect of your work. Some of them sound like truisms, and to a degree they are, but they are the truisms worth remembering throughout everything you do online.

1. The more others promote your content for you, the more trustworthy your content will appear to be.

2. The more open you are with others, the more people will be open towards you.

3. The more real you are online, the more engaging you appear.

4. The less you give yourself to do, the less you are likely to make mistakes.

5. The more interesting you are, the more people will find you interesting.

Content

Having looked at what online engagement is and some of the basic principles behind it, let's consider some of its elements in more detail, starting with content.

Almost more than any other type of work, online engagement is reliant on good content, be it words, pictures, sounds, videos, games or anything else that can appear online.

Sometimes, all an online engagement exercise has is content. Someone may see something funny online, and so send it to their friends or post it on forums, causing more people to become engaged with the content. Never underestimate the power of something as simple as this example. Done well, simple but effective content can deliver massive returns.

Now, nine times out of 10 when this sort of thing happens, it wouldn't be seen as 'online engagement' as such, as no-one intended it to be, it just happened. However, we're looking at principles in this book, rather than learning what just happens to happen today. Purely in principle, a piece of content that accidentally becomes popular online is just as much 'online engagement' as a campaign funded and run by an organisation.

So, what is good content? Well, if I or anyone could sum that up in one sentence, they'd rule the Internet. Asking what good content online is, is like asking what good music is. Everyone's going to have a different view, and very few people are going to be able to create it. Like music though, you can pull out a few general rules, and in terms of finding it in the first place, here a few clues to the form good content takes.

- **It's clear**

  Not just clearly written in plain English, but clear to understand in and of itself.

- **It has an overarching theme or narrative**[54]

  Good content tells a story that people can understand, and even relate to themselves.

- **It's interesting**

  Or at least, if it can't be interesting overall, certain parts of it are interesting[55].

- **It's relevant**

  Content may only be relevant to a few people of course, but the more people to whom it is relevant, the more people will take the time to engage with it.

- **It has an end goal or action for the user to take**

  Now, strictly speaking this last point isn't necessary, but if you're taking the time to engage with someone, you may as well use the opportunity to get them to engage with you a little more, even if it's just giving you their email address so you can send them information more frequently and directly. Alternatively, when you're running a project that involves participation, this end goal can take on huge importance, and represent things like people submitting responses or publishing regular content to your site.

---

[54] Again, just as you might when hosting a party funnily enough, although you don't tend to dress up to use the Internet.

55 For example, consulting on how a local authority spends its budget overall is generally pretty dull, asking whether to save money by closing local schools will be far more engaging.

Beyond principles such as these, there are a few different ways of defining, segmenting or chopping up the content in order to understand better the role it needs to play. The one I usually work with is whether the content is coming from the perspective of an individual or from the perspective of an organisation.

7.2 Personal vs organisation based content

One way of defining and segmenting content is between personal content and 'organisational' or non-personal content. Lots of people have a Facebook profile these days, but when they post things through it for others to see, do they only post personal content, or do they post content to do with their business or professional activities as well?

Often, the safest approach is to keep the two entirely separate. For example, some people have a Facebook profile where they share content about their personal lives, and a LinkedIn profile for their business 'life', in effect treating the person as an organisation or business. Nearly every time an organisation develops a presence online, especially in the world of social media, the content is kept entirely separate from the personal lives of those administering it.

Personally, I think this is a shame, and various signs point to this being true. Whilst you're less likely to post something damaging to your organisational reputation if you separate the two, the additional credibility and respect you gain for being open in this way is both considerable and important.

Look for example at some famous people using Twitter, indeed people whose fame is now in part synonymous with Twitter. Former British Prime Minister's wife Sarah Brown has one million individuals following her on Twitter[56,] and has achieved this following by being herself on there, not sticking to just a work related theme, and by replying in a personal way to

---

[56] see http://twitter.com/#!/sarahbrownuk . Also note this is not the same as 1 million people reading each message she posts. She could well be hidden from display by a number of people, and the number is specifically about the number of Twitter accounts following her, many of which may be inactive or rarely checked.

messages sent to her. Former spin doctor Alistair Campbell mixes his personal and work lives on Twitter excellently as well[57].

It may seem risky to take this approach, but it's actually quite easy, as long as you realise that there are some personal things that should probably not be posted online anywhere anyway, and that it's not the end of the world if someone happens to criticise you. After all, the aphorism that 'the only thing worse than being talked about is not being talked about' is very true indeed when it comes to getting people to notice you online.

Tools for online engagement

I promised myself when I started this book that I wouldn't write about specifics tools or platforms and how to use them. Too many people nowadays are getting trained in how to use specific tools like Twitter or Facebook, and forgetting that these tools can change over time, rendering the training obsolete. Instead, I want you to learn the principles behind how to use these tools, so you can easily adapt to the changes as they happen.

However, I'm well aware that before people know anything at all about digital engagement, it can seem both obvious and tempting to learn about Facebook, Twitter and a few other websites then just get stuck in. So, I think it is worth looking at some individual tools and how to use them here, but more as case studies that bring out various universal principles than as things to use in and of themselves.

7.3 Using email for online engagement

First of all then, email.

Now, I can almost picture the look on your face as you read that, puzzlement mixed with disappointment I'd wager. After all, everyone uses email the whole time, it's just what we do nowadays. It's hardly anything interesting, let alone digital engagement.

---

[57] http://twitter.com/#!/campbellclaret

Well, as well as saying that it is interesting, and that it definitely is digital engagement, I'd also say that it's one of the most important digital engagement tools that there is.

For this view I am indebted to long time digital engagement advocate Steven Clift in the USA[58]. Steven runs a well subscribed email list about e-democracy and digital engagement, and constantly points out to those who run after the latest social media trend that email is far more widely and more regularly used than social media, and indeed always has been.

I suspect the reason most people overlook email in the field of digital engagement is partly that it's so regularly used that it's almost become second nature, and partly because it's never really changed or done anything that looks exciting. There may also be in there a bit of a fear of spam, not wanting to contribute to a problem that everyone hates by using email more than necessary.

The fear of being seen to be a spammer is well founded, but spam is no more welcomed on social media platforms than it is on email, so it's not as if email is any more risky to use than social media in that regard.

But if you want to get a message to somebody and have them read it, emailing it to them is probably one of the most effective methods you could possibly use. That's not to mention the other things you can do with email that most people don't seem to know about, like seeing if that person reads you email, seeing if they click on any links inside it, seeing who they forward it to and so much more.

Nearly everyone uses email these days, and if you can get their address, get permission to use it then send them content they find interesting, you have an extremely powerful online engagement tool at your fingertips.

____

[58] Whilst most of us in the UK were still completely unaware of the Internet, Steven was already developing the field of e-participation over in the US. See http://stevenclift.com

How to use email for online engagement

Whilst I hope this book makes things nice and simple as far as it can, I'll not make it so simple that I describe how to use email. If you don't know the basics of how to write, send or read an email, then ask the person next to you right now. What I do want to do though is tell you some of the principles you need to know to use email as an effective tool for online engagement, and some of the principles that sit behind this.

Getting addresses

Before you want to start thinking about using email for online engagement, you need to have addresses to which to send your email. If you're serious about engaging people online over any length of time, you almost need to become obsessive about gathering people's email addresses, and gain a sense of satisfaction every time you get hold of a new one.

The thing is, of all the contact details you could have for someone, email is the best. If you get their postal address, you lose them when they move. If you get their home phone number that too will change as well if they move. You could get their mobile number, but again, people lose their phones and/or change their numbers more often than you might think.

Someone's personal email address on the other hand, generally being free and accessed from any location through the web, tends to stick with them for life[59]. Note I say personal email address here, as a work address for someone may well cease to reach them should they change jobs.

So, how do you gain someone's email address? Well, there are lots of ways to do so, but not all of them are that useful. Many websites people join will display their email address if you've a mind to go looking for it, and you can even buy huge lists of email addresses under licence for very little money indeed. However, as we will see below, for an email

---

[59] I still have and check an email account I set up 15 years ago, which uses a name I first thought up when I was 12. I've heard many similar stories from others too.

address to be of any great use to you for online engagement, you have to get people to give it to you voluntarily.

There are as many ways to do this as there are to exchange any sort of information, and as many opportunities to do so too.

First of all, let's look at the ways to collect it. As I say, there's theoretically no limit to the way this could be done, but some tend to be more simple and effective than others. It is easier to collect an email address using a web form than it is to have it sent to you via carrier pigeon after all.

Web forms

Probably the most common way of collecting people's email addresses with their permission is to use a web form. This is commonly a single line text box and a submit button, asking the user to type their email address into the box and click submit.

The advantage of this approach, apart from being very simple for the person entering their address to use, is that it generally places that email address straight into some manner of email storage system, which can then be used to manage and send out emails to the people who have signed up.

In addition, any other location online where people might enter their email address can be used to collect addresses. For example, if someone signs up to a discussion forum, you could offer the option of joining your mailing list as part of their signing up. Often companies take email addresses from their online order forms and use them to send out regular newsletters.

Email based signup

Apart from having people enter an email address online somewhere, another way of collecting addresses is to use some prebuilt mailing list management software. This allows people to sign up to a mailing list by sending an email to a dedicated email address. Emails sent to this address are not read by humans, but rather by software, which takes the address of the sender and adds it to the mailing list automatically.

Less common than they once were, these mailing list management programs used to be extremely popular, especially for running discussion communities by email, to which we will return later.

They are though still available to use these days, and some well known popular ones include;

GNU Mailman[60] - http://www.list.org/

Majordomo - http://www.greatcircle.com/majordomo/

Listserv - http://www.lsoft.com/products/listserv.asp

You probably wouldn't want to use this mailing list management approach as your primary method for collecting email addresses, but it can have useful applications still. For example, how good would it be to invite everyone you send an email to to subscribe to your mailing list? Well how about putting the following in the signature you attach to every email you send?

To be kept updated about the work of my team, click on this email address and hit send - anything@example.com

As you've written the email address in full there, it should be recognised by most email programs and become a link for the reader to click on. When they click on it, their mail program will open a new email with that address in the 'To:' field. If you've set your mailing list management program to add to your mailing list the 'From:' address of every email it receives, then you've just created a simple two click process for everyone you email to sign up to your mailing list.

Written forms at events

Given most of what happens online stays online, it is often all too easy to overlook instances where an online process can integrate with an offline process, and this is just such an instance.

---

[60] GNU Mailman is open source software.

If you ever hold public events, or have physical locations where the public can access you, then why not put out a paper form and a pen, so they can write their email addresses down for you. After all, if they've made the effort to come and connect with you in person, it's perfectly possible that they will be interested in connecting with you online as well.

Once you've collected email addresses in this way, then it's just a case of sitting down and typing them all into your the file or program you use for managing the email addresses you are collecting.

To help get you started, I've included two template email sign up forms for you in the appendices of this book as examples.

Using email addresses

So, when can you use an email address? Well, there are two factors to consider here, one moral, one legal.

First though, as a rule of thumb, when carrying out online engagement, always think the following:

"You can only send an email to an address when the owner of that address has given you permission to do so"

First of all, the moral reason for this is quite simple. Receiving unsolicited emails is annoying, no-one likes it, and it could be considered at times to be impolite. Following quickly on from that, it almost goes without saying that if people find receiving such unsolicited emails annoying, they are hardly likely to engage with or look kindly on their contents.

Second though, there are various legal reasons behind this too, at least in the UK. However, being legal issues, there are inevitably various different scenarios to consider, each with their own rules about when you can and cannot email people. I am not a lawyer, and so won't try to offer any specifics here. However, if you stick to the rule of thumb above, then you're very unlikely to fall foul of the law.

In addition, as with any other data you may collect from people, it is important, and often legally required, to provide a statement connected to the email sign-up process stating who is collecting the email address, what they will use it for, and any other information relevant in the individual circumstances. As long as you have this in the 'terms and conditions' part of your website, and link to it from where you are collecting the email addresses, then you should be fine.

Finally, if you've got a set of email addresses you're allowed to use, how often should you use them?

Well, a lot of this can be trial and error, as each different type of audience will tolerate different frequencies of emails being sent out. For example, if you signed up to the mailing list of a website about celebrity gossip, you might be happy to receive an email from it once a day. However, a daily email about the latest consultations on traffic regulations in your area somehow seems less appealing.

Have you spotted something there, something that might be used as a tool for judging how often emails can be sent to different groups? If you thought 'it looks like it depends on the content', then 10 points to you.

In the two examples above, the email that can be sent more often without people minding is the one with the content people find more interesting. As a good guide, if you think the people you're sending the email to will be interested to see it, then you're probably ok to send it.

This is not by any means to say that you have to send an email as soon as or every time you find something interesting to send people. Often you can add to the impact and engagement of your emails by storing content up and sending it at regular intervals, for example in the form of a monthly newsletter.

The advantage of putting lots of different content together in one email is that if they are interested in it, recipients are more likely to dedicate a period of time engaging with the content, rather than skimming over it onto the next email. Because a periodical mailout only happens, well, periodically, you also dedicate a period of time on your side to putting it together, meaning you are more likely to do a good job of it.

In practice, it can be nice to mix up the two. If all you ever send out is a monthly newsletter, people can soon start to glaze over and ignore it. If you send out occasional emails on specific topics between newsletters from time to time, you're more likely to be towards the front of the recipient's mind when your newsletter does arrive.

Writing good content for emails

Before we come onto the content specifically, we should have a quick look at the two different ways you can send content via email. Most people only ever think of emails that appear as plain text, but there are actually two different types of email you can send, plain text and HTML.

Plain text is the sort of email you most commonly see, comprising of a (usually white) screen with just text on it. There might be the occasional link included in the text of the email, but when it is it is written out in full.

HTML on the other hand is an email that has been written in HTML code, the language used by web browsers to display webpages. Just as with a webpage, when the recipient sees the email, they don't see the HTML it contains, and instead see whatever the HTML is designed to display. This may mean the email displays images within it, possibly even videos too, as well as generally containing words that have been turned into clickable weblinks.

Whilst most people have seen HTML emails at one time or another, it is nearly always as a recipient of them, which is a shame really. Creating an HTML email really isn't tricky, there are loads of templates out there on the web you can use to get you started, as well as a fair few helpful sites that will teach you all you need to know[61].

HTML email can be really effective and turn your content from looking mundane into something really professional. There is though one quite major problem. Lots of the programs that people use to read their email prevent HTML emails being delivered to their recipients, or even where they are delivered, they do not display correctly.

One of the major reasons for this is the fact that sending HTML directly to people's email programs can represent a significant security risk, as the

---

[61] Try checking out the links at http://bit.ly/noMlAz for a start.

HTML can contain code that is run as soon as the email is opened, code which could have less than friendly intentions towards the recipient.

So, you could put together the loveliest HTML email the world has ever seen, but it could end up being read by very few people indeed, and you could be none the wiser that this was happening.

What you can do though is send the same email in both ways, and let computers work out which type goes to who, based on who will be able to see HTML email and who will not. We'll come on to that in the next section.

So, what makes good email content? Well, good content is that which is interesting to those that receive it. Only you can be the judge of that, but there are a few things you can do to make your email interesting.

- Make sure the email has an interesting subject line that describes its contents and entices the reader to open it.

- If the piece of content you want to share is particularly long, consider placing it on your website instead, and just using the email to provide a brief synopsis of it and a link people can click to read more[62].

- If sending an HTML email, put a small relevant image next to each piece of content to bring it to life.

- Include one or more 'calls to action' in the email, content that invites the reader to do something as a result of reading the email, for example visiting your website or taking part in a new consultation.

- Run the email through an online spam checking system. Many email spam filtering systems will 'read' the content of the email and

---

[62] This also gives you the bonus of getting more people looking at your website.

block it from being delivered if it believes it to be spam[63]. Spam filters can be extremely sensitive, and trigged by things as simple as the email containing words such as 'click here' and 'unsubscribe'.

That's probably about as much as needs to be said with regards to creating good email content. Once you've got the basics right, it really becomes an art not a science, and only by watching how well your emails do will you be able to learn more about what works and what does not.

Incidentally, from all my years of looking at which articles in a large newsletter people click on, I've never noticed where the article appears within the newsletter to make much difference. If it's interesting content, people will notice it and read it, wherever it is.

Finally, there is one vital piece of content that you must include in every email you send out to your mailing list, and that is some text making the reader aware of their ability to unsubscribe from your mailing list, and ideally a link to click to be able to do so. This may seem like a silly thing to include, after all, you want to get more people on your mailing list, not start letting people leave it. However, not only is including this content more likely to keep people happy[64,] it is also a legal requirement in many jurisdictions.

If you do receive a request to unsubscribe from your mailing list, then you must act on it as soon as possible, both as good practice and also to comply with legal requirements. Many mailing list management packages you can use will handle people unsubscribing for you automatically, just by them clicking on a link in the email. If you have this functionality available, do use it, it really can save lots of headaches further down the road.

---

[63] This can also help resolve another issue you may unexpectedly encounter, known as the 'Scunthorpe Problem' - http://en.wikipedia.org/wiki/Scunthorpe_problem

[64] Every email you send to someone who has decided they no longer wish to receive them will only make them more and more annoyed at you, and likely to tell other people of their annoyance to boot.

Sending and tracking emails

So, how do you send emails? Well, I said at the start of this section that I wasn't going to be as simplistic as to describe the basics of sending emails, but there are some ways of sending emails which are far from basic, and are well worth getting to grips with.

First of all, who do you send the email from? Generally it is best to use a real person's email address wherever possible, as this adds greatly to the trustworthiness and impact of any email sent. This email address should contain their name, often in the format 'firstname.lastname@'. Note that the email address is not necessarily the same as the name that appears next to the email itself when it arrives, as this can often be specified separately. Again, always try to make this name relate to a real person.

For the last part of the email address, always try to make it the URL for your organisation or of the website you are promoting. For example, my email address is gez@gezsmith.com. Giving people your domain name in your email address not only helps promote it, and thus leads to more visits to your site, but it also adds a sense of security to any messages sent from it, in comparison with 'disposable' and free email addresses created using third party systems such as Googlemail or Hotmail.

This is not to say that you should always use a real person's email account for all of your communication. Sometimes it is easier to create a generic one, especially where you are using an address over a long period of time, when you want the address to remain the same regardless of the turnover of the staff who administrate it. It can also be useful to have and promote a generic address for your organisation as a whole, in case people have general enquiries and don't want to spend the time researching the right member of staff to contact about them.

Even in this case however, you can make this generic address more engaging and real for people in order to build trust and appear more approachable. For example, the Samaritans in the UK use 'jo@samaritans.org' as their generic contact address, whilst other organisations use things like 'hello@' at the start of their generic addresses.

Apart from the above reasons, often the most simple way to carry out online engagement with email is to use the email system you use for sending email from day to day. If you want to email a small group, and especially if most of the members are known to you, this can often be a good approach. After all, coming straight from your email account, the email seems more personal, and recipients can easily reply directly to you at the click of a button.

If you do use your email account though, how should you send the email? Well, first of all, never put all of the recipient addresses in the 'To:' field. This will likely mean that all of the addresses appear in the header of the email for anyone who opens it, causing a distraction. A good way around this can be to put your own address in the 'To:' and the recipients' addresses in the 'CC:' field. This provides the added advantage of giving you an email confirmation that the email has been sent successfully and correctly, as you will receive a copy of it too.

However, and this is very important, only use the 'CC:' field if you have or can reasonably assume permission from each of the recipients to have their email addresses shared with one another. It might be that the group you are emailing are all known to each other, or 'cc'ing' people has become the standard method of group communication between members.

In every other scenario, use the 'BCC:' field.

If you put all of the recipients' email addresses in the 'BCC:' field, no recipient will be able to see the email address of any other recipient. If you fail to do this, you are effectively sharing the personal data of every recipient with every other, potentially a breach of the law, especially if you do not have permission to share their data in this way. I have seen this done before by the consultation team of a UK local authority, and they very narrowly avoided being reported to the data commissioner for a breach of the law.

If you are using your own email account for sending emails, making sure recipients' addresses are all in the 'BCC:' field is something you should become utterly paranoid about, and rightly so.

Alternatively though, you don't necessarily have to use your email account for sending emails to your mailing lists, as there are some extremely good software packages available which will send your emails for you and a whole lot more.

It's worth noting that pretty much all of these systems have been developed to help businesses market their products and services, and so aren't specifically tailored to the needs of digital engagement. That said, the needs of the two different areas aren't so dissimilar, and for most purposes, these systems can be an incredibly useful asset in conducting online engagement.

Firstly, they will send their emails for you. If you're sending emails to large mailing lists, then this can be a real bonus, as you will be using someone else's server and bandwidth instead of your own, keeping yours freer and less stressed. As part of sending them, they can also check your emails against the workings of various major spam filters, warning you if your email is likely to be filtered out as spam and allowing you to alter it accordingly[65]. As mentioned before, they will also be able to tell which of your recipients can receive HTML emails, and send them that version, whilst sending all of the others a plain text copy of it.

If you want to be really clever, you can set these systems to do what is called 'split testing' for you. In a split test, one sample of recipients is sent an email with 'content A', and another a different email containing 'content B'. The system may then leave it an hour or two, and see which of the two emails performed the best in terms of being opened or any other criteria.

Once a winner has emerged, all of the remaining recipients will be sent the email with the 'winning' content. To give a practical example of this, split testing can be a great way of working out which subject line for an email most encourages people to open the email itself. If you do split testing like this on each email you send, you can learn what works and what doesn't for your particular audiences much more quickly.

---

[65] You'd be surprised just how sensitive these spam filters can be. I know I was.

Once the emails have been sent, these systems will then track what recipients do with the emails. For example, this can include how many people open the email, who these people are, which links they click on in the email, how many times they click on them, who unsubscribes, and so forth. It is likely that the system will also collate these individual pieces of data into some manner of overview for you, so you can see at a glance how your email has gone down, without any of the recipients having to have any actual contact with you.

Unfortunately though, as with every godlike power, nature has imposed a limitation upon it. Here, it is that these systems generally rely on HTML code for tracking recipient actions such as these, so any emails sent as plain text won't be able to have any tracking done on them.

Using emails to run discussion communities

There is another way in which email can play a role in digital engagement, and it is here that I and the aforementioned Steven Clift differ.

As touched on above, 'in the olden days of the Internet', people used to use email to run discussion groups. Using these, participants would send an email to a single address, which would then forward the email on to all of the other members of the group. To reply to the group as a whole, all participants would have to do is click reply, write their response and send it back to the same address. To prevent different conversations getting mixed up with each other, each email on a new topic would be sent with a new subject line.

If you wanted to track the discussion, you could just read down an email and see all of the conversation that had gone on before. Well, not all of the preceding conversation, rather most of it, depending on which email you read and whether anyone had deleted anything before replying for reasons of email size.

Therein, to my mind at least, lies the reason why email groups got superseded by discussion forums and are no longer really worth using for online discussion. With a discussion forum, each comment made by a participant is displayed in date order on a page that anyone can view. It is thus really simple for someone to come along to the forum, read the entire discussion that has taken place so far, and get stuck in. You just can't do this in a nice and usable way using email lists. That said, many email discussion lists also store a copy of each message for viewing online, but if you're using them that way, why not go the whole hog and switch over to a forum anyway?

Email strategy

The above covers the some of the specifics of using email for digital engagement, along with some of the principles behind it. But there is one more element supporting the successful use of email for digital engagement that we have yet to cover; the email strategy.

Does your organisation have an email strategy? If pressed, I would guess that most of you would say no to that, or perhaps more likely 'I have no idea'. To my mind, that's a real shame.

Not only does creating or reading an email strategy make you take time to think about how you use email and how you could use it better, having a well-read email strategy should help you avoid some of the legal problems that can arise through using email for digital engagement and more.

The thing is though, I almost hate myself for recommending every organisation has an email strategy, as it creates the risk that can arise with any strategy. Namely that someone thinks it should contain a big list of things people must not do. Strategy documents that just tell you not to do things, especially those that threaten you with disciplinary proceedings if you do, just make people feel nervous, risk averse and ultimately disinclined to do anything much at all, in case they get it wrong.

An email strategy instead should be written as something everyone can sign up to and take pride in making sure happens. Keep it short, set out how things should look when all is going well, add in some tips on the best ways to do things, then include a contact name and email address in case there are any questions. Make sure the person acting as the contact is a friendly and personable sort, so they encourage people to try new things, rather than just telling them they can't whenever they try.

When you've written it, stick it up online somewhere for everyone to see; it should hardly be a secret. Do make clear though that the strategy doesn't contain any performance measurements against which you can be held accountable. Not only will this save you hassle from those determined to cause it; including performance indicators in a document rarely makes people more inclined to read it.

Despite my encouraging you to keep your email strategy short and fun for people to use, there are no right or wrong answers as to how it should look or what you include in it. To give you some ideas though, here are some elements it could include.

- Name and contact details of strategy owner.

- Overview of the tone of any emails to be sent on behalf of organisation e.g. helpful, friendly, personalised to the recipient and correctly spelt.

- Information on the sorts of email that may need to be checked and signed off by someone else e.g. legal responses, Freedom of Information requests.

- The format all email addresses will take.

- What content should be contained in any automatic signatures placed on the bottom of the email.

- How to set up your email to deal with your times of absence e.g. holiday, sickness.

- The acceptable use of email for personal/non work purposes.

7.4 Text messages and mobile phones

Perhaps understandably, nearly all of the focus in digital engagement is on computers, but let's not forget that digital engagement can refer to the use of any electronic device for participatory purposes.

One important device to consider, other than a computer, is a mobile phone[66]. Now it used to be that mobile phones were of use for just one purpose in this field, and that purpose was text messaging. Not that you couldn't telephone people on their mobile as well, but it was generally assumed that telephoning people was long established as an engagement method, so it was generally left out of the field of digital engagement.

Nowadays however, with mobile phone technology having advanced to the point where they have become more like mobile computers than telephones, there are a few more issues that need to be looked at when it comes to using mobile phones for digital engagement. That said, let's start with text messaging shall we?

Text messaging

Text messaging, more properly called 'SMS'[67], was one of the great white hopes of digital engagement in the UK when it kicked off around 2004. All sorts of pilots were run involving text messaging, but sadly they were generally complete rubbish. The problem was that people tended to get stuck thinking inside the digital engagement box, and so generally used it to alert participants to content they may wish to look at online.

Now using text messaging like this suffered from the same problem as offline advertising[68] in that the recipient had too many steps to go through in order to convert the receipt of a text message into undertaking an action online. Once they have received the text message, they have to

---

[66] My apologies to American readers, as, being English, I'm going to talk about them as mobile phones in this book. Feel free to think 'It's called a cell phone you moron' every time you read it.

[67] Which stands for Short Message Service.

[68] See Chapter 9 for more on this.

remember it the next time they are at a computer, read it again and type in the URL it contains manually in order to complete the intended action.

Generally this didn't happen, and indeed it seems the general populace were far more aware of this than the so called experts from a very early stage. Whilst working at Delib, I trialed allowing people to sign up to SMS alerts about newly published consultations with a few different clients, and each and every one of them saw next to nobody sign up to the service. People just weren't interested. Sadly this idea still seems to be kicking about in certain places, so you still see tenders for digital engagement software that include the ability for people to sign up for SMS consultation alerts as a specification requirement. If you're ever tempted to do the same thing in your procurement processes, please don't, as it really is a complete waste of time.

So, SMS is just useless for digital engagement then? Well, not quite, as there are two important things you can use it for, one quite old and the other still emerging and in need of further testing.

For helping me discover the older purpose, I have to thank the Housing Department of Bristol City Council. When I worked at Bristol as a consultation officer, we had at our disposal a bulk text messaging system, provided to us by a third party. We'd had no joy using it for anything, and had pretty much given up on it, until some officers from Housing got in touch and asked if they could use it for contacting council tenants. To my surprise, they came back a few weeks later delighted with how well it was working. Instead of thinking them quite mad, I had a chat with them about what they'd done, and it really was quite ingenious.

Instead of using the system to alert people to online activity, they had decided to use it to complement their offline activities instead. A problem they had been struggling with was getting council tenants along to their regular tenant feedback meetings. They sent them letters a couple of weeks in advance, giving the time and date of the meeting, but this just didn't seem to create the sort of attendance figures they had hoped for. So, suspecting that people were reading the letters but then forgetting about them over the intervening fortnight, they used the SMS system to send a text message to each tenant, reminding them about the meeting half an hour or so before it took place. As the meetings are located so as to be close to the tenants they are aimed at, this timely reminder seemed to be what it took to refresh people's memories about the meeting and spur them to come along.

So, again we see another crossover between digital engagement and offline activity, using the former to complement and augment the latter. Truth be told, I've not yet seen enough examples of this sort of work to be 100% certain that it will work every time, but where it does work it seems to be extremely effective. So, if you're minded to use text messaging as part of your digital engagement activities, then why not use it to send time sensitive content to people, encouraging them to get involved in an offline activity?

After all, if you think about it, this approach actually contains very few different steps for the participant to complete, viz;

1. Receive text message

2. Decide to go to meeting

3. Go to meeting

There's likely to be more work needed here to try out other such uses for text messaging as a digital engagement tool, but already a picture has emerged about what works and what doesn't.

Incidentally, whilst we're looking at text messaging, it is worth noting that mobile phones don't just have to be used for texting. Blackberry mobile devices for example possess the ability to 'broadcast' messages across groups of other Blackberry users. Indeed, during the riots that took place in the UK in Summer 2011, whilst the media was busy getting all excited about the role of social media in provoking and co-ordinating rioting, it was actually Blackberry group messaging that was being used for these purposes. It appears social media had next to nothing to do with it[69].

---

[69] For more information on this, see
http://www.guardian.co.uk/media/2011/aug/08/london-riots-facebook-twitter-blackberry

7.5 Using mobile apps

I've got to admit, I'm not a huge fan of the word 'app'. Sure, it's an abbreviation of the correct word for small, often single purpose software applications, but it has been somewhat hijacked by the more clueless for the purposes of marketing larger software packages, meaning it's harder than it needs to be to know what truly is an 'app' and what is actually something larger.

Still though, the prevalence of small software applications for a wide range of different purposes is now vast, and, as the saying goes, whatever you need to do, there's likely to be 'an app for that'.

Although they don't have to be, apps are generally used to refer to small pieces of software that are used through mobile phones. Combine this with some of the other interesting functionalities built into mobile phones these days, such as automatic image recognition through built in cameras, GPS location data and so on, and you get some really interesting possibilities for developing digital engagement tools that people can carry around in their pockets.

Already, we see excellent websites like www.fixmystreet.com being complemented by downloadable apps for a range of different mobile phones, allowing people to report problems to their local council whilst they're out and about, just by using their mobile phone. I suspect there are many more such applications mobile phone apps could be put to just waiting to be discovered.

Now I'm not necessarily the person to go thinking of them, but because the more successful apps are generally so simple, anybody could come up with an idea for a really useful digital engagement app. All it takes is a spark of inspiration.

So whilst I'm not going to suggest a range of ideas for mobile apps you could develop and / or use, I would say this. Why not get in touch with your local community of software developers and ask them if they have any ideas, perhaps offering to fund the development of the best ones? Building an app shouldn't cost too much.

You could also combine this approach with your work on open data[70.] Why not open out as much of the data you hold as you can, and see if any of it can be used for developing useful little apps for your local community? After all, if you put useful information together with something as convenient and readily available as a mobile phone, then the chances are you could end up creating something very useful indeed. If you do create something useful or interesting using this approach, let me know about it, and I'll include it in the next edition of this book.

The mobile web

No longer just a thing of mobile phone marketing brochures, there are millions of people out there now with the ability to access the Internet through their mobile phones. Indeed, they can not just access the web, they can do so at speeds resembling those they might achieve on their home computer. So how do you make best use of that fact?

Well, for the most part, you don't have to. Many mobile phones use exactly the same web browsers as a normal computer might for accessing the Internet, and as long as your website has been built by someone half competent, it should work on a phone browser just fine. That said, there are some browsers that have been built especially with mobile phones in mind, and it is always worth checking that your site does indeed work correctly on those. However, checking that your site works on every possible mobile phone browser out there would be an arduous task with diminishing returns, so I would say it's only worth checking it on the most widely used of them.[71]

Given the fact that the Internet risks being accessed at lower speeds on mobile phones than on static computers with their direct connection to a telephone line, you can also help people to use their phone to access your website by minimising the use of images and other content that will take a long time to download. Indeed, some websites provide an

---

[70] See Chapter 11 for more on open data.

[71] UK Government policy for example was to ensure their websites work on any browser with over 2% market share. If you want to find out what market share each different browser currently has, http://en.wikipedia.org/wiki/Usage_share_of_web_browsers should get you started.

alternative version of themselves specifically for use on mobile phone browsers, for example http://m.facebook.com or http://m.guardian.co.uk. This approach is probably a step too far for most organisations to be worrying about, but do keep an eye on the feedback you're getting from your users, in case there are sufficient numbers of them wanting to use your site through their phones to make creating a specific mobile version worthwhile.

Finally, there is one direct application of mobile phone based Internet access that should not be overlooked. If you're doing any form of offline engagement with your target audiences, then why not use your phone to facilitate this?

For example, rather than interviewing people and collecting their responses on paper forms, why not set up an online survey to collect the data, and access it via your phone in order to enter people's responses directly into a results database? There are companies out there marketing dedicated handheld devices for doing this sort of work, but as Internet enabled smart phones become ever cheaper and readily available, I suspect their days may be numbered.

7.6 Running discussion forums

I love discussion forums. They're how I first got interested in how people interact and communicate with each other online, and they were the first ever online project I designed and ran all those years ago.

Whilst you can learn a lot about it, I still believe that forum moderation is primarily an art, not a science. It takes a wide array of qualities to make a good forum moderator. Patience, compassion, a thick skin, a good memory and a severe addiction to the Internet all help someone keep an online community chatting away happily.

So, if it's about people rather than hard and fast rules, perhaps I should be up front about my time as a forum moderator, to give some context to the things I suggest and the reasons behind why I suggest them.

Back in 2001 I was doing a masters in International Relations[72] which unfortunately I discovered I had absolutely no interest in about halfway through the first seminar. Still though, I'd signed up to it, told everyone I was doing it, borrowed a lot of money to pay for it and, most important, had little idea what else to do with my time anyway.

So, I stuck it out. The thing was, whilst the content of the modules themselves just seemed like a load of needless academia made up to justify funding bids[73], September 2001 was a fascinating time to be around a politics department. September 11th had just happened, war with Afghanistan was looming and those in the know were already pointing to an invasion of Iraq. However, the media just wasn't reporting what I was hearing from inside the department, but I wanted to know more, so I turned to the Internet.

On there was a plethora of discussion about the international political situation. Not just information on what was happening, but more important, analysis of why it was happening and what was likely to happen next. Suddenly I found I had access to hundreds of different minds, all able and willing to share their views in discussion with each other.

I got pretty addicted to discussion forums at that time, and so, when I made the inevitable leap into party politics that anyone who spends too long studying politics is bound to do[74], I was amazed to find there wasn't any equivalent discussion space online for 'politics with a big P'.

I'd joined the Lib Dems, and got involved in the youth wing[75], so persuading them to set up some party political discussion forums seemed like an obvious step to take, with one section restricted to party members only, and another open to anybody. After all, liberal people love debate and discussion, right? Well, it seemed not, as people were paranoid. Paranoid that someone might post something online that might harm their

---

[72] Like studying politics, just the politics of abroad.

[73] Most modern academia sadly still strikes me this way to be honest.

[74] Don't worry, I leapt back out of the whole thing many years ago now.

[75] Called Liberal Democrat Youth and Students at the time, or LDYS for short.

career. Paranoid that someone may let slip some vital secret to the opposition. Paranoid that it would just give our 'opponents' an opportunity to attack us.

Still though, I pressed on, and around the start of 2003, the first political party discussion forums in the UK were born. I moderated them every day for three years, and that's what's led me to the following conclusions;

- **Discussion forums are a very real living community**

  This is one of my biggest bugbears in digital engagement over the last 8 years, that all sorts of organisations have been sold 'discussion forums' as a piece of technology, and then sat there and watched tumbleweed blow through them as the expected hoard of eager participants failed to materialise. You need to put work into building your community over time, and into keeping it happy in the long term.

- **Discussion forums should be free**

  If you've ever paid money for software to run discussion forums, you've almost certainly wasted your money. Perhaps because forums have finally provided a way for geeks to communicate with other geeks without having to leave the house, the geeks have given their programming knowledge to the world for free.

If you want a set of discussion forums, you can download the software for free, install it on a server somewhere and you're ready to go. Personally, I've always liked and used phpBB (http://www.phpbb.com/), an open source and very well made piece of discussion forum software, now used by so many people that myriad different configuration options are available for free as well. There are other free forum packages out there, but I'd recommend phpBB if you're just starting out, or even if you want to stop paying someone for your forums.

So then, the software's simple and free, but how do you actually turn your forums into lively bustling places full of conversation and debate?

What's your point caller?

The title above is a tongue in cheek phrase sometimes used in reply to forum posters who don't seem to have said anything relevant to the conversation, but it's also an important consideration for anyone setting up discussion forums. As, before anything else, your forums should have a point.

Now, with the LDYS forums I set up, there were some clear points to their existence. We wanted to encourage our organisation's membership to talk to one another, we wanted to replace our email list groups that were being used at the time, and we wanted to encourage political discussion amongst young people in the UK more generally.

One of the reasons you see discussion forums languishing without anyone taking part in them is because the forums themselves have no clear purpose, or perhaps not enough of a purpose. Providing forums 'to allow people to discuss things in our local area' isn't a clear enough purpose really, especially when there will already be other places in which people can do that. Before embarking on any discussion forum project, see if you can write down three clear reasons why the forums should exist. If you can't, don't set them up until you can.

The reason having a clear purpose or purposes to discussion forums is so important is that that same reason has to entice people to join. With the LDYS forums, we had people wanting to join to talk to other members, people wanting to join to attack us as a party, and people wanting to join just to find out a bit more about politics generally. The purpose is also the reason people will stay using a discussion forum over time, which in turn will lead to a community developing around it and the forum growing sustainably.

Let people know you're there

Once you've got your purpose(s) clear and the forum software set up, the next step is to tell people about it. I won't got into this too much here, as the principles for promoting discussion forums are by and large the same as for any digital engagement website, and are covered in more detail in Chapter 9.

However, with the LDYS forums, we found that the best way to start them going was to get the 'already engaged' using them first. These were people who were already using our email discussion list, to whom we simply emailed the URL for the new forums, as well as to other people for whom we had email contacts. We actually did a 'soft launch' of them first, inviting a select few to start using them, so that anyone arriving to them after the official launch would see others already taking part. It's hard to overestimate the importance of seeing others taking part to encouraging new people to join in.

Again, think back to the idea of digital engagement as a party. If you wander into a room at a party and there are just two people in there talking to each other, you're most likely to walk straight out again and go somewhere else. On the other hand, if you go into a room and it's full of people chatting away to each other, you're more likely to stick around and join in a conversation yourself.

'From little acorns mighty oaks do grow'

If you've followed the above steps correctly, then you should start to see the forums developing, new members joining and conversations taking place. That said, you need to put in a lot of work to keep people taking part, stopping them losing interest or being forced out of the forum by other members.

To refer back to the analogy of a party once again, it's not enough to invite lots of people and then have them turn up. As a host, you need to work the room, keeping conversations going, introducing new people and making everyone feel at home.

To do this, you need to be a participant in the discussions yourself. I despair at the amount of times organisations have seen discussion forums as a 'them and us' type of scenario, used purely to allow people to talk whilst the authority watches. To keep your forums growing, you need to join in too. Not only does this help build respect for you as a moderator[76,] but it also demonstrates to people that someone is listening and perhaps even acting on the conversations that are being had.

Now the extent to which you get involved in discussions is a tricky one, and has to be down to your personal judgment. In the LDYS forums, as well as looking after them, I was also angling for promotion within the organisation, so I was regularly on there debating and arguing with others, setting out my stall ready for the next set of annual elections[77].

However, if you're representing an organisation, you have to be more careful about this. This is especially true if you work for an organisation run by elected figures whilst you are just an officer carrying out their instructions. In this situation, it is probably best to stay well away from getting involved in debates themselves and expressing your own personal points of view.

This is not to say though that you should never post on your forum yourself. There will be many situations when all that is needed is a simple answer to a question someone has raised, or perhaps a correction to a demonstrably incorrect viewpoint. At the end of the day, it is exchange of information between people that keeps a forum interesting, so whilst you may not be adding information on your opinions, you can still add all sorts of factual information into the forum that will make it richer and more interesting for all of those taking part.

General housekeeping

As well as taking part in the forums here and there, there are two other useful roles that you can play as a moderator. One is moderation, which we'll come to in a bit, but the other is what might be termed 'housekeeping'.

---

[76] Hopefully, at least.

[77] I actually did this a little too well, ending up as National Chairman of the organization and a Deputy President of the entire party nationally, despite never winning a contested election.

If we think back to the party analogy once more, it is often the role of a host to go around during the party clearing away empty plates and glasses, sweeping up spillages and generally keeping the place looking nice. The same is equally true of discussion forums.

For example, imagine one day a news story breaks that is of relevance to your forum. In all likelihood, someone will go to the forum and start a new thread about the topic, to which others will reply with their thoughts. If the forum's running well though, someone else might excitedly go to the forum and start another thread on exactly the same topic. Now, having two or more places to discuss the same thing can get confusing for people, and lessen the quality of the discussion in both threads, so most forum software will let you merge threads together, placing the posts from one thread into another, keeping the discussion in one place.

It may also be that people start threads that are of no relevance to the forum whatsoever, so again, to keep the place tidy, you can step in and move the thread to a non public section of the forum[78]. Sometimes even, and this is a little more cheeky, you may wish to use your powers as a forum administrator to go into someone else's post and correct typos and spelling mistakes for them.

Be warned though, doing any of the above too zealously will annoy people and drive them away from the forum. However, the right amount of housekeeping here and there will keep the forums nice, tidy and welcoming for members both old and new.

---

[78] Do not ever delete any thread or comment though, the reasons for which will be covered below.

7.7 Moderation

So then, the most important part of your work as a forum moderator or administrator, moderation itself. Moderation is the act of making sure all the posts made on the forum are within the forum rules, removing any that are not, and even sometimes warning or banning posters who fail to keep to the rules.

It's a thankless task in many ways, and because much of the work can involve removing posts from the site or sending users warnings, much of a moderator's activities are never noticed by the majority of forum users. But what sort of people make good forum moderators?

Who should be a moderator?

First, at least one moderator should be someone who owns, or is happy to take legal responsibility for, the site. Make no mistake, no matter the size or type of discussion forum, someone can be held legally liable if someone breaks the law on it. Given the global nature of the Internet, it is sometimes a moot point as to whether that legal liability can be upheld, and there are things moderators can do to limit their liability, but to ignore the legal status of today's forum moderators is to invite potential catastrophe.

Don't let this legal issue worry you though, there's still no official 'moderator licence' needed to do the job (nor should there be), and the chances of things going wrong are remote unless you really aren't paying attention or doing your job properly. However, do bear it in mind in all the moderating decisions you make, and use it to give you more confidence in enforcing your position as a moderator, and in upholding the moderation policy at all times. At the end of the day, it's your forum, you're responsible for it, you're quite possibly legally liable for it too, and so you can do whatever you see fit to keep yourself and the forum safe.

This is not to say you should rule with an arbitrary rod of iron, forums tend to die when people do. Like bees, the users will swarm and migrate to a more pleasant location. But you should always be clear in your mind that it is your responsibility, and you are in charge.

One thing you always want to try to incorporate, at least once the community is up and running, is some level of community involvement in the moderation process. Now this can take any shape you choose. On one end of the scale, you could just encourage the community to take pride in the forum, be nice to one another, pull people up when they break the rules and alert moderators to problems; all the sorts of things a good forum moderator should be doing every day. Having the users of the forum as your 'eyes and ears' for things going wrong can make your job an awful lot more simple in so many ways.

On the other end of the scale, you could make members of the discussion community moderators too, with all of the ability to delete, move, edit and hide posts that that contains. This can be useful, but it brings with it its own hazards. So how should you choose new moderators from the forum community?

Well, the first thing I tend to do is discount anyone who is overly eager to do the role, or seems to have their own personal ego or advancement at the heart of why they want to moderate. Look for people who want to do it to help others, not themselves[79]. However, in order to do a good job, a moderator has to want to do the work involved, so it can be best to pick from those who say they would be happy to do it if called upon, or those who don't take much persuading to say yes. Do check though that they clearly have the maintenance and improvement of the community, rather than their own ego, in mind.

Another important factor to consider, and sometimes a way of deciding who to appoint, lies in the personal reputations of forum users. Moderators have to take tough decisions sometimes, and have to hold the respect of others, even the majority, in order to be able to make tough calls.

Now reputation online can often actually be something quite specific, rather than the more intangible quality it holds in the offline world. Many

---

[79] The irony is of course that moderating a forum is generally a position of no consequence whatever outside of the forum itself, meaning those who are desperate to do so to enhance their personal reputation are generally rather odd.

websites use some sort of software based reputation system in order to support users interacting with each other.

Perhaps the best known one of these is on eBay, where a need exists to build trust between people who will never meet, in order to give security to the process of buying and selling. On eBay, anyone buying or selling has to register a profile, and every transaction they make creates an opportunity for both parties in the transaction to rate each other; ratings that can then be viewed by others. The better your rating, the more trust worthy you appear to be and the more likely people are to trade with you.

On discussion forums, various different reputation or rating systems can be put in place, often to serve a similar purpose. The closest one to the eBay example exists through the ability to award a user 'reputation points' when they post something you agree with or support. These points then get displayed next to each post made by that poster, allowing people to make a degree of judgment as to the truth, worth or trustworthiness of any of that poster's future posts.

Often these sorts of mechanisms are tempered with a few restrictions to stop them running out of control, such as allocating each poster a set amount of reputation points they can award that day, or preventing a poster from giving too many points to one individual without giving any to others as well. Some setups allow people to award reputation points only, whilst others allow people to award them to or delete them from each other.

Despite controls such as these though, I tend to find reputation systems like these on a discussion forum add little to the experience of the users, and if anything just create more problems. From time to time, people on forums won't get along, and will follow each other around arguing and generally bringing each other down. Giving them a user reputation system to attack each other with just tends to make these problems worse. As with being a moderator, gaining a high reputation score can become an aim of the socially tragic, a score that they then use to throw their weight around against others.

Above all, regardless of these problems, I tend to think that the anonymity provided by a discussion forum acts as a great leveler, allowing different people to interact with each other in a way they would not be able to face to face. A reputation system often only serves to cancel out this beneficial leveling effect, so unless you've got a strong reason for putting one in place, then you might be better off not doing.

If you're looking for a moderator drawn from the community then, you should judge your possible applicants by their less tangible but no less important reputation amongst other forum users. Look for those users who already step in to calm arguments, help others, and start new threads for discussion. In essence, a good moderator will already be doing some of the moderator's role before they are appointed.

So, that's who to choose, but what sort of role should you be giving these people? Everyone works better when they know what is expected of them, and the same is true of moderators. There are a few different components that add up to make the work of a moderator, which could be summed up as follows;

"a moderator is someone who has to apply the same rules to a wide range of people in a wide range of ways"

So, to look at the work needed from a good moderator, let's take things in that order, first looking at the rules, then the people then finally the methods.

Rules for forum discussion and moderation.

You need these.

It may sound obvious, but it's surprising how many projects are launched without remembering to include terms and conditions of site usage. Not only do they make for easier moderation and better discussion, but since forum owners can in many instances be held legally liable for defamatory or illegal content being posted to their site, a lack of terms and conditions can present a very real risk.

These terms and conditions need not be onerous, but unfortunately no common standard for them yet seems to have evolved. The information presented in this book is in no way meant to act as final and definitive guide to the specific terms and conditions that may be required by a website of any kind, and it is strongly recommended to consult professional legal advice on this issue where necessary.

In essence, terms and conditions need to set out the following points as a minimum;

- Guidelines for what is and isn't acceptable in terms of content. Repeating the purpose or purposes of the forums that you have already written (see above) can help make this clear.

- A prohibition on posting content that breaches any applicable laws, not only in the country in which the discussion is based, but potentially with regard to international law as well[80].

- An absolute reservation of the right of moderators and administrators to administrate posts made and users registered at all times, including deleting both from the system at their absolute discretion.

  Seriously, this is your party, your venue and your rules, so don't feel bad kicking out anyone who is messing things up. It's all too easy to get into endless and tiring discussions over what should and shouldn't be posted on the forum, so just be firm and get on with it. However, remember that you can only kick so many people out before you have no one left.

- The rules by which posts and members will be judged in terms of moderation and deletion/removal, clearly and simply set out.

- Any appeals process you may wish to put in place if posters have grievances with your work as a moderator.

- In all cases, where user registration is present, users need to agree to these terms and conditions as a condition of registration or participation.

---

[80] As touched on elsewhere in this book, It is important to know where your forum is being hosted, as often it can fall under the laws of the country in which it is being hosted, even if these differ from the laws in the country in which the discussion is being held.

However, whilst these terms and conditions are essential for legal purposes, you don't want to make them too legalistic and difficult to understand if you can avoid it. The main point of them is for every user to be able to understand and make use of them on a day to day basis. If only a few can understand the rules, this few will hold more power than the majority who do not.

A generic example of a moderation policy and terms and conditions for online discussion can be found in the appendices of this book, which you are welcome to use under the Creative Commons licence.

Situations and 'personas'

Ultimately, moderating an online discussion is a matter of experience, which very often means knowing your community of users, their quirks, foibles and habits. Successful forums are made of real people having real conversations, and each will over time develop their own in-jokes, approaches and well-known personalities.

However, in all my years of using and running forums, I have noticed that there are a number of different types or 'personas' of users, and an awareness of these can make the task of moderation a good deal more simple. Here are the types of people I've met online so far.

The ideal poster

This person would be great. They would be friendly, participative but not dominating, eager to help out but in a collaborative way, would never break the rules and would write clear and compelling posts like a best selling novelist.

Sadly, I've never come across an ideal poster. Indeed, I wouldn't even call myself one. Instead, you're likely to meet the following.

The dominant poster

One of the most common poster types, especially on new forums where a community has not had time to develop, is a poster who dominates the conversation. Often this will be not just in terms of the way they respond to other postings made, criticising or correcting them, but also in the sheer volume of postings made by this poster. The more they post, the less worth each of their posts will contain, and ultimately others will become tired of reading this person's opinions on everything and stop reading the forums altogether.

The best way to deal with such posters is initially through a polite and friendly private message to them, pointing out that what they are doing is stopping or putting off others from joining in.

If this does not work, it can be worth reiterating this advice to them in public on the forum, although often other posters will do this for you first. If all else fails, it is worth looking at putting in place a small 'acceptable usage' policy for that particular poster, allowing them a set number of posts per day, and, *in extremis,* banning them if they continue to breach this.

Sometimes dominant posters do not realise that they are coming across as overly dominant, and certain dominant posters are actually just over eager and/or have too much time on their hands, leading them to reply to every post made. Pointing issues like this out to them can quickly stop the problem.

Ultimately however, it is important to keep an eye on and take action against overly dominant posters, as they can quickly kill an online discussion for other people.

The 'conversational couple'

Leading on from this, another often unwittingly dominant habit can occur when two posters get into a conversation or argument with one another. These situations usually develop quickly, with both posters online at the same time, and a moderator can return to a discussion to find a thread has grown by many pages in their absence, consisting solely of a conversation between two posters.

Whilst these conversations can be interesting, especially for the participants, if others aren't joining in or clearly are not given opportunity to, this is a situation that should be dealt with. Often a polite public post addressed to both parties asking them to 'take the conversation to PM' (the forum's private messaging system) can work well.

Alternatively, splitting the posts that form a conversation between two people into a different thread and giving it a new title can leave the conversation both as an interesting archive for others, as well as a space for the conversation to continue, whilst leaving the original thread unencumbered for others to continue to participate.

As with dominant posters, conversational couples can often be oblivious to what they're doing, so caught up are they in the conversation. Such conversations can often turn into argument however, as well as being off putting to others, so they must be watched closely.

The abusive/aggressive poster

One poster making the occasional rebuke to another is generally fair enough on a forum, as long as it's not breaching the terms and conditions of the site (no offensive language, no libel, etc.). Sometimes people just don't get on, and there may be nothing a moderator can do to alter that. Productive discussions are often born from tension and opposing views, so don't worry too much about disagreement occurring.

There are three types of abusive poster though, which go beyond the bounds of acceptable behaviour and must be looked at by a moderator.

The Troll

A troll is a poster on the Internet, not necessarily just on a discussion forum, who is there just to cause trouble and argument. There is a lot of information about the different types of troll available elsewhere online, but generally trolls and their behaviour (known as trolling) post little but abuse, or strongly and deliberately contradictory comments to whatever any posters say.

Trolling can be a hobby, and people can undertake it purely for the amusement of watching others become irate or upset at what they are saying, safe in the (supposed) anonymity of the Internet. It is interesting that trolling is more uniquely an Internet phenomenon, nourished by anonymity, as it is difficult to imagine someone successfully trolling a real life conversation for any sustained period of time.

Trolling and a judgment on its severity is always a judgment call for the moderator at the end of the day, and should be evaluated on a case-by-case basis. It is important not to let personal prejudice cloud one's judgment in dealing with a troll. Just because someone disagrees with the majority view does not make them a troll per se.

There are a number of ways of dealing with trolls. Generally the approach should start with a friendly comment or private message pointing out that their behaviour in the conversation is more destructive than constructive. If the situation persists, this can then be followed up with a warning, which can then be turned into a ban from the discussion, either on a short term or permanent basis. Sometimes however, trolling immediately breaks the rules of the board to such a degree that it can and must lead to a ban straight away.

The Unwitting Troll

Sometimes trolls are not trolling because they want to cause trouble, but their behaviour can come across in a similar manner when they persistently disagree with and criticise others without adding anything constructive.

This can often occur on a topic basis, where someone has strong feelings that run contrary to the majority view, and, rather than discussing them with others constructively, they just keep on reiterating their point again and again. This can become especially frustrating when others provide links to evidence contrary to the individual's view, whilst their response remains one of 'don't confuse me with facts, my mind's made up'.

To deal with such situations, it is often worth having a word with such an individual via private message, to point out that their behaviour is preventing others from holding a constructive conversation on the topic, and suggesting that if such a topic aggravates them so much, perhaps they might be better to avoid it in the future.

The 'Bull In A China Shop'

When a forum is on a topic of some potential controversy, and has been running for some time, a new poster can arrive, bringing with them a selection of firmly held convictions on the topic. Such posters can dive straight into the debate, without taking the time to read the conversations that have already been had, and start aggressively criticising the topic, the existing posters, even the host organisation for the conversation.

A sign of a well established forum community is when such posters are immediately taken to task and asked to engage in a more constructive manner by the existing posters. Indeed, when I ran the LDYS forums, the occasional poster would turn up from another political party and immediately start trolling the forums as a way of attacking their political 'enemy'. It was pleasing when this happened to see other forum members from the troll's own party slap them down, telling them that these forums were a place where people from different parties talked to each other in a civil manner.

However, in the earlier stages of a forum's life, it is up to the moderator to point out that all views are open to being heard, but that there is an expectation that posters listen to the views of others too, and converse in a constructive and friendly manner.

It is surprising how disarming and engaging a friendly response to an initially aggressive poster can be. At the end of the day, everyone wants to be listened to, so if you can demonstrate that you are listening, then often people will find it difficult not to start listening in return.

The Lurker

Too often, forum moderators are concerned with managing those who post on the forum, and forget that there may be an even larger community of people 'lurking' on the forum, a term which means reading what is being posted but never posting anything in response.

It would be imagined that lurkers are more common on forums that can be read without the need to register (as all forums should be unless very good reason otherwise can be found). However, even on forums where registration is required in order to 'lurk', many people do register just to read the conversations of others. It is not at all unknown for people to lurk for many years on forums without ever posting.

Reasons for lurking vary, and people should always have the right to do so. However, it is surprising how many lurkers can be 'brought in from the cold' through simple methods.

One of these is to have a prominent thread in the discussion 'stickied' or 'pinned' at the top of the forum (so it always appears on the top of the forum regardless of the last date someone posted in it) inviting lurkers to join. A similar outcome can be achieved through having a dedicated thread for new members to introduce themselves.

However, if this latter approach is taken, then it is important that at least the forum moderators, if not community members themselves as well, reply to such introductory posts with a warm welcome. Imagine introducing yourself to people at a party, only for them to look at you blankly before ignoring you completely and carrying on their existing conversation. There is little more off putting than an introduction that is met with tumbleweed.

Similarly, it is worth remembering that some people lurk as they do not feel they have the confidence or expertise to take part in the discussion at the same level as the other posters. A little hand holding and encouragement of such users as they find their feet can work wonders here. If moderators hold and promote the view that everyone's contribution is equally important, regardless of background or specialist knowledge, this can soon suffuse through the ethos of the entire discussion community.

The Leaver

As with any community, over time people come and go. This is natural, and as long as the community membership is generally on an upward curve overall, then there is little to worry about in this regard.

However, there are a couple of things that can be done to bring back leaving posters. One simple one, contained in many standard forum platforms, is an all member messaging facility. If you have gained the permission of members to be contacted occasionally by the system upon registration, then do make use of the system to send occasional messages to all members, perhaps updating them on the outcomes of conversations that have been held already, or on the topics of interest that are currently being discussed. The Internet is a large and busy place, and sometimes people just forget about a part of it they used to visit, so a friendly email reminder to members that the discussion is still ongoing and is still interesting can work wonders.

Alternatively, when a community is more established, forum members often take it upon themselves to find former posters and encourage them to come back to take part, particularly when an issue arises in which their opinion or expertise would be valued. There are few things more enticing than the knowledge that people are keen to hear what you want to say. Equally, a moderator can seek out former members and get in touch with them encouraging them to come back and take part if they think it would be of use and interest to the wider community.

Be careful though not to confuse the leaver with...

The Flouncer

A flouncer is someone who announces for all to read that they are leaving the forum, often starting a whole new thread to inform people of just this fact. Nine times out of 10 they will take a day or two off from visiting the forum before returning to post as they did before. Once someone has flounced like this, they are far more likely to flounce again.

I've never done this, so I have little insight into the mind of someone who would, but from what I have seen, flouncing is almost a cry for attention, respect or love. Full of melodrama, the flouncer's 'final post' will be filled with how they have been grievously wronged by the community or the moderators, and how they will never return. In response to this, they hope for people to leave heartfelt messages bemoaning their departure and wishing it were otherwise.

The amusing thing about flouncing is that, as a forum moderator, you can generally check the last time someone visited the forum and the threads they looked at when they did. If someone is flouncing, rather than truly leaving, they will often regularly revisit their flouncing thread to see who has replied and what they have said, even if they don't post on that thread again.

Flouncing on a forum is of little problem really, unless their 'final post' contains content that breaks the site rules. Generally I don't ever feel the need to stroke the flouncer's ego by replying, and I would encourage you to do the same.

The Sockpuppet

Identity in real life is usually straightforward, but can be troublesome. People can claim to be someone they are not, or pretend knowledge or a background that they do not actually have. On the Internet, this can be even more difficult, as there are not the normal human means of distinguishing people from each other, such as appearance, voice and so forth.

This leads to the creation of 'sock puppet' accounts in an online discussion, where one person holds more than one login or user profile within the site, and uses them for a variety of purposes[81]. Sometimes sock puppet accounts are used to argue with one another, allowing one person to give the impression that there is tension amongst the community. Alternatively, sock puppet accounts all present the same view, giving the impression that there is a majority view in one direction, when the truth may actually be different.

Sockpuppeting on the Internet is usually grounds for an immediate and permanent ban, at the very least for the sock puppet accounts, and in most cases for the user who created them as well.

Spotting them can be a fine art, and often intuition is a good guide here, when posting styles and tone of language all seem similar, or support a vested interest that normally would not be so well supported. A lack of

---

[81] As you may have guessed, the name comes from the practice of putting a sock on your hand and using it like a puppet. Remove the sock, and there's the real person underneath.

comprehensive background for an individual poster coming across in their posts can also be a sign.

From a technology perspective, a good piece of forum or discussion software will allow IP addresses to be searched within the system, and will highlight where and which users are all posting from the same IP address. These can then be investigated further if sockpuppeting is suspected.

It is worth noting that sockpuppeting has gone on for years in offline media as well. The practice of campaigners writing letters to newspapers under assumed names in order to support their cause is quite possibly as old as the existence of newspaper letters pages themselves.

The Astroturfer

Astroturfers are in a way similar to sock puppets, in that they purport to be genuine posters, when actually they have an ulterior motive behind their comments. The term 'astroturfing' is explanatory of this, in that often the practice is used by campaign or lobby groups to give the impression that there is a grass roots movement of support in one particular direction, when in fact such grass roots are fake, or 'astro turf'.

Astroturfers can be harder to spot than sockpuppeters, as they are often genuinely individual people only using one account. They can be harder to deal with too, as accusing someone of astroturfing when they are not can be highly offensive and lead to wider anger amongst the community.

However, often astroturfers will often only post on one issue, will post the same message with the same style or wording as each other (as they have been given a series of prompting points by the campaign or lobby group) and will not engage in the wider discussion on other topics in the same way a more disinterested poster may.

Astroturfing can be an offense worthy of a warning or a ban on occasion. However, often it is best dealt with by the community itself, sometimes even through ridicule. Once again, this persona flags up the need for time and work to be allocated towards building a successful online community discussion approach, and highlights why short term discussion forums for consultation purposes can be ineffective and troublesome.

The Tin Foil Brigade

The great thing about the Internet is the fact that anyone can use it. As a result, one of the most interesting things about the Internet is some of the people who do so.

If you're running an online discussion space for any length of time, you are likely to come across people who hold radically different views from what may be considered to be the mainstream, and some of these views can be pretty odd indeed.

I refer to these types of poster as the 'tin foil brigade', after the old idea held by conspiracy theorists that global governments are trying to control people by beaming messages directly into their brains, and the only way to stop this is to wear a tin foil hat as a barrier.

Sometimes these people will wander into your online discussions. Indeed, they seem to use the Internet for spreading their messages of global conspiracy and shape shifting space lizards more than any other medium, making them not too rare a persona to encounter.

There's not a lot you can do about them, and most of the time they cause more amusement than harm. However, do be careful not to let people promoting conspiracies without providing facts to back them up dominate your conversations, as this can become very off putting to more evidence based participants.

It doesn't have to sound crazy to be a conspiracy theory either, as we're all prone to retelling myths as facts without supporting evidence from time to time. Use the idea of these people to remind yourself that all serious discussion online should be able to be backed up with links to supporting evidence. If it cannot be, it may have no worthwhile place within your discussion community.

The Spambot

Nowadays, most people are all too aware of spam arriving in their emails, unwanted messages promoting often dubious goods and services. Indeed, in 2009, spam was estimated to make up 90% of all the emails sent across the world[82].

However, spam does not just affect emails, but also appears in discussion forums and anywhere else comments can be posted online. There are two main reasons for this.

The first is reasonably obvious. Just as spam emails rely on a percentage of emails sent to lead eventually to money changing hands, so spam is posted on forums in order to promote opportunities to spend money. This sort of spam is so obvious when it appears that it often stands little chance of surviving in public view for very long, as long as someone is checking the forum on a regular basis.

The second though is perhaps more sneaky. Part of the way search engines decide what results to display when someone searches for a term is to count how many pages link to a certain page, as well as the words used in the links themselves. For example, if lots and lots of pages linked to my website, www.gezsmith.com with the words 'saviour of the known universe', then a search for those words would likely return me as the top result[83].

So, what forum and comment spam aims to do is to post comments containing the search terms being targeted, and include within it links to the website being promoted as well. The more of these comments that appear online, the more search engines are likely to place the page being promoted higher up in the search results.

Now of course, the true picture is somewhat more complex than how I've just described it, but this in essence is the point behind people posting spam comments online. Only I've just written a deliberate mistake, as

---

[82] http://news.cnet.com/8301-1009_3-10249172-83.html

[83] At the moment, Flash Gordon seems to be the top result for this search, curse him!

very often it's not people posting these comments, but computer programs.

Many programs have now been written that scan the entire Internet for opportunities to post comments. When they find one, they can register themselves with the site if necessary, log in and post a comment, all automatically. Pretty clever stuff no?

It is, but it's very annoying at the same time. Even more deviously, nowadays the comment spammers try to make the comment posted look genuine, and contain the sort of content that people are unlikely to delete, normally congratulating the site owner on an excellent website, blog or post.

Here are a couple of comments pulled at random from website I built [84].

| web maintenance services itwebxpert.co.uk/web_design /website-maintenance.h... | Submitted on 2012/04/19 at 11:02 am

great posting. was good to see We appreciate, result in I found precisely what I was looking for. You have ended my four day long hunt! Our god Bless you guy. Have a nice time. Bye I'm generally to blog and i really value your content. The article has in fact peaks my curiosity. I'm going to save your site to remain checking for brand new details. | Guy Lloyd's Beyoncé Mission For Glastonbury 2011: Part Two

View Post |

This one's attempting to flatter me into leaving the comment live for others to view, but the use of English really is quite bonkers.

You can see what's going on on the left of the comment though, the 'name' of the commenter contains the keywords they want their site to rank highly for in search engines, and below it is the address of the site itself.

---

[84] www.worthyfm.com

This one's not quite so clever as the previous one in terms of the comment, but they've tried to hide the fact that it's comment spam by using a more realistic sounding name, and again, if I didn't know better, I might be flattered by their comment and leave it live for the world to see, and for search engines to count when deciding how to rank different websites against each other.

This sort of comment spam may all seem pretty innocuous, but it does have some real downsides for a website's owner. First, it makes the site look to others as if no one is looking after it, reducing its credibility and making it appear like a potentially risky place to hang out. It's not unknown for viruses to lurk in comment spam. Second, it can actually confuse real site users. Most regular web users are aware of comment spam these days, but I've sometimes been amused to see unwitting people reply to comment spam and try to engage the 'poster' in conversation, not realising that they're talking to a piece of software that will never even read their reply.

There is also a more dangerous form of comment spam, or at least there was a few years ago, as admittedly I haven't seen any online for a while now. This spam, rather than posting a 'realistic' sounding comment, would just post embedded pictures and videos in the forum or blog, generally of a pornographic nature. As a forum moderator, there was little more alarming to get up in the morning and find the a whole load of new forum posts had been posted, each displaying an eye watering range of sexual enthusiasm.

Comment spam is a well known problem these days, and there are a number of things you can do to prevent it. For instance, have you ever been asked to type a couple of words into a text box before clicking submit? That's there to prevent software submitting content, as the idea is that only humans can read the words on the screen and type them into a box.

Also, just as with email spam, there are automated processes available to detect and filter out comment spam before anyone even sees it. These processes are constantly changing and being refined as the spammers themselves change how they operate, like a constant game of cat and mouse.

Ultimately, like email spam, it is unlikely comment spam will ever fully be prevented, but once you know about it, you can at least be sure to check your site for it and remove it wherever it appears.

Incidentally, comment spam sometimes is written by real people, usually to promote a specific event or piece of online content. Most website owners are generally fine with allowing this sort of human written content to be posted to their site, as long as they have been asked for permission first and/or the person posting it is otherwise a regular site user.

However, if someone registers with your site and posts an advert for their event or content straight away without asking, it's best to take a zero tolerance line in order to make it clear this sort of behaviour is not acceptable. Delete what they have posted and ban them from the site.

Moderation methods

Now we know the sort of people we're likely to encounter when running a discussion forum, or a blog that allows comments, we should look at some of the tricks you can use for keeping everyone posting away happily and within the rules.

Splitting and merging threads

If a forum is healthy and growing, it is likely that people will start to return to it to discuss news and ideas as they emerge. Alternatively, it may be that a discussion on one topic leads to a whole new discussion on another topic starting up within the same thread. In both of these cases, you may need to split or merge threads.

This is quite a simple process built into the moderator's abilities within all good discussion forum software, and one that allows you as a moderator to keep the forums clear and tidy for all to use.

Splitting a thread is when you select any number of posts within the thread, create a new title for them and click submit. This will then create a new thread in the forum containing the posts that you have selected. Splitting threads like this can be a good way of keeping the original thread on topic, by pulling out the posts that are to do with another topic and placing them in their own thread so that discussion can continue on them elsewhere.

There's no need to be over zealous with this, a few off topic posts within a thread is no big deal, and indeed if the posts you're splitting don't make sense when put together, it may be best to leave them where they are. It is also good manners to add a short note at the top of the first post in the new thread explaining that this thread was split out from another thread, as well as giving a link to the other thread for reference purposes.

Merging threads is the opposite of splitting really, and is most useful when two or more threads are all started on the same topic around the same time. You should always encourage your forum users to search the forums for a topic before deciding to start a new thread about it, but sometimes the search doesn't pull out the right results, or they just forget. Merging threads on the same topic together helps keep the discussion of that topic lively and in a single location, as opposed to everyone's comments being scattered across the forum in different threads.

Alternatively, if you see a new thread start on an existing topic before anyone else has posted in it, it can be as well just to reply to the first post with a link to the existing thread on the same topic and then 'lock' that thread so that no-one can post anything more in it. There's no point merging in content from other threads if it doesn't add anything to the thread you're merging into after all.

Again, good discussion forum software should contain the ability to merge threads together without too much difficulty. Most of the time you just need to select the threads to merge and click 'merge'. A simple note at the start of the new merged thread should be used to keep people up to date with what you've done.

Deleting content

Pretty regularly on a forum, content will appear that should not. It could be personal information, comment spam or something so wildly distant from the topic of the forum that it has no place remaining there.

In such instances it is tempting to delete the post from the forum and let that be an end of it. Indeed, it is well within your powers as a moderator to do so. However, I would recommend you do not.

Instead, I would create a new section of the forum and set it so that only moderators and administrators can view it and its contents. Whenever a post appears that you would like to remove from view, use the forum's functionality to move that post into the hidden forum. This means the post is now only visible to moderators and administrators, and serves the following purposes;

- It allows you to keep a record of what has been said in case it needs to be used elsewhere, for example in the event of legal action.

- It allows other moderators to see the objectionable content and who has posted it, information which can sometimes prove useful in future decisions.

- It also allows future moderators, and if the forum lives any great length of time then it is likely there will be some, to see the sorts of content that is required to be removed from the forum, as well as the track record of any objectionable posters they may need to know about.

Posting kittens

This is perhaps a silly trick in a way, but it's one I came up with once that seems to work pretty well.

Sometimes, two or more people posting on a discussion forum will just not get along. Thanks in part to the anonymity of the Internet, and the misunderstandings that can arise through non verbal communication, certain posters will take any opportunity to argue with each other, sometimes even following each other round on a forum just to be critical and insulting. Alternatively, discussion of just one topic can get particularly heated, and descend into argument every time it arises.

In this situation, you can try to ask people to keep it calm and reasonable, but often they just won't. After all, as far as they're concerned, someone is in the wrong and must be told so repeatedly until they mend their views[85].

In this situation, post kittens.

Seriously, if you find an argument or feud is going on, and just won't stop after a polite request, find a picture of a kitten online, and post it in whichever thread the argument is taking place. At the same time, tell people you'll keep on doing so until the argument stops.

Perhaps it plays to some deep part of the human psyche, perhaps it just makes people look silly, but there is something about pictures of cute fluffy kittens appearing throughout an argument that makes it practically impossible for the argument to continue. It's also quite a fun thing to do, so after a while you may find other posters joining in with you whenever they see an argument, in another example of a discussion forum being a living community where people look out for each other.

Incidentally, it's exactly this effect caused by pictures of kittens that led me to choose the cover image for this book. Have a look at the front cover now. Doesn't it make you feel better about the world, and by inference this book?

Banning posters

Sometimes, someone may become so disruptive to an online community over a period of time, or break the rules in such a comprehensive manner just once that there remains no option but to ban them from the site.

---

[85] I love this cartoon, which sums up this sort of situation perfectly - http://xkcd.com/386/

First of all, don't feel bad about doing this. It's your site, you're in charge of it, and you could close the whole thing down tomorrow if you wanted to, effectively banning everyone. In that context, a ban seems less severe.

On most forum software, you get the option to ban an individual poster, an act which generally preserves all of the posts they have made up to that point, but puts the word 'banned' next to their username on each post. Where it exists, be sure to use this option instead of deleting the poster's account. This makes it clear to all that a banning has taken place, and serves as notice to all site users that the site rules are being actively enforced. Banning a user can often generate a huge amount of extra work for a moderator however if their friends start questioning the decision and asking for it to be reconsidered. Try not to get involved in any debate here. If it is questioned, just set out clearly the rule the banned poster breached for all to see, and leave it at that.

Never, under any circumstances, let a permanently banned poster return. Unless they can prove they were banned unfairly (in which case you need to be looking into the circumstances of the ban quite closely), letting a banned poster return essentially shows that the moderation system in place is weak, and can start to be ignored. It doesn't just show this to the banned poster themselves, it shows to the entire community, and can lead to an escalation of problems.

If you're feeling particularly keen to add to your workload, then you can put in place a system of temporary bans for users, and some forum software will even let you set the length of the ban, automatically reinstating the user's account on the appointed date. However, over many years of dealing with situations like these, I tend to work on the principle that a ban is a ban, containing within it no shades of grey or room for debate.

Keeping a moderation log

I've got to be honest here, I'm about to recommend something that I'm personally pretty rubbish at doing, because I've yet to find a quick way of doing it. Still though, my personal failings don't make it any less of a valid activity.

The idea behind a moderation log is to keep a written record of each activity you undertake as a moderator, for example each post you have deleted, each poster warned or banned, as well as the reasons behind each action and the date you carried it out. It's an onerous activity at times, but it really can be useful if or when people challenge something you do as a moderator. It can also be useful to remind yourself which posters have been warned before, in order to decide whether their latest transgression should result in a ban or not.

If you want a more simple life, there are automated moderation log generating programs built into some of the various forum software and platforms that are available, but I've still yet to find one that allows me to record information in quite the way I need it. I'll keep looking though.

7.8 How to use Twitter for online engagement

For a website that's not been around all that long[86,] Twitter has certainly made a big impact, at least in the popular consciousness. In many ways, this is because Twitter exemplifies some of the best qualities of successful digital engagement. It's a very simple idea that is equally simple to use, and one that meets a clear need that people have, that of sharing information with each other quickly and simply. The fact that it's free to use makes a big difference too.

The problem with Twitter is that it has got caught up in some of the trends that swirl around the Internet, which are most evident in how the media reports on it. A Twitter account has in many ways become a 'must have' status symbol. After all, everyone else has one, so so should you. Now I don't know about you, but I've never heard a poorer reason for using a piece of engagement software. Sure, if everyone was using it, then it might be a suggestion with some relevance, but let's not forget that, when compared with email and search engines, Twitter is still relatively small in the scheme of online communication methods.

However, the world of digital engagement is just as prone to fashions as any other. As a result, for many, having a Twitter account is an essential

---

[86] Twitter was launched in July 2006.

part of any digital engagement strategy, to the point that you may appear not to know what you're doing if you don't take part in it.

Now, that's all well and good, and the trendiness of it will hopefully fade over time, but I have to say I'm not one to share the view that Twitter is an essential part of digital engagement. At the end of the day, Twitter is just another tool you can use if you want to, but just as with any other tool, unless you're going to dedicate the time to using it well, then you might be better leaving it alone.

Personally, whilst I've used it a lot on behalf of organisations I've worked for, I've never found the need to use it much for myself. I've already got opportunities to connect and converse with others using Facebook, LinkedIn, discussion forums, email and my mobile phone, which seems to be just plenty to keep on top of for now. I've got a Twitter account[87], and I may end up using it some more one day, but for now I've got no real purpose for it.

So why are there 175 million registered accounts on Twitter then?[88] Surely there must be some purpose to it?

Why to use Twitter

To work out why you should use Twitter, we should first look at what it does.

On Twitter, you can post any message you like, as long as it's not more than 140 characters long. It's this character limit that makes Twitter what it is in many ways, as you're forced by the system to keep your message as short and to the point as possible. Indeed, if ever proof were needed of the importance and impact of keeping your online content as succinct as possible, the global success of Twitter provides it more than amply.

---

[87] http://www.twitter.com/gez_smith if you're interested.

[88] http://twitter.com/about . Note however that some estimates of regularly used and active Twitter accounts fall as low as 56 million.

You can include what you like in your message, so it could just be some text, or it could incorporate links to other websites, abbreviations or a phenomenon that has been developed by the Twitter community itself called hashtags. We'll come on to the language and content to use on Twitter shortly, but first let's look some more at some of its applications.

When you publish something on Twitter, unless you have set your account to be private, it is there to be viewed by the whole world. As such, Twitter has become a useful information sharing and publishing tool for individuals and organisations alike. Nowadays, if a journalist wants to add some colour and context to an article on a breaking news story, they can just visit Twitter and pick out some relevant quotes from tweeters, without even having to ask their permission. Next time you read an obituary online, check the end of the article. Chances are you will see some responses to the person's death from various celebrities, taken directly from their Twitter accounts.

Each tweet posted on Twitter has next to it a 'timestamp', or information on when the tweet was published. This is a really useful way of getting round one of the more common problems in online communication, that of knowing whether the information you are reading is up to date.

So, taking these facts into account, Twitter can be a really useful information sharing tool, and due to the timestamps, the information shared on it can be immediately assessed in terms of its timeliness. As much as I don't really tweet myself, I must say I do use Twitter if I am looking to find the most up to date information on news or events taking place. Given that a tweet is necessarily a short piece of information, many people find it the easiest way to share up to date information with the world, rather than having to go into their existing website, add a new article or page to it and then type the information out in full.

In addition to broadcasting to the world, you can use your Twitter account for two way communication with others as well, either by sending them a private message on the system, only visible to you and the recipient[89], or

---

[89] Only possible when both parties are following each other to help prevent abuse of the service (spam, etc.).

by including their Twitter username in your tweet with an '@' symbol placed in front of it[90]. In this way, Twitter is following on from a convention already understood through email, that information containing the '@' symbol is directed at somebody or something. If you put someone's username with '@' in front of it in a tweet, your message will be flagged up to that person next time they log in. Remember though that, unless you use Twitter's private messaging system, your conversation will be visible for all the world to see.

In a move also found in Facebook, different Twitterers can follow each other, resulting in the content of a user's default Twitter feed showing the latest tweets from those they follow[91]. An interesting netiquette has built up around this, with the more followers you have than you yourself are following, the better you look, a phenomenon expressed more simply as follows;

Followers > following = good

Followers < following =bad

I suspect there are two reasons for this. First, that it is also general etiquette when someone follows you to follow them in return. This way everyone artificially boosts their follower numbers, making them look more popular. However, people can abuse this kindness by following as many people as they can, purely to receive a fair proportion of those followed following them in return.

However, because not all Twitter users will follow in return, you can spot these sorts of people, as they will have similar numbers of both following and followed, although the following will always be slightly larger. So if someone has more followers than people they are following, you can be reasonably sure they're not trying this reputation-building game.

---

[90] @ stands for the word 'at'.

[91] Very similar to Facebook's 'add as friend' functionality, although more open, allowing you to follow someone without their explicit permission, unless they've specifically made their account private.

The second reason I suspect is because it demonstrates that you are an interesting and reliable source of tweets. Just as it's always more attractive in Covent Garden to go and watch the street performer with the biggest crowd, so on Twitter the more followers you have, the more people will want to follow you. You could say there's a bit of the wisdom of crowds going on too.

The really nice thing about Twitter that, to my mind, sets it above the rest at the moment is the well known ability to publish someone's tweet on your own Twitter account for your own followers to see. The exciting new media reason for this is that it allows you 'to share wisdom across the globe' or some such, but I suspect 'using other people's tweets to make yourself look better' or just 'to provide some free content' are also up there as reasons why people do it.

Anyway, this practice is called, sensibly enough, retweeting, and it's always clear when someone has done this, as the identity of the person they are retweeting appears in the retweeted tweet. Retweets are, after all, what cause revolutions and riots across the globe, or at least that's what overexcited journalists who don't use Twitter tell us anyway.

In addition to publishing, sending, receiving and sharing information with other Twitter users, Twitter also has an excellent and simple search functionality built into it, meaning you can search it for anything you like, and quickly see a page full of tweets containing that information. Twitter isn't much good at longevity though, as you can only search the most recent tweets that have been published, generally from around the last week or so. In addition, Twitter limits how many times you can search it per day, and will block you for the rest of the day if you search it too much.

Much like the method we looked in Chapter 6 on unstructured consultation, Twitter also uses a form of tagging to display information. On Twitter, this practice is called 'Trending', and instead of being controlled by site users directly, it is calculated by a mathematical algorithm built into Twitter. The results calculated by the algorithm are displayed as a 'top ten' on the Twitter homepage, and provide an at a glance method of seeing which are the most popular topics currently being discussed on Twitter.

You can change the top ten you see by location as well, so you can see what the top ten most popular topics being posted about on Twitter are globally, then narrow it down to see the topics from a more local area. Whilst everyone would like to get more traffic to their Twitter account, or sites they link to from it, through becoming a trending topic, Twitter are wise to this. At worst, can ban you from the site for trying to manipulate or cash in on trends.

There are a few more things you can do with Twitter too which we will come to in a moment, but that covers the basics for now, and if you want to learn more, Twitter has an excellent online help section at https://support.twitter.com which will tell you all you need to know.

How to use Twitter

So, how to use Twitter then. First of all, I would suggest lurking for a while before starting to use it yourself. Visit Twitter every day for a short while, have a look at some trending topics, do a search for the name of where you live and see what people are saying about it. Only when you feel comfortable that you know what's going on there should you go to http://twitter.com/ and create yourself an account. Don't worry too much about your username when creating your account by the way, the days when it mattered to have your own name attached to a profile you use online are long gone.

Once you have an account, link it up to the other places online you are using for your engagement activities. There are many different ways in which you can do this, so I'll just give you some of the more obvious ones for now.

Link your Twitter account to your website and vice versa

On your Twitter account, you can enter a small amount of text to be displayed on your profile when people visit it. Put in here the URL of the main website you would like people to visit to find out more about you, along with anything else you think people might find it helpful to know, such as who you are and whether your tweets are representative of your organization, or whether they are instead only your own personal views.

You can also get your website to display the content you post on Twitter if you want. There are many different ways of doing this, but most web content management systems now have a plugin you can install into your site that will display your most recent tweets in a tidy and usable manner, generally linking back to your Twitter account when clicked on.

Link your other social media tools to Twitter, or vice versa

If you want to save yourself some work, and you're confident that the content you post on one site will be appropriate for the others, then you can link up the different sites you use with Twitter in a variety of different ways.

For example, when I run a blog, I generally set the blog to post a link to any new post I publish on it to Twitter. When I write a new blog post, I want as many people to see it as possible, but having to copy the URL for the new post, go to Twitter and paste it in as a link before publishing the tweet is a bit of a hassle. Most blogs can now be set to publish a new Tweet announcing the new content on the blog automatically, and setting the blog to do this can save you a good deal of time.

Alternatively, if you're using Facebook, then you can integrate Twitter with it, so that each tweet you publish automatically gets published on your Facebook profile or page as well. Again, this saves you having to duplicate work to make sure your content is visible to the widest possible audience.

These are just a few of the ways you can integrate Twitter with your other online presences. The chances are, if you can thing of a way of integrating it, someone will already have developed a quick and simple way of doing so, so have a hunt around!

A note about Twitter links

One interesting side effect of the development of Twitter has been the rise of link shortening services. For many various reasons, the URL of any given page on the Internet can often be quite long, and cause you problems if you try to incorporate the whole thing within the 140 character limit Twitter allows.

However, you still want to be able to share links to other pages using Twitter, to drive traffic to your site or gain respect from others by alerting them to a useful site elsewhere. As a result, there are various websites you can use to convert your original long URL into a shortened one. The shortened URL these sites give you may not necessarily be that pretty, but it saves you so many characters that you have much more space to write engaging content to go alongside the link.

Three good sites you can use to shorten URLs include;

Google URL Shortener - http://goo.gl/

Bitly - http://bitly.com/

Tiny URL - http://tiny.cc/

Twitter language

Just as with any other digital engagement activity, the most important aspect of how you use Twitter is the content you put on it. We've already seen that Twitter forces you to think a bit more than you normally might when writing content, as it limits you to only 140 characters per tweet. However, like any living community, Twitter has developed its own language styles and conventions, which it can be extremely useful to learn.

It's not as if Twitter is unique in this regard. Discussion forums and instant messaging have also developed their own languages, and as with text messaging, these have mostly been acronyms to save typing. 'LOL', 'BRB' and 'IMHO' are all just foreshortened forms of existing phrases after all[92].

On the other hand, some forum language seemed to arise through a combination of brevity and technical requirements. There are, after all,

---

[92] 'Laugh out loud', 'Be right back' and 'In my humble opinion' respectively.

phrases you may wish to say online that word-filtering software might stop you posting, so 'WTF' and 'OMG' become the safer options to post[93].

With Twitter though, a new language has been developed very quickly, as the text entered into it essentially has two functions. The first is one of communicating with people using a limited amount of words, the second is one of communicating with the software itself.

Before, with a discussion forum for example, you would post a reply to somebody in public, which they would only read if they returned to the forum to view it. Alternatively, if you wanted to send them a message directly, you would use the private messaging system within the forum, which would often then send a message to your email to notify you that a new private message has arrived.

Twitter mixes these two elements though. As already noted, you publish a message to someone publicly, but by putting '@' in front of their username within the message, you also send them a notification that they have a message. Similarly, conventions have arisen to group content together with hashtags, placing '#' in front of a term to denote it as a topic, which others can then click on to find other tweets that contain that same hashtag. So, whilst on a forum, you may have said;

"Hello Jim, fancy watching the football later?"

On Twitter you get;

"Hello @Jim, fancy watching the #football later?"

It can look a bit silly to the untrained eye, but it's not that unreadable. However, problems can arise when you start wanting to spread your message far and wide.

Twitter is a popular mass communication medium, so link spamming, or promoting content to as wide an audience as possible, regardless of whether they want it or not, is a real issue. There's no need to go into this

---

[93] 'What the f***' and "Oh my god'.

too much, but on Twitter it involves people posting messages '@' popular people, or messages that contain hashtags which are highly viewed but possibly unrelated, so messages quickly become crammed with '@'s and '#'s. For example, if you see that the term #football is currently trending, then you can bet that lots of people will be looking at tweets containing that term. So you may be tempted to put #football in your tweet, whether it has anything to do with football or not[94].

The natural desire then, is to use popular hashtags and other terms people may search for to promote your message. Since there is a 140 character limit on Twitter though, this desire can see normal English dispensed with, in favour of what is more akin to code. So in this case, the above message might become;

"@stephenfry @Jim football later? #football #bristolcitysuck"

This whole issue with Twitter posts getting filled with technical and unintuitive language has over time got a whole lot larger too. Twitter Data[95] is a project that's as interesting as it is inevitable, in that it adds a whole new layer of software communication to messages posted.

For example, by using the '$' symbol, you can mark parts of your message on Twitter as being for other software systems to read. For example, the Twitter Data site itself once had a vote on some proposals it made, which could be voted on through your own Twitter account by including '#twitterdata' and '$vote -1' or $vote + 1' in your message. This may be interesting and sometimes useful, but ponder for a moment on what you understand from the following type of tweet Twitter Data suggests its methodology could bring about.

"@toddfast driving $mph 65$, oops just hit a wall $mph 0"

---

[94] As mentioned above, Twitter rightly can and does ban people for doing this. It can also turn into a significant PR disaster for those that try it, just see this example from the (now bankrupt) Habitat chain in the UK - http://www.digitaltip.com.au/index.php/how-not-to-use-twitter-habitatuk-as-a-case-study/

[95] http://twitterdata.org

Didn't make much sense did it? Still, it would make sense to the software behind Twitter Data, so why does it matter that real people find it hard to understand?

Well, as covered repeatedly in this book, information and/or content is the most crucial element of any online project. It has to be easy to find, and easy to understand once it is found. Information on Twitter is easy to find, certainly, but it currently seems to be heading further and further towards only being expressed in its own language, one that tries to meet competing, almost mutually exclusive, goals of talking to people and machines at the same time.

Worse still, the unique style of language on Twitter can easily start to spread across the rest of the web as well, to areas where it will be even less understood. Integrate your Facebook status with your Twitter account, and you risk starting using the language designed for one community in the middle of another. Linking Twitter, or even just its language forms, up with blogs can make the latter look odd as well. The Lib Dem Members website, Lib Dem Voice, was terrible for this at one time, starting posts titles with phrases like 'CommentIsLinked@LDV'. How engaging was this for the non tech savvy? [96]

But am I just being a luddite here? Shouldn't a phenomenon as big as the Internet start to influence the language and behaviours of those who use it? Well, I personally wonder if this is really the way we want to be heading. After all, can we seriously include Twitter in the list of new technologies that increase and widen engagement when it is already moving away from commonly understood communication conventions?

My hunch is that democracy and society would be far better served by focusing on improving communication between individuals, rather than trying to make machines understand what those people are saying.

---

[96] See http://www.libdemvoice.org/commentislinkedldv-chris-huhne-the-implicit-media-prejudice-against-the-lib-dems-16581.html for an example. To their immense credit, the site owners responded to a blog I wrote about this and changed their headline formats to remove this problem almost straight away.

Anyway, rant over, other than to say a few words about my own personal experience of Twitter which I'm increasingly hearing chiming with that of others too. Twitter is a great communication tool, and the speed at which messages can travel through it, as well as the distance they can travel, is pretty much unbeatable at the time of writing. It's absolutely awesome at giving people time-limited news or the latest updates, without taking too much time away from your other tasks, such as handling a crisis. Having someone sitting on a computer just to operate your Twitter account should be an essential component of your 'war room' when a high profile website goes down[97].

Of course, there's also a huge social aspect to Twitter, with an enormous volume of data constantly being churned out by millions of people. Quite apart from the volume of conversation going on on there, there are all sorts of ways of tracking the human behaviour contained within it. However, I'd always be a bit careful not to infer too much from Twitter posts, as it restricts its participants to short statements, which is hardly natural behaviour. It easy is easy to get the wrong end of the stick from a written message compared with one conveyed face to face, and this problem only gets worse when the message has to be truncated.

As mentioned elsewhere, I've never seen the need to throw myself massively into Twitter on a personal level, perhaps because I already used other websites for such purposes by the time Twitter came along. However, I've found it immensely useful and enjoyable to run Twitter accounts on behalf of other clients, and one tip I'd recommend to those struggling to get to grips with a Twitter account, other than delete it if you're really not going to use it, is to try automating your content publication.

Now, that may sound like something technical, but it's really not. It's basically a way of looking as though you're using a system on a regular basis even if you're not. Using some free software, you can write a load of content for your Twitter account in one go, and then queue each piece

---

[97] See Chapter 10 on 'protecting your reputation online' for more on this 'war room' approach.

of it up to be published one at a time over the coming days or even weeks.

I've used this approach when blogging for a long time now, either to keep fresh content being published when away from my computer for a few days, or to ensure that a piece of content goes live as soon as it is allowed to but no sooner, for example if it is a piece of embargoed news. I once wanted to publish a blog about the opening of an exhibition at an art gallery as soon as the doors opened, but not miss the opening myself. So I went down during the afternoon before it opened, took photos of all the pieces in the exhibition and wrote them up into a blog. This blog was then set to be published at 7pm that evening, the exact same time as the doors opened, giving people online the same opportunity to see the pieces as the people there in person. Indeed, when the blogpost went live, I was already down at the show, and arrived back later that evening to find a few thousand new views of my blog.

Of course, if you do use this approach on Twitter, you still have to keep an eye on your account fairly regularly, or else you risk ignoring people who may have sent you a message or mentioned you in one of their tweets, and look rude in so doing. However, you can get Twitter to email you alerts when things like that happen if you really can't bring yourself to keep an eye on Twitter itself.

If you're still not getting to grips with it after a few months though, it may be an idea to post a tweet saying that you're taking a break from Twitter and leave it alone for a while. Be careful not to delete your account altogether and free up the Twitter name you were using though, as it may turn out that you can't get it back later.

7.9 Facebook

Facebook, a website so well known that they've even made a movie about it[98]. With nearly 850 million active users at the time of writing[99], the conventional wisdom is that everyone who's anyone is using it, and if

---

[98] http://www.imdb.com/title/tt1285016/

[99] http://newsroom.fb.com/content/default.aspx?NewsAreaId=22

organisations wish to engage with people, then they should be on there too.

Well, it's certainly a popular site, and it doesn't look like going the same way as Myspace just yet, but of all the social media platforms you could use as an organisation, I just can't shake the feeling that Facebook is probably the last one you should think about using.

One of the key reasons behind this is the sort of social space that Facebook is. Whilst other social media platforms have become well known for being inhabited by a mix of businesses and private individuals, Facebook still very much has a truly social quality about it, being the place where you go to catch up with friends, or at least flick through their latest photos in a somewhat voyeuristic manner. If organisations are on Facebook, then they are often there as advertisers, the sort of thing one tolerates in return for usage of the site being free.

This isn't just my impression either. I have heard of a variety of different surveys undertaken with young people by the UK public sector, where the young people have very clearly said that they don't want their local council or health service to use Facebook, as it is 'their space', a site they go to to get away from authority and be amongst friends.

Indeed, if you think back to the analogy of a party that runs through every aspect of this book, an official organisation using Facebook is akin to someone from that organisation going into a pub, plonking themselves down someone's table and starting to join in with their conversations. An act which is hardly likely to receive a warm welcome. Since we definitely have places in the real world where we go to get away from authority, it is hardly surprising that we should find the same happening in the online world as well.

However, this is not to say there is no point in using Facebook at all. Whilst it may not be much good for organisations to use as a two way communication channel, it can still be a very powerful tool for broadcast communication. This is because Facebook, like Twitter, works on the concept of a 'feed', where the latest content posted by your friends, by groups you have joined or pages you have 'liked' appears on your homepage when you log in. Having your news and other content appear in as many Facebook feeds as possible is an excellent idea, especially if this content links back to other sites that you use for receiving feedback or engaging in two way conversation.

So, let's look at Facebook from the perspective of being an information publishing medium first, as for such a simple to use site, there are actually many ways to get things spectacularly wrong.

Profile, group or page?

There are three main ways you can exist on Facebook. You can have an individual profile, containing your information, latest news, photos and so forth; you can have a group, which is more of a collective space for you to run in collaboration with other group members; or you can have a page, which is similar to a profile, but is more designed for the needs of businesses and organisations.

Choosing the right method of appearing on Facebook can be crucially important. Partly because you want to make sure you have access to the sorts of functionalities you most require, but most important, because if you get it wrong, Facebook can and will delete you.

I had to learn this one the hard way myself a couple of years ago. As a hobby, I had set up an increasingly successful blog on the topic of street art and graffiti[100]. In order to widen the reach of the blog, I set up a profile on Facebook for it, using the name of the blog as the name of the profile. One day, I went to log in to the profile, only to find Facebook had without warning deleted it, meaning the 800 or so people who had by that point added me as a friend suddenly stopped receiving the latest blog content I wrote. There was no way of recovering a list of those friends I had accumulated, so that was that; 800 useful contacts gone.

In order to keep the site tidy, Facebook insists that individual profiles are only used to represent real people, and if the profile looks as though it's for an organisation or website, they will delete it without warning.

---

[100] I've always been an observer in this field rather than a participant by the way. I can barely write with a pen, let alone draw with an aerosol.

So, unless you're going to use Facebook as yourself, don't set up a profile on it. That leaves you with two options, creating a group or creating a page. Now, it's tempting here to give a big list of the pros and cons of groups vs. pages, but Facebook is forever tweaking its functionality, so rather than risk becoming out of date, have a search on Google for 'Facebook group vs. page' and read some of the articles that come up.

Personally, unless Facebook adds some new form of profile into the mix, I'd say that the best option is always to create a page. Regardless of the better functionality for organisations that pages offer at the time of writing[101], there is also the more simple intuitive point. Most organisations are not groups of people, at least not in the legal sense, rather they are individually constituted bodies, and it makes far more sense to say that you 'like' an organisation on Facebook than to say you have joined it. As ever with digital engagement, the answer that seems more intuitively right to you will also most likely seem most appropriate to others as well.

Using Facebook as a broadcast channel

As mentioned above, if I were to use Facebook on behalf of an organisation, I would primarily use it as a broadcast channel rather than a space for building customer interaction. Not just because that is how potential customers are most likely to wish you to use it, but also because the more channels for feedback or two way communication you have open, the more likely you are not to notice messages that people send you, and thus the greater the risk of creating dissatisfaction, albeit unintentionally.

However, using it as a broadcast channel, you create a simple way for people to be updated on your news and content every time they log into Facebook, rather than relying on them visiting your website.

Developing Facebook as a broadcast channel needn't be a difficult or time consuming task either. Just as with the examples we looked at with

---

[101] Appearing in search engine results, the ability to view your page's visitor statistics and customising your Facebook URL to name just three.

Twitter above, there are a number of different ways to integrate Facebook with other platforms and services.

Firstly, if you are running a page on Facebook, you can set the page to pull in content automatically from another website, for example a blog. If you do this, every time you publish a new blog post, a synopsis (typically the first few lines) of the blog will appear on your Facebook page, and so in the newsfeed of every individual who 'likes' your page, along with a link to the full blog article on your site.

Alternatively, you could keep your website and Facebook separate, and use the latter on its own to broadcast specific types of information most relevant to your Facebook audience. After all, not all the news you create will be of equal interest to everybody, and if you start publishing too much information of little relevance to Facebook users, then those users will start to click that little 'x' that appears next to each of your posts and hide you from their newsfeed.

Another way to use Facebook as a broadcast channel is to pay for advertising on it. As with all free to use websites, Facebook has to generate revenue somehow in order to keep functioning, and selling advertising space on the site is an effective means of doing this.

Like any web advertising, buying Facebook ads isn't just as simple as deciding what you want your advert to say and how long you want it to appear for. Of course you have to do both of these things to start with, but then you can decide other factors, such as who to target the adverts at in terms of their demographic profile and location. This ability to target adverts at specific audiences often makes Facebook advertising much more effective than other advertising locations, and exists as a result of Facebook collecting detailed demographic information on each registered user.

In addition, like most good web advertising, Facebook adverts are run on a 'cost per click' basis, meaning you only pay money when someone actually clicks on the link in your advertisement, rather than alternatives such as 'cost per impression', where you pay money each time an advert appears on a page someone is viewing. To prevent your budget running out of control, you can set the maximum you are willing to pay per day, and once enough people have clicked on your advert to spend that money, your advert will disappear until the next day.

I've used Facebook advertising a few times now on behalf of clients, and whilst it can be a bit hit and miss, I've seen some really impressive results occur when the content and the targeting of it have been right. However, I've also seen some adverts generate literally no clicks, despite a significant budget being put behind them.

This may be because, as mentioned above, people see advertising on Facebook as a necessary evil that exists to keep the site free for them to use, rather than something interesting that keeps them abreast of the latest trends. As a result, it often takes some real thought to build a successful Facebook advertising campaign, but it's work that's worth doing if you've the time and inclination.

7.10 Integrating your different engagement channels

There are numerous different ways in which you can get sites to integrate with each other, but here's an overview of a typical integration setup to get you thinking. Each of the arrows represents content moving from one platform to another.

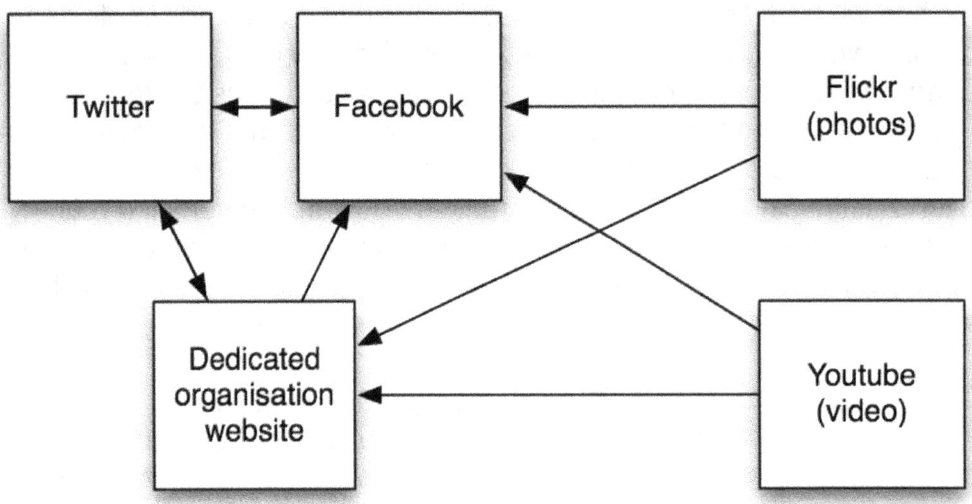

In this example, the following is happening;

- All content first published on the organisation's own website is being automatically published onto the organisation's Facebook page, with a link back to the original website.

- All content appearing on the organisation's Facebook page is automatically published onto their Twitter feed, with a link back to Facebook or the relevant page on the organisation's website.

- Content on the organisation's Twitter feed is embedded in the organisation's website, with a back link out to Twitter.

- Photos and videos are put on Flickr and YouTube respectively. Both of these types of content are automatically embedded in the organisation's main website, as well as being shared on Facebook.

When you're dealing with many different platforms for digital engagement at the same time, it is often important to map out the different journeys your content will be taking, and refer back to it from time to time. Otherwise it can be very easy to forget what is appearing where, and start to publish inappropriate content on some of your channels.

7.11 Who can talk online

We've spent a lot of time in this chapter looking at the different ways you can use online tools to build engagement with your target audiences, and how to integrate them with each other in order to save time and effort. There remains though one final point to consider. If you are looking at undertaking this work as or on behalf of an organisation, as I suspect many of you will be, who should you allow to create content for it?

Now, there is no right or wrong answer to this question per se. Obviously, if you're wanting to communicate a core set of messages to your audience, it is best to have an individual or small group of individuals take responsibility for this, to make sure that everyone is 'singing from the same hymn sheet' as it were. But if you're looking at entering the field of online engagement, then you're looking at working in an extremely unstructured area, where your audience can often set the agenda and choose the topics of conversation they want to engage you in, rather than you being in control.

In this case, it is unlikely that having a single individual responsible for responding to these conversations will actually be that good an idea. For unless that individual is some sort of polymath with regards to everything your organisation does, all they are going to have to do is pass on the questions being posed to the people who can answer them before replying to the original questioner. This will inevitably leave the response seeming somewhat stilted, and also risks introducing errors into the response in the way long chains of communication often do[102].

So given these facts, the rule should generally be that the less structured the engagement activity being undertaken, the more people on your side it is appropriate to involve in participating and responding. But with this rule comes a problem. Especially if you're using social media for your engagement activities, following this rule risks creating a conflict with a policy as common as it is banal, the policy that staff may only use the Internet for work related matters.

Now this rule in and of itself shouldn't stop you getting lots of people on your site taking part in your online engagement activities, but the way it is applied often does. For the simplest way to make sure staff only use the Internet for work is often seen to be to restrict which sites they can and cannot access from their work computer. As a result, access to Facebook, Twitter, blogs and a whole host of other websites gets blocked, meaning that however much they may want to engage with your audiences online, your staff or colleagues simply cannot[103].

Personally, I have always thought that blocking staff from accessing any part of the Internet on work computers is a faintly ridiculous idea. If you can't trust people to do the work they are supposed to for fear of distraction by social media, then you have a bigger HR issue to resolve,

---

[102] Just like the game Chinese whispers -http://en.wikipedia.org/wiki/Chinese_whispers
[103] I shall spare their blushes, but I do know of one UK local authority that was extremely proud of the work it was doing using a blog based platform as a base, only to find that no-one else in the authority could see this engagement website, as their IT team had blocked all access to websites based on blogs.

not an issue that can be solved through the application of IT. We are all perfectly capable of wasting time in a wide variety of ways when we're not interested in our jobs, and you can't block each and every distraction people may find in the course of their work.

Even if staff are not blocked from accessing these sites, prohibitions are often written into corporate policies or individual employment contracts, forbidding employees from talking about their employer online. To my mind, this is generally as unacceptable as it is foolish. Unacceptable, as if you can't trust your staff to say nice things about you, then you're once again trying to turn an HR issue into an IT issue, and foolish, as it makes the Internet pretty unique in terms of the communication methods your staff can use.

After all, if someone emailed a member of your staff to ask them a question, would you forbid them from replying? What if they asked their question by telephone, would you insist your staff hang up immediately? Should they be forced to bin every letter they receive in the post because they can't post a reply back? If the local media made an incorrect statement about your work, would you just ignore it and allow the inaccuracy to become considered an unchallenged fact?

The answer to all of these questions should be of course not. So if that's the answer with regards to those communication methods, why is it not the answer when it comes to someone asking you a question or making an inaccurate statement about your organisation online?

Your staff or colleagues are the people best placed to make sure that your customers have all of their questions answered quickly and politely, and are also best placed to look out for and correct any untruths that may appear. So instead of banning them from talking about their work online, make best use of their capabilities in this area and encourage them to go out and be online advocates for your work. You'll soon get to hear if any of them start to get things wrong or make things worse, and again, this is an issue you fix using your HR process, not IT.

7.12 Blogging

I've mentioned blogging repeatedly throughout this book, often in the context of something else, and this shouldn't come as any surprise really. Blogging is one of the oldest and most widely used online engagement tools currently available on the web. Personally, I started blogging back in 2002, and I could have been using Blogger, my original choice of blogging platform, from as early as 1999.

In case you've not come across blogging yet, it's quite a simple process. The word blog is derived from the words 'web' and 'log', and as these words suggest, the original idea behind blogging was to write a regular log of your activities, a kind of diary really, and publish it for others to read online. The problem was though that most blogs along these lines were crushingly boring, as only a few people have lives that are truly interesting to others when written down in detail.

So nowadays, the concept of a blog has expanded somewhat to encompass news, information and commentary on both of these more generally. In fact, there is practically nothing that couldn't be used as content for a blog, the only criteria for success being that the content is interesting to others, just like many other online engagement tools.

The other main problem encountered with blogging is the perseverance and stamina of the person writing the blog. No matter how the good the intentions are when starting the blog, most bloggers will admit that retaining the enthusiasm to write blog posts week after week is difficult, and this is before you factor in the additional work that blog popularity can bring with it. Comment moderation, answering emails from readers and responding to other bloggers can all add to your workload to the point that something has to give.

I have my own experience of this that may serve as a case study. In 2007 I started writing a blog about graffiti in Bristol. I'd been interested in and photographing graffiti in my hometown since the early days of Banksy back in the late 1990's, and wanted to learn more about the graffiti scene and the artists involved in it. So I embarked on a bit of a learning journey, and used the blog to help me. In part it helped me find out more, because if I didn't know something, I could write my question into a blog post, and a reader would generally leave a comment answering me.

In another way, the blog helped me to keep learning, as I'd made a commitment to write at least one new blog post per day, so I had to keep learning new things in order to keep the blog going. Behind all of this, I figured that the hundreds of photos of graffiti I'd taken over the previous 10 years or so would mean I'd always have ready made content to fall back on if daily life got in the way from time to time.

The blog grew steadily over the next two years, averaging 1000 unique visitors per day at its peak, and I even got some exclusives, such as announcing that Banksy was to return to Bristol for an exhibition at Bristol Museum months before the 'secret' was announced in the mainstream press. However, aside from the work involved in going out to art galleries, events and regular graffiti spots to take photos, the blog also created a lot of work dealing with enquiries from the media, students doing research projects, and the occasional threats of violence from people who claimed to be graffiti artists[104.]

Put all this together, and I was doing around two hours of work on the blog per day, pretty much taking up every evening I had. Sure I enjoyed it. I got to go to some great events, I fought and won some mini campaigns here and there and met some fascinating people. But over time it all got to be too much. My enthusiasm waned, and I stopped blogging in 2009. After all, since I'd made an editorial decision to write the blog anonymously and accept no money or gifts from anyone in order to keep the content objective, I was putting in lots of work for little reward.

So, if you're thinking of starting a blog, do bear my experiences in mind. I had great fun doing it for a while, but the workload involved in building and maintaining a successful blog should never be underestimated. In many ways it is problems like these that have helped define what creates a successful blog, so let's have a look at how to do just that next.

---

[104] I have my suspicions about who these threatening people were, and they're certainly not about anyone involved in graffiti. Rather I suspect they were from people who want to stop graffiti happening, pretending to be graffiti writers themselves. A prime example of 'sock puppeting', explained elsewhere in this book.

How to blog

Despite the vast majority of blogs failing within a month or two of being set up, successful blogging isn't actually difficult. Indeed, I suspect those blogs that fail are the ones that make it more difficult that it needs to be, the blogger setting themselves up to fail through their own self imposed complexity. If good blogging is all about keeping it simple, so too should the explanation of how to do it be simple. Here's a step by step guide.

Choose your weapons

There are many different software platforms you can use for blogging, and the good news is that they're pretty much all free. Now, there are two ways you can use this free software. Platforms such as Wordpress allow you to download a copy of the software for free and install it on your own website, making your blog just one part of your wider site. This can work well, and provide a reason to keep people visiting your site on a regular basis in order to read your posts. However, on the flip side of this, if your blog starts gathering dust from lack of blogging, then it can make your site, and so your image, look worse than if there were no blog on there in the first place.

Alternatively, most blogging platforms will host a blog for you, typically giving you a URL that contains their URL too, for example www.yourblogname.wordpress.com Since the URL you use for a site now matters far less than it used to, there's no shame in using a domain name like this, and indeed many very popular blogs do just this[105]. If you're uncertain as to whether you're going to take to blogging or not, then taking this approach gives you a zero cost way of dipping a toe in the water, without risking damaging the reputation of your website if anything goes wrong.

For examples of some free to use blogging platforms currently available, see section 12.3.1 of this book.

---

[105] For example, one of the UK's most read political blogs used to be written by Iain Dale, and lived at http://iaindale.blogspot.com/

Choose your topic and audience

As covered elsewhere in this book, when creating any website, you should give consideration to what it is going to be about and who you would like to use it. This is especially important with a blog though, as some of the most successful blogs are those which pick a specific topic to cover and stick to it. Indeed, some bloggers who want to write about different topics will set up individual blogs for each one.

Whilst this may seem like overkill, it is now necessary to do this, as readers have come to expect to be able to use blogs to meet their own niche interests. If you blog about too broad a range of topics, then not only will the specialist attention to detail of your blog suffer, but no one audience will be satisfied by every post you make. Dissatisfied audiences soon become smaller audiences.

Of course, it could be that you want to return to the original idea of blogging and blog about yourself and what you get up to. If you're a person likely to be of interest, such as a celebrity, organisational figurehead or elected official, this may well be no bad thing. If you're not though, then going down this route is likely to result in a dead end.

Given blog posts are typically short and about current events, many organisations use blogging as a way of publishing their news as it happens. Using a blog platform as a place to publish media releases isn't strictly speaking blogging as such, as blogging generally contains thoughts and opinions about news, rather than just news itself. However, given blogging platforms provide a quick and simple means of publishing content online, there is no harm whatsoever in using them for this purpose. If you're not allowing people to leave comments on your news though, then it is best that you do not call this part of your website a blog, as for many people, the ability to leave comments is what separates and defines blogging from the more general publishing of content online.

Keep your blog posts short

We already know that people read less text on a screen than they do on a page. Add to this the fact that your blog will be competing for attention with myriad other blogs already out there, and the need to keep your blog content short and simple is extremely important. Two paragraphs of four lines each will generally suffice.

I must confess that I'm terrible at this myself. If I think of something interesting to blog about, I end up writing six or seven long paragraphs, and my audience figures suffer as a result. Of course, I could edit it all down once written, but this takes time, and I generally find that the best way to keep myself interested in blogging is for it to be a fun, spontaneous and ultimately quick activity as part of my daily routine. An overly considered blog post, whilst shorter, can still be quite boring.

To get round the problem of my extraneous verbosity when blogging, I use the following trick.

Use an image in every post

Images are great online, and the different ways of using them are considered in Chapter 4 of this book. However, they're especially good in blogging, as if you want to keep your blog post short, an image can often convey the same information you would otherwise convey using words.

For example, if you see something funny, irritating or downright stupid whilst you're out and about, rather than writing about it, why not take a quick photo of it using your mobile phone or digital camera, post that photo on your blog and add just a couple of lines saying what it is, where you saw it and what you think about it. If people are interested in it, they will leave a comment on that post, and you can then get into more wordy discussion about it in the comments.

On the other hand, if no-one leaves a comment, it may well be that you're the only person that found it interesting, and so you've just saved yourself from writing more about something everyone else finds dull.

Share some link love

Blogs are one of the areas of the web where the hyperlink comes into its own. First, if you see something online and want to write a blog post about it, then linking directly to what inspired your post can save you having to write it all out again. A blog post like this could thus take the format of "I just saw this <link>. I think it's stupid because X. What do you think?". One nice, short and simple blog post. Job done.

In addition, most blogging software contains functionality called trackback. When one blog post links to another blog post, trackback will cause the post which is being linked to to display a link to the post that is linking to it in its comments[106]. So, when you write your post and link to someone else's blog in it, the owner of the blog you are linking to will be notified of your post, and all of their readers will see a link to your blog on the post you're linking to too.

Often, this can be a good way of getting an interesting debate going between blogs, and it can also be a good way of gaining web traffic from another blog that is perhaps better read than yours, as readers of the better read blog click on the link in the trackback you have created.

If you're better at understanding pictures than words, here's a diagram explaining how trackbacks work.

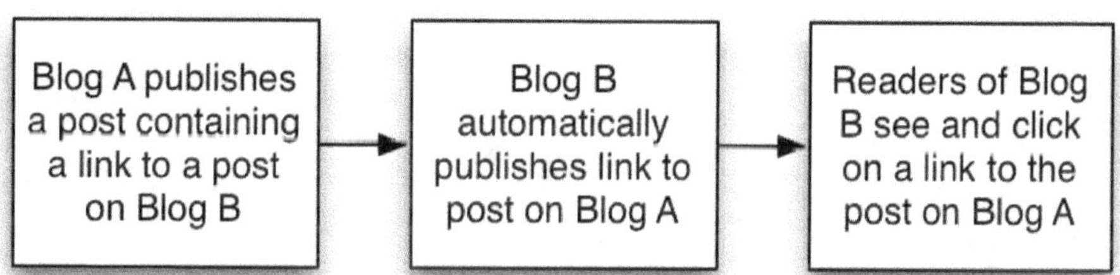

In addition to this specific piece of blog functionality, including links to other sites in your blog posts is also good practice for a couple of other reasons.

First, because if people see you are linking to them, they are more likely to link to you in return. Second, because links provide access to other interesting content for your readers. By doing this, your are in a way providing a news and editing service for your readers, reading a range of content and linking to the best bits you find, saving your readers the trouble of searching through content themselves.

---

[106] That is, assuming the blog being linked to has trackbacks enabled on it, as it can be turned off if the blog owner so wishes.

UK political blogger Iain Dale used to have a very good approach to this, having a daily blog post called the 'Daley Dozen', which just contained links to the 12 most interesting blog posts he had read that day. His readers thus always came straight to his blog to find interesting blogs to read, giving him more traffic, and the blogs that he linked to benefitted from the traffic this gave them, making them more inclined to link back to him in return. A win-win situation for all concerned.

As long as you've got the points above covered, then blogging really isn't, and indeed shouldn't be, any more complex than that. You need to keep it simple in order to maintain your motivation for keeping it going. Keeping it simple keeps it fun to do, and if you enjoy writing your blog, you will write the sort of content that others enjoy reading. The more people read what you write, the more you will enjoy writing it, and so on and so forth.

Chapter 8. How to analyse data

One of the great advantages of any digital engagement project is that analysing any data it generates, whether it's customer feedback or a formal consultation, is made a whole lot easier by being collected in an electronic format. With other consultation and engagement methods, you can face sometimes significant overheads from tasks such as data entry, data collation and physical data storage, all of which are generally just not relevant to digital engagement.

In addition, since you're collecting it in an electronic format, you can tailor that collection format however you want, to make generating understanding from the data collected as simple as possible.

Again here, we see synergies between online and offline processes, for both offline and online data can be collated into and analysed in software based packages. However, analysing offline data using software would not be considered to be digital engagement, as the participation itself isn't happening using electronic methods. So in looking at data analysis options in digital engagement, it is with this requirement in mind; that the data must have been created by the participant using electronic methods in the first place.

8.1 Data analysis formats

There are a great many different data analysis packages out there, so it is perhaps unsurprising that there are also many different formats in which data can be stored. This does not mean formats in the visual sense of how the data is arranged and laid out when you look at it, but rather formats in the sense of the type of file, for example a Microsoft Word format as opposed to a plain text file format.

The good news is that most of the time you don't have to worry about variety in the latter sense of file format, as there are some file formats that can work universally across them. Indeed, were it not for these universal file formats, I probably wouldn't bother bringing up this entire topic, as I would only be able to talk in terms of specific pieces of software. However, since these formats exist, it is well worth knowing about them.

The first is .csv format. CSV stands for Comma Separated Values, and it stores data as plain text, with each individual item generally being separated from its neighbours by a comma. There are in fact a number of different types of .csv format, which can cause some compatibility problems from time to time, but in the vast majority of cases, data stored in .csv format can be opened, read and manipulated in a wide range of different software packages.

Most commonly, when you double click on a .csv file, your computer will by default use Microsoft Excel or a similar spreadsheet program to open it, and this gives a clue to the more common usage of .csv format files, that of storing data in a spreadsheet. Indeed, one of the easiest ways to create a .csv file is to enter the data into a spreadsheet package and then use the 'save as' option to save it into a .csv.

For the purposes of digital engagement, and data storage online more generally, a .csv file is an excellent means of transferring data between both people and systems. So much so that I generally assume that any data storage system I might want to use should contain the ability to export its contents in .csv format as standard, and so should you.

The other major data format group contains formats like .txt and .rtf, standing for 'Text' and 'Rich Text File' respectively. These types of file are most commonly used for storing text as opposed to spreadsheet data, and generally allow you to do very little formatting of the text in the file. Again, these file types can be opened by a wide range of different software programs, but in this case it is more typically word processing programs that are used to open them by default. As they contain very little to no formatting on the text, these files are typically smaller in file size than a word processing document containing the same text.

So between .csv and .rtf/.txt file formats, you have a wide range of ways you can store data and use it in a number of different software programs, even when those programs would normally save data in their own proprietary format. In most sites I've worked on, as long as one or both of those file formats is available for exporting any data the site collects, I've not found the need to have other file formats supported by the site's export process.

8.2 Data analysis tools

There are many different pieces of software you can use for analysing any participation data you collect, and there's no point in giving you a blow by blow account of them with their strengths and weaknesses. However, they do fall into a few basic categories, so it is well worth being aware of the different sorts of tools out there, and some of the interesting things you can do with them already.

Don't feel constrained by these though. To my mind you can have some real fun with how you analyse and present data to make it interesting. Not forgetting that the more work you put into your data, the more you get out of it.

8.3 Quantitative analysis

Sometimes, you just want to turn your data into data or statistics, and give people the numbers. If you're looking at things that can easily be measured in that way, then no problem. It's good to know if people are more satisfied or dissatisfied with what you do, and indeed a form of this calculation, called an election, is used to run democracies across the globe.

Getting to grips with calculating and working with statistics isn't something worth going into here, as there are plenty of other books out there that can teach you this. All I would say is not to be put off by the idea of learning about it. I'm utterly hopeless at mathematics, but pretty good at the sort of statistics you need to do market research. Also, whilst I've sometimes used reasonably sophisticated stats software, I generally find that most calculations can just as easily be done in a spreadsheet program like Microsoft Excel or similar. Something as simple as a calculator can even do everything you need to at times.

Of course, it could well be that the digital engagement software you are using has statistical analysis functionality already built into it in one form or another. In which case the most useful thing you can have is the ability to generate 'top line stats' (simple counts and percentages of the raw data) and the ability to cross tabulate data (compare one set with another). Anything more than that you can usually do more easily in a spreadsheet program than on the software itself. After all, the spreadsheet software has probably had far more money invested in being usable than an analysis tool that only forms one part of a bigger package.

So much for dealing with the numbers you may collect, what about analysing the words?

8.4 Qualitative analysis

Before anyone tells you otherwise, can I please assure you that the ability for software to be good at recognising and analysing language for its meaning, good enough to be statistically reliable, is still a fair way off. If it does exist at all, it is hardly on widespread release. I have no doubt it will exist one day, but at the moment there are just too many nuances between dialects and people to have software understand and interpret free text responses reliably. In a world where hot can mean stolen and cool can mean fashionable, we still encounter problems of understanding between fellow humans, so how we expect a computer to do it perfectly I don't know.

So, if people are writing you comments, you still have to read them in order to get the most out of them, and afford the same courtesy of time to the person who took the time to write to you. However, you can make large amounts of comments more usable as you read them by coding them, or grouping them into categories, with each category being given a single word or set of words to group them together. The more observant of you will have realised this is just what your site's users are able to do themselves on unstructured consultation sites of the types discussed in Chapter 6.

Once you have coded up data in this way, you can start to run quantitative analysis on it, for example 'How many people said plate tectonics was their number one daily fear?'.

However, there are some clever tools online which will run this sort of analysis for you automatically, counting how many times any given word occurs across an amount of text, and presenting the results in the form of a word cloud. In case you've not heard of a word cloud before, it's very similar to the tag cloud we looked at in Chapter 6, except rather than acting as links for information, words in a word cloud are generally just static words. Like tag clouds though, the words are all sized differently, where the larger the word, the more times it has appeared in a piece of text.

So, you can't always be guaranteed of being able to understand the sentiment of what is being said by creating a word cloud from your free text data, but you can often gain an interesting sense of what it contains and what people are talking about.

Word clouds can also look really good in presentations by the way, partly because they convey relevant data in an interesting way, but also because not many people have seen them before, making you look cool.

If you fancy creating a word cloud for yourself, a good free site for this, at the time of writing at least, is http://www.wordle.net, and to show you what they can look like, here's a word cloud made of all of the text in this chapter, created using http://www.wordle.net/create.

Chapter 9. How to get people to visit your site

The one thing you want to do, having set everything up, is to have people visit your site. Now we've touched on this quite a bit already at various places in this book, and doing so is sort of inevitable, as there are so many things that influence how many people visit your site and what sort of people they are. In this chapter however, we are going to look more specifically at the tools and techniques you can use to build the number of visitors, commonly called 'traffic', to your website, as well as some of the ways in which you can judge whether they are working or not.

First of all, if you're feeling at all uncertain of being able to do this sort of work, please don't be. It's actually some of the easiest work you can do in digital engagement, and in most cases it is simply a case of the more work you put into it, the better the results you will get. Given there's only so much work you can do at any one time, this is also an area where the longer you work on it for, the more visitors you will get. In essence, as we will see in a bit, building website traffic is just a big numbers game, the more people you tell about your site, the more people will look at it.

There are three areas of work that we need to consider in making sure people visit your site, one is active, one is passive and the other is a mix of the two. In essence, we need to look at how you invite people to your site (active) and how you allow people to find your site for themselves (passive), as well as those activities which sit between the two.

Common online channels for building visits, from active to passive

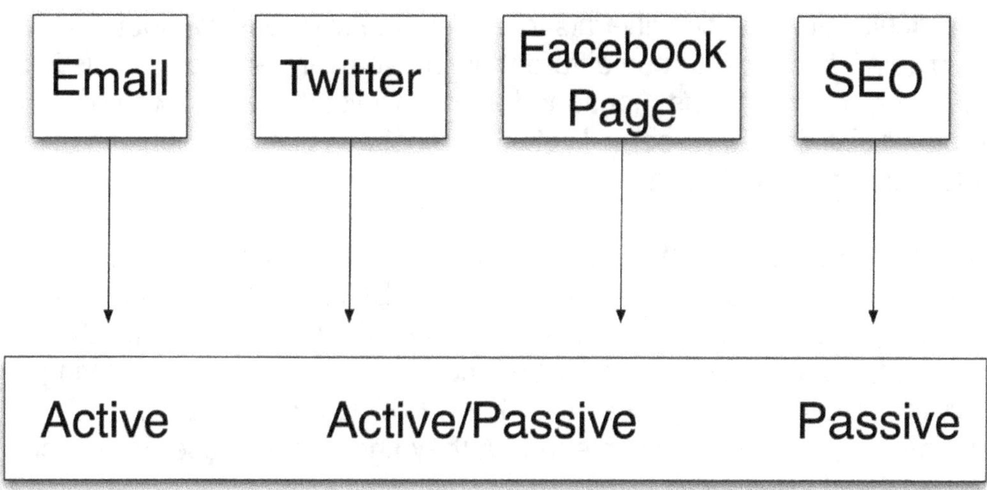

As can be seen from the above, there is no activity that could be said to be 100% active or passive without at least some element of the other creeping in. Even the act of sending someone an email, whilst in and of itself a purely active method, could see that email and its content being found and read by someone else later without you knowing. Equally, whilst being found through Google is passive, actively carrying out Search Engine Optimisation (SEO) to make sure people find you through there gives SEO at least a bit of an active element.

However, this is not to say that active and passive aren't useful categories for understanding online marketing work, neither is it to say that all work should be lumped together into the 'Active and Passive' category. When I talk about an area being active or passive here, it is on the understanding that the majority of that area works either actively or passively to draw people to your site.

So then, let's have a look in a bit more detail at these two main forms of work for getting people to visit your site, as well as those activities that fall neatly between the two extremes.

9.1 How to let people know you're online through active promotion

It's difficult with a section like this to explain the methods, without once again going over how to use different online software and tools. This is a pity in some ways, for as mentioned above, whilst there's no way of telling for certain yet, it seems likely that most specific communication tools online are short lived.

It's all very well to learn how to use Facebook to get people to your website, but how much longer will Facebook be one of the pre-eminent forces in people communicating online? Even if it does survive for the long term, it's almost certain that it will continue changing and evolving over time. So when people say they know how to use Facebook, remember that they actually mean that they know how to use Facebook *as it works at the moment.*

Two prime examples of this are Myspace and Geocities. In the mid to late 2000's, Myspace was huge. In 2005, Rupert Murdoch bought the company who ran it for $580 million[107]. Its name was almost synonymous with social networking, and if you wanted to find people to tell about your website, you'd go there. Now, in 2012, it's said to be worth around $20-30 Million[108], and as you can see from the chart in section 9.5 on passive means of building web traffic below, it doesn't even get 1% of the total Internet usage market, against Facebook's 44%.

Similarly Geocities, which brought the idea of having a personal presence and your own page on the web to millions of people, is now closed and offline, almost like an entire global city and network just disappeared forever, along with all of the information people had uploaded to it[109].

So whilst it would be silly to try to talk about this sort of work entirely theoretically, I've tried to keep the examples of active promotion below in broad themes and areas, rather than getting too attached to any one

---

[107] See http://news.bbc.co.uk/1/hi/business/4697671.stm
[108] See http://news.cnet.com/8301-1023_3-20075167-93/myspace-sale-nearing-end-with-low-$30m-price/
[109] I suspect and hope history will not look kindly on a mass deletion of public data such as this.

piece of software. That way, I always feel you're more future proof than if your fortunes are tied to the fate of any one company's platform.

Email campaigns

When it comes to promoting websites and online content more generally, you really can't beat the power of the email.

Email is much more than an active marketing and promotion tool though, it is a tool which quickly progresses into a two way conversation between yourself and those you are emailing. As such, it is as much an online engagement tool as an online promotion one, and for best results it should always be approached from that perspective. If all you intend to do is send emails and never reply to them, you're straying into the world of spamming, a world that is best avoided at all costs.

So do have a read of the section on emails in Chapter 7 if you want to look into email as a channel for marketing your website, as with email, the line between marketing and engagement quickly starts to blur.

Blogger/website outreach

One great way of building traffic for your own website is to tell other website owners about it, and get them to link to your site. For not only does this lead to more traffic coming directly from the readers of the linking site, it also encourages search engines to rank your site more highly in their search results, giving you a passive marketing win as well as an active one.

Now, I've tended to find that once your site reaches a certain critical mass, people will start linking to it of their own free will. Quite what this critical mass consists of, I'm not sure, but I suspect it comes about when your site contains good content, plentiful content and a certain number of incoming links; all things that will generate enough visits for the people likely to link to you spontaneously to start finding you.

However, to get to that point, you often need to give people a bit of a nudge, and start creating links to your site yourself, or at least encourage others to do so. Way back in the early days of blogging, 2002 or so, I was a bit cheeky in this regard. A very well known New Labour leaning blogger at the time wrote a blog post criticising bloggers of other political persuasions, and on this post I left a comment stating that I was a Lib Dem blogger, so would this person please come and criticise me too? My comment of course contained a link back to my blog.

Immediately, I started noticing an increase in traffic coming through the link left in that comment, and even better, the blogger then wrote a whole new blog post criticising me and my views, containing yet another link to my blog, causing my traffic to rise even higher. The blogger openly thought me a moron for inviting criticism from him, but it helped take my blog traffic up another level, and I must have been doing something right, as that level then became my new daily average for a while. Of course, I then wrote a post explaining why I'd left the comment in the first place, and thanking the blogger for bringing my thoughts to an even wider audience.

I doubt such a tactic would work in quite the same way these days, as people would see it for the spam that it pretty much was. However, the point behind it remains. If you want people to find your site, one of the best ways of doing it is to go and leave comments on other sites, and include a link to your site somewhere in them. At the very least, the site owner will most likely check out the link you have left, and if they like your content, they will keep reading, and sooner rather than later start linking to your site in new content that they publish. That is, of course, if your content is interesting, which flags up again how crucial interesting content is to building a successful website.

Another means of generating traffic for your site in this way, rather than using comment functionality, is to approach the site owners directly and ask them for a link. Now, you don't get something for nothing in this world, so you have to be a bit more sophisticated than just emailing someone to ask them to link to your site. Instead, you have to give them something that is useful to their site in return. If you're just launching your site, then perhaps you could give the most prominent or most read blogger in the relevant field an exclusive on your site's launch, to give them the kudos of being first with the news.

Alternatively, if you've got some interesting news to share, why not send it out as a media release to relevant bloggers [110]? As covered elsewhere in this book, regular blogging can become an onerous and time consuming task after a while, so most bloggers are happy to be sent new content to publish that doesn't require them to do much additional writing[111].

Also, don't forget that blog post always look better with images, and in fact some bloggers will only post something if they have an image to accompany it, so it's worth sourcing and attaching an image or two with any media release you send out.

I tried this once with the online component I ran of a national environmental consultation for the UK's Department of Energy and Climate Change, where we produced some content and images about the consultation specifically written for bloggers, and sent it out to a couple of hundred of them across the UK. We didn't receive tons of traffic on this one, as the restrictions of government language at the time made it hard to make the consultation all that interesting sadly, but we definitely engaged a good few bloggers in the work of the department more generally, and gave them a good base to build on for future consultations too.

Of course, sometimes you don't need to do any engagement work towards the media and other sites at all. If your content is interesting enough, such a high percentage of visitors will start to share it with friends and colleagues that the sites you want to target will pick it up pretty quickly anyway.

This happened with a consultation game project I worked on back in 2005 called 'Pimp My Party', which was designed to work around the UK Conservative Party leadership election which was running at the time. The party was pictured as a clapped out old car, which people playing the

---

[110] All news information like this nowadays should be called 'media releases' rather than 'press releases', as news now comes from a much wider source than the printed press.
[111] Most traditional journalists are the same to be honest, which is why I've never seen how PR can be seen as a particularly tricky job.

game could customise, choosing things like who should be driving the car (i.e. leading the party) or what the bumper sticker should say (i.e. choosing the party's core message). These choices were then collected and analysed to give some insight into the views of the general public.

The game was such an oddity, with such obvious topical and visual appeal, that we hardly had to tell anyone about it before it was picked up by news channels such as the BBC Daily Politics and Channel 4 News, leading to even more traffic.

Social media promotion

As with email, a lot of the content on social media platforms in Chapter 6 covers what you need to know to start promoting yourself and building web traffic through social media.

I would only offer two additional pieces of advice when approaching social media from a purely traffic building and marketing perspective.

The first is that in this area, more perhaps than in any other, you run the risk of looking inauthentic and like a spammer, so be careful what you do. In fact, I might go so far as to say that the best marketing you can do through social media is in fact through doing online engagement work, actually getting out there and talking to people directly. This does mean you have to be on there regularly, interacting with people and being a 'brand ambassador'[112].

The second is to consider the speed your marketing message will travel and how long it will stay visible. In offline media, this was sometimes referred to as 'tomorrow's fish wrapping', in the sense that today's newspapers would be used tomorrow by fish and chip shops to wrap people's meals, meaning the news they contained would just be thrown away and forgotten.

---

[112] Or at least what a 'brand ambassador' used to mean before it became a new word for unpaid intern.

In online media, the effect is far more virtual and potentially a whole lot faster. Post something on Twitter using a popular hashtag one minute, and the next minute it will have disappeared from view thanks to all of the new tweets containing that hashtag too. So with these high speed channels, it's all very well to say 'I've posted it on Twitter', but that information may only have been easily visible to your target audience for a few minutes. Not to say you should then start posting the same message over and over again, as you'll look like a spammer straight away, but it's certainly something to bear in mind when choosing your social media marketing channels and how best to make use of them.

9.2 Promotion activities that are both active and passive

One form of promotion for your website that sits across both the active and passive methodologies quite well is offline promotion, by which I mean physical assets such as posters, leaflets, newspaper advertisements or written letters. They're active in that they have a large active element to them, given that you have to write, print and distribute all of the promotional materials, unlike a similar but more passive activity of online advertising or search engine optimisation, where many of these active work elements aren't necessary. However, they're also passive, as once your active work is done, you have no further input into who sees them and/or acts on them, again unlike online advertising.

Sadly, when it comes to the idea of promoting your website using these means, I can offer only one piece of advice; don't bother, it doesn't work.

To be fair, saying it just doesn't work is a bit of a simplification really, as it's not as if no-one will ever be inspired to visit your site after seeing it promoted offline, but compared with online promotion, this approach has one major drawback, shown by the following image.

Comparison of steps to site visit from online and offline promotion

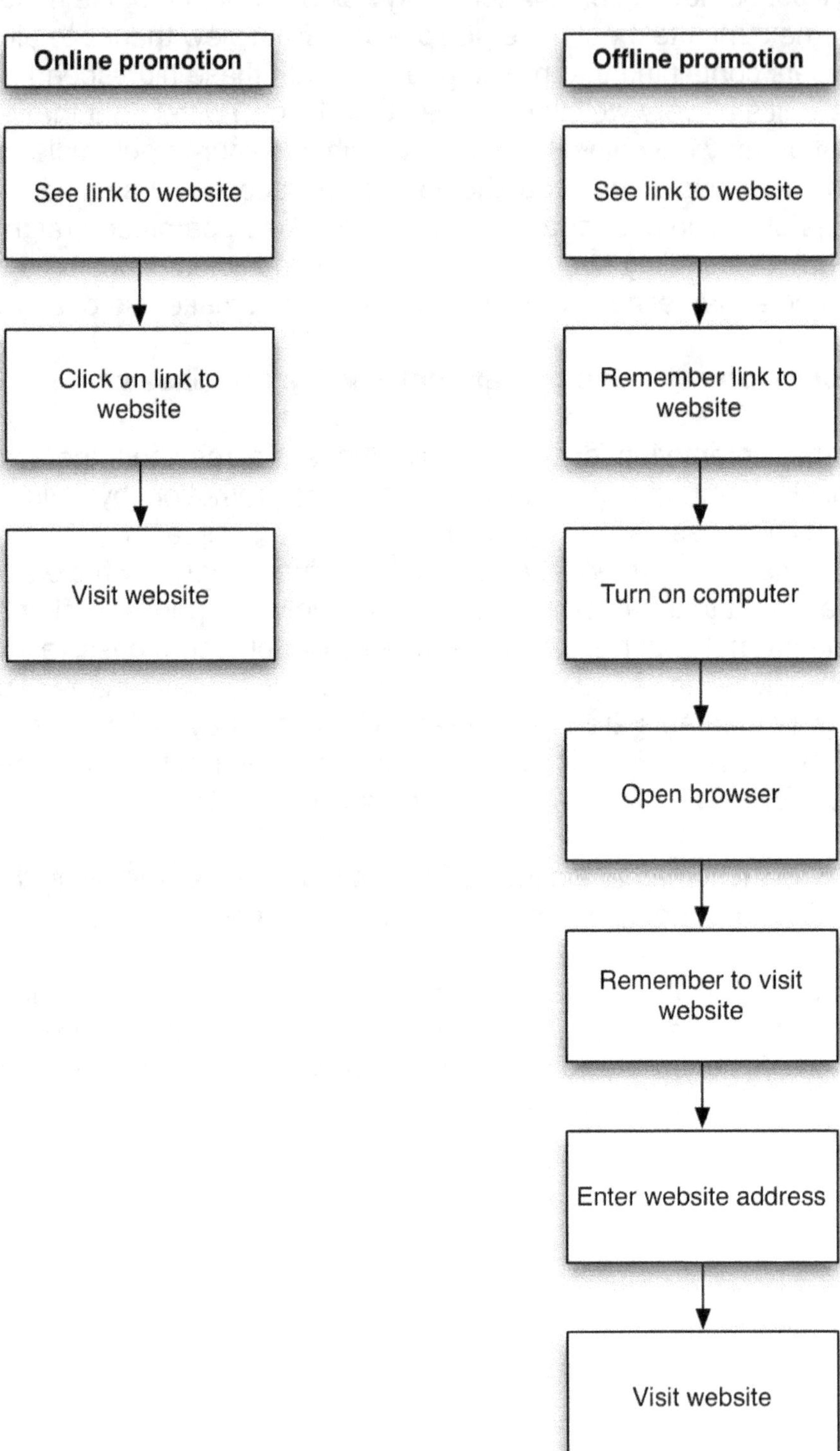

As you can see from the flowchart opposite, there are many more steps between seeing a link to or an address for a website offline then actually visiting it, compared with seeing a link to a site online. As each of these steps represents a stage at which the user could become disinterested or distracted by something else, it is clear that promoting a website offline is likely to lead to a much smaller return on promotion investment than promoting it online.

The world of offline marketing is, of course, well developed with its own set of rules, and it is clear that not all offline promotion of a website is a waste of money. Indeed sometimes it can act as a reinforcement for the promotion of the site, acting as a reminder for people who had already heard of it, or a way of adding credibility to the site more generally.

However, if you're on a limited budget (and even in the darkest days of UK Government's carefree 'piloting' expenditure, I've only ever seen one project that wasn't), then focusing on online promotion first must be your priority. It is from there that you will see bigger returns on your time and money, and find some of the quickest wins also.

9.3 Passive promotion activities

There are three golden rules to getting more traffic to your site through passive means, and these are presented below.

1. Make the content interesting

2. Have interesting content

3. The content must be interesting

Ok, so that may seem a bit of an exaggeration, but the point still stands. So many times, I've worked with clients, lovely people, who get all excited about doing their project online, and want to draw people to their website as part of that work. I write them a big plan for how to do it, they agree it, then present me with the content for the site which turns out to be as dull as ditchwater. Or if it isn't, it's presented like it is, and they can't get anyone on their side to agree to changing how it's written.

At that point, my heart sinks. But it's just the same truth as we see everyday all around us. It doesn't just matter whether something is any good. For people to 'buy' it or engage with it in some way, it has to come across as being good. Online, the primary currency for whether something is 'good' or not, at least when people first see it, is whether it's interesting.

There are so many reasons why having interesting content on your site is good for building passive traffic it's hard to list them all. However, some of the big ones that stand out include;

1. If someone finds something interesting online, they are more likely to send it to someone else, who may then do the same. This is truly what 'going viral' means, although it's sadly a much abused phrase these days.

2. If someone finds your content interesting, they are going to keep coming back to your site to check for new interesting content. If you keep providing it to them, then they will keep coming back, keeping your site traffic high. Indeed, repeat visitors are one of the main ways to build very high site traffic over sustained periods of time.

3. If content is interesting, it is generally written in such a way as to be easy to read, making it more engaging to a wider range, and so a wider number, of people.

4. It is not just humans who like interesting content. Search engines tend to rank sites better when the content is clear and well written, and also rank them better when lots of other sites link to them, which they are more likely to do if your content is interesting.

Writing interesting content for the web is covered in more detail in Chapter 7 of this book, but let's have a look at some of these things that flow from having interesting content in a little more detail.

9.4 'Going Viral'

Viral marketing is big business these days, with entire companies being based around carrying it out for people. However I can barely resist the urge to put the phrase 'going viral' in inverted commas, as it's become such an abused term.

The real meaning of something 'going viral' is very organic. Typically, something amusing is found online by someone, who then sends it to someone else. This person finds it amusing too and sends it on themselves, and so on from there. This does happen, and when it does, the content it is happening to can become very well known very quickly, and the site it's hosted on can suddenly get hit with tons of traffic out of the blue too.

As a result of it being sent on organically between people who know each other, truly viral content can often be a real boost for the reputation of its originator too, as content sent between friends is generally seen as more trustworthy than content promoted through advertising or the like.

However, just as we saw above with practices like astroturfing, content that is seen as 'viral' very often isn't, as the people actually sending it around and posting it on forums and social media are PR companies, desperate to boost their client's reputation through making them appear to have viral content.

To a degree, there is an acceptable element of cross over here, as if you want to create something viral, and there's no reason why you should not, then you have to put it online and tell a few people about it in the first place, or else it's over before it started. This practice is called 'seeding', and true to its name, involves placing the viral content on a few popular places, relevant to the target audience, around the web. These seeds then hopefully grow into mighty trees spreading roots and branches across the web.

When good content is seeded, it will often then go viral, with lots of people all sending it to each other. If bad content is seeded though, it is unlikely to take off, and this is when some of the more dodgy claims of virality start emerging. If you place content in lots and lots of places online, it will inevitably be seen by lots of people. This doesn't mean that it's gone viral though, only that you, or the people you have hired, have artificially tried to create a natural phenomenon.

It's an odd analogy perhaps, but I sometimes think of it in terms of salmon. A true viral grows and travels in the wilds of the Internet by itself, just like a truly wild salmon. Just like a truly wild salmon, a true viral is also extremely rare to find. A seeded viral is like a salmon that has been hatched and raised in a fish farm, until it is old enough to fend for itself, at which point it is released to travel the wilds of the oceans or the Internet alone. A fake viral is a farmed salmon raised on hormones and chemicals. It can look very similar to a wild salmon, but it's pretty artificial and can leave a bad taste in your mouth[113].

The other thing to remember about viral content is that, again like a wild salmon, you can't control where it goes. I once was involved in a very successful viral campaign involving a short online game people could play. The client was delighted with it receiving tens of thousands of visitors, but was a little perturbed to see a few of those thousand were playing it in Poland, well outside of the client's target market and intended audiences. No harm was done, but it flags up the importance of differentiating how successful a piece of content has been in absolute terms, and how successful it has been within the audience at which it was aimed.

One final thing worth saying in this brief section on viral marketing, an area which again you can learn more about online if you've an interest, and that's about the 'send to a friend' idea.

Back when the Internet was younger, people very quickly noticed that people were sending content to each other, and the benefits this was creating. So, in an attempt to promote this happening, they built 'send to a friend' functionality into their websites, allowing you to enter a friend's email address into a ready made form and click submit. This would then see an email being sent to that friend with a link back to the content being shared.

---

[113] Thank you very much, I'm here all week, do try the fish.

This was all well and good, but you'd be surprised how rarely people actually do use this functionality. Very often, people could not break the habit of using their emails, and if they wanted to send content to someone else, they would instead copy and paste the link to the page into an email and send it to a friend themselves.

Nowadays of course, this sharing of content has got even easier, with people being able to share content they find with their friends on sites like Facebook and Twitter at the click of a button. As a result, I rarely see the need to include an email based 'send to a friend' element in any website, and judge people who do so with suspicion, especially when they promote it as some sort of effective viral marketing tool.

9.5 Building repeat traffic

It is sometimes easy, in the rush to get as many people to look at your site as possible, to forget one of the easiest ways to build site traffic, which lies in generating repeat traffic. Repeat traffic is caused by people who have come to your site once, and have found the content so interesting that they keep checking back on it regularly, in order to see if new content has appeared. Now, of course, some of this repeat traffic these days is taken away by the use of RSS readers and similar tools (see section 9.10), but not everyone uses these, and even if they do, they count as repeat traffic of sorts, albeit one that's more difficult to measure.

Once you start thinking about building repeat traffic, you almost necessarily shift your focus from promoting your website to making sure what's on your site is relevant and interesting to your target audience. Indeed, my standard strategy for launching any new website generally works along the following lines;

1. Build site

2. Populate with interesting content

3. Promote site to others

4. Focus on writing engaging and interesting content from then on

In this model, the promotion is almost a one off activity that comes fairly early on in the process, and is then left alone, as it is repeat traffic I want to build from then on. I may occasionally go and let a specific site or two know about a specific piece of content if I think they might miss it, or I want to be sure that I'm seen to have got the exclusive on a piece of news. Otherwise though, I stay focussed on providing interesting new content on a regular basis, and let the promotion look after itself after that.

The reason for taking this approach is quite simple really. If you want to maintain high levels of site traffic, you have to think of it like building a brick wall, where the bricks are people who may view your website. There are a finite number of people in the world, so there is, by definition, a finite number of bricks your wall can contain. If you add new bricks to your wall, it will grow higher. But unless you can keep those bricks in place, it will never be able to grow as high as it could do over time. Otherwise, for each new brick, or view, that you add, an equal number will be taken away, likely never to return.

The most successful websites become so because they steadily build up a group of regular viewers over time, with each promotion activity adding new members to this group. Websites that fail can often have high viewing figures at the start, but these viewers decide not to return, leading to an ever dwindling number of new viewers, and an overall decrease in total viewers.

Finally, it is worth mentioning that what may look like repeat traffic may actually be new traffic coming to old content. Indeed, once your site has a lot of content built up, and especially if that content is starting to be well ranked by search engines, you will start getting a lot of traffic to your old content, which can sometimes confuse your figures.

For example, one blog I used to write was very well read, that sometimes received over 1000 unique visitors per day. I stopped writing the blog in March 2010 and haven't posted to it since, but as the graph below shows, the old content on the blog is still receiving a good deal of traffic to this very day.

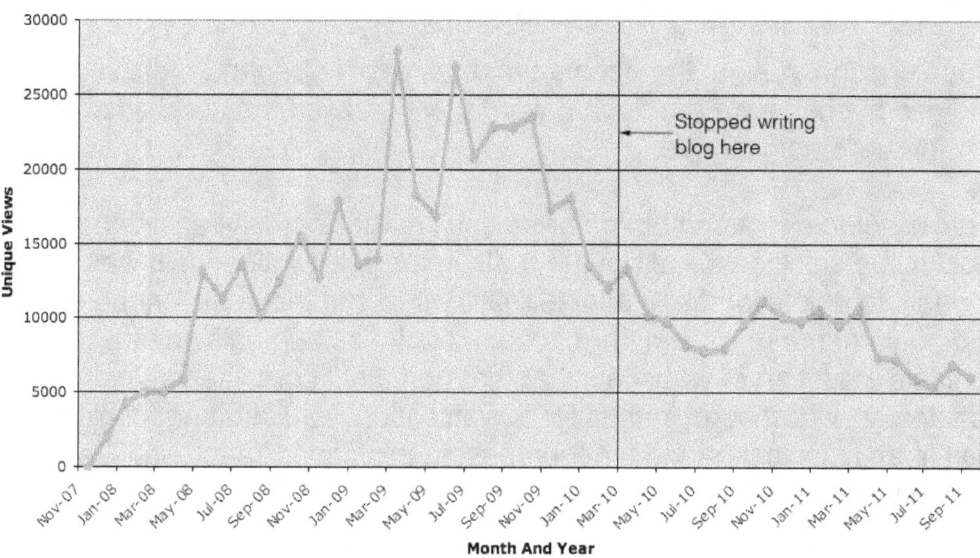

9.6 The myth of the domain name

When the Internet was first booming, being found was seen as being all about the domain name, the address for the website itself. After all, that's how people had always been found before, by knowing their address, except with the Internet people could guess your address for no cost, so having one the same as your name or brand was seen as important. As a result, huge bidding wars started off in a mini gold rush to own the right domains names. At one point silly money was being shelled out by people to own a domain name, literally millions of dollars[114], but, apart from the occasional flare up, things seemed to have calmed down somewhat these days.

In the end though, like with anything with lots of money flying around, some of this domain name bubble ended up in court, with rulings that some people had more right to a particular domain name than the people who had bought it. Indeed, policies have even been put in place to regulate domain name ownership, such as the engagingly named

---

[114] http://en.wikipedia.org/wiki/Domain_name#Resale_of_domain_names

'Uniform Domain-Name Dispute-Resolution Policy[115]' run by the Internet body ICANN[116].

Soon enough though, the bubble burst, as people began to realise that the odd hyphen here or relevant word there allowed the creation of tens of similar domain names.

This is not to say a domain name doesn't matter entirely, as it can still hold some significance, if not the traffic generating influence it was once thought to hold. Not many people realise this, but the suffix on the end of a domain name (the .com, .org, .co.uk, etc.) was originally meant to indicate what sort of website sat at that domain. '.com' stands for 'company', whilst '.org' stands for 'organisation', whilst other suffixes such as '.fr' and '.ca' can stand for countries, in this case France and Canada respectively.

The suffix is still meant to fulfill this role, although it's not as tight a system as some might once have envisaged. For example '.com' is often seen as a generic suffix to describe any website, even if the site isn't about a company. However, I've noticed that in the UK especially, charities and other not for profit organisations tend to use '.org' or 'org.uk', perhaps in a keener desire to be seen as distinct from the private sector.

As touched on in Chapter 7, the domain name is now used more for the reassurance and security of the site visitor, in that if the domain name is that of the organisation and is clearly owned by that organisation[117], then the site is more likely to be genuine and not malicious.

Mention of malicious sites brings us on to one important area of the domain name though, that of preventing domain squatting. If a domain name provides security and credibility, then it doesn't take much for any group opposed to you to buy a very similar domain name and put a website there to attack you. Not only can this help the attack site be found in search engines to a degree, it also raises the surprisingly common

---

[115] http://en.wikipedia.org/wiki/Uniform_Domain-Name_Dispute-Resolution_Policy
[116] http://en.wikipedia.org/wiki/ICANN
[117] You can look up who owns what domain name at sites like http://www.whois.net/

occurrence of someone seeing the attack site and believing it to be yours, or linked to you somehow. As a result, misleading information could well end up being seen as the truth.

Another form of this practice worth mentioning is typo squatting[118], where someone buys a domain name similar to yours, but perhaps in the plural, or with a common typo that might be made with your domain name, such as www.paypla.com. Sometime this can have very unintended consequences indeed, such as the difference in content between www.hotmail.com and www.hotmale.com (the latter is very much Not Safe For Work (NSFW) by the way).

As with this Hotmail domain name issue, problems can arise when you choose a domain name that is similar to something else already online, especially if the other site is of an opposite purpose to your own site. Very often this comes about because projects are initially designed offline, with the web presence for the project only coming as an after thought. I suspect this is what happened with a famous example from UK Central Government a few years ago.

In early 2010, the UK Government's Department of Children, Schools and Families (DCSF) launched a project for children called 'Buster's World' on the Government's DirectGov website, only to find that that 'Buster's World' was also the name of a very well known gay pornography site. Indeed, if you typed 'Buster's World' into Google, the porn site got returned as the first result. Thankfully the rest of the Internet picked up on it and alerted the DCSF, who then took the site down and gave their suppliers a shouting at by the looks of things[119]. It just goes to show though, if you're looking to promote a project online, then you need to think about your naming strategy for it pretty carefully first.

Having checked that a domain name was going to work and not introduce any additional risks, I always used to advise clients on more high profile projects, or those with a risk of being attacked online, to buy up all the

---

[118] http://en.wikipedia.org/wiki/Typosquatting
[119] There's more on the story at
http://www.theregister.co.uk/2010/02/05/directgov_busters_world/

domain names similar to, or even sometimes just related to, the domain name they were actually going to use. Generally we then just set each of the other domain names to redirect visitors to the main domain name automatically, encouraging them in rather than just preventing domain squatting.

Of course, you don't necessarily need the domain name in order to be able to run an effective attack site like this. I was once on the receiving end of an online campaign against some consultation proposals, one that was so vociferous and successful that it even saw local councillors elected on that single issue. The domain name that campaign chose was related to the consultation, but in no way passing itself off as it, and its success sprang mainly from the effectiveness of the copy writing and content, no doubt helped by the involvement of a national journalist who lived locally, so I was told.

However, I suspect the main reason that the domain name bubble burst was a more gradual and pernicious one, and lay in the area of Internet search engines. The domain name became less important in finding content, not because people had stopped needing to find things online, but because search engines provided a much better way for them to do so, when compared with guessing the domain name.

Let's have a look at search engines then, how they led to the demise of the domain name, and how you can use them to make sure people find your website above those of your competitors.

9.7 Search Engine Optimisation

Over the last 15 years or so, search engines have risen from niche websites to become a hugely important means of finding content online. From the beginning really there have been a few different search engines for the entire Internet out there, although some have come and gone. Google is now pretty much seen as the default search engine of choice for the majority of Internet users, but let's not forget Altavista, Inktomi, Lycos and all those other old school engines of choice.

An interesting thing about search engines, and this still holds true to this day, is that they were, and are still, responsible for much more than just searching for things online. Google provides a huge range of free online software for users, and has even launched a competitor to Facebook in the form of Google Groups. Indeed it strikes me that one of the reasons that search engines like Yahoo are still around in the face of Google is due to the communities that still use them, with things like email lists (Yahoo groups) and access to other content on other sites Yahoo has bought, such as Flickr.

So looking at the start of it, many search engines played the role in the development of early social networks too, ideas that then grew so popular that they shifted to a new 'social network' sphere all of their own. Indeed, I would argue that in many cases it is still necessary to include platforms like Yahoo and Google in social networking or social media work, as they still allow peer to peer community interaction just like the other sites people think of as 'social media'

However, it's not just the social network angle of the big 'search engines' that people need to consider, it's how many people use them compared with other platforms as well. After all, the more people use a search engine, the more people there are to find your site in the course of their searching.

The graph below makes this point quite well I feel.

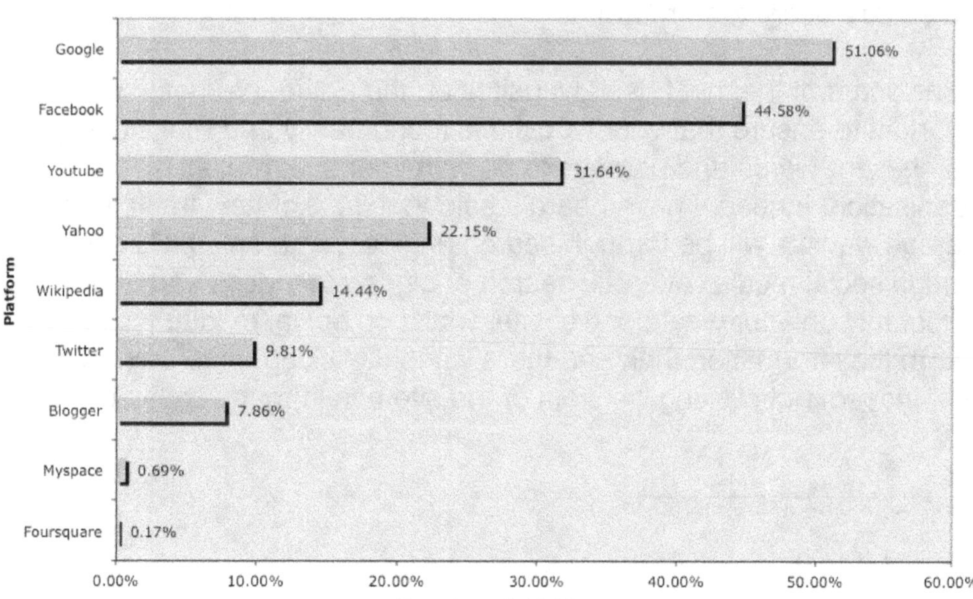

The chart above shows the percentage of the worlds Internet users[120] that used each of the sites listed on the 25th April 2012. The data in it is taken from www.alexa.com, a website that tracks and publishes information on the usage a great many different websites receive.

Over half (51.06%) of the world's Internet users used Google that day, a pretty cool figure to boast about if you're Google. Facebook wasn't far behind though with 44.58% The interesting thing is that the next 4 sites in terms of percentage (YouTube, Yahoo, Wikipedia and Blogger) are all ones not considered as traditional social networking websites.

Twitter's the next biggest social media site there really, with 9.81%. The death of Myspace looks confirmed with it only now being used that day by 0.69%, and I've put Foursquare in there as an example of social media nonsense. Some people include Foursquare into lists of important sites to consider targeting in online engagement campaigns, but it was only used by less than a quarter of one percent of the world's Internet users on the 25th April 2012. I personally wouldn't worry about it just yet.

The data above may change of course, but the message from it is clear. When building online engagement campaigns, consider the sites that will reach the most people across all demographics first, and treat much smaller sites as channels for targeting niche audiences. For example, if you do online engagement using Foursquare, expect a load of Foursquare users to turn up.

So, as some of the most used websites on the entire Internet, it is hugely important to ensure that your website is found easily and ranks highly in searches for words and phrases to do with your site, project or organisation. Indeed, I have heard it said that 80% of new traffic to an average website will be through search engines, with only 20% coming through social media. After all, search engines are places you go to temporarily on your way to a website, whilst on social media, you can absorb the information then and there without clicking on to anywhere else. Indeed, not clicking links out of the site has in many cases become

---

[120] Not population!

a habit for users of some social media platforms, although of course there are exceptions to this like Twitter.

If your main presence is on social media, then all this is no problem to you of course. But if you want people to come to a site you own and run, then you might well be better making sure search engine users can find you before you worry too much about social media audiences.

So what does it mean to be able to be found by search engine users? Well, to understand this, you must understand the different steps involved in someone finding a website through a search engine, which I've set out as a simplified user journey below;

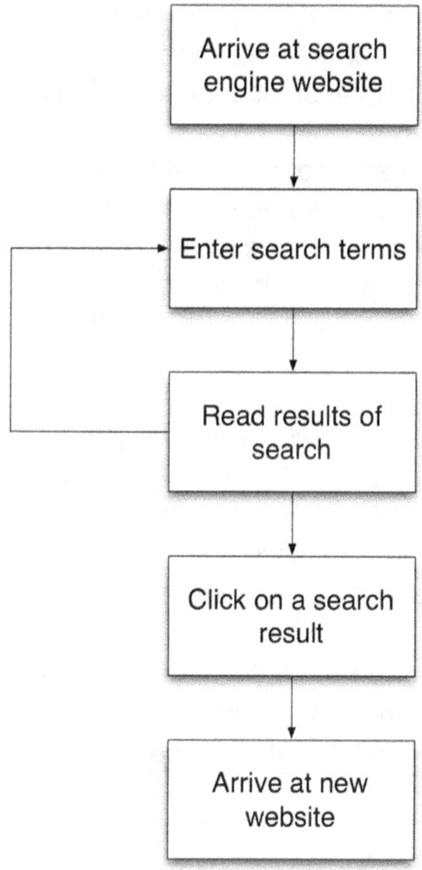

The first and last parts of that user journey are self explanatory really, but it is in the middle three that the wonders of the world called 'Search Engine Optimisation' can be found.

Entering search terms

First of all, the way people find sites through search engines is by typing words into them and pressing a button marked 'submit', 'search' or similar. So far so obvious. But this way of operating defines the very heart of being found through search engines, in that you are found through words.

Now these words could of course just be your name or the name of your project, and unless that name is shared with someone or something already famous, it's usually something to worry about if you're not appearing in searches for you own or your project's name. But the skill in getting the most out of search engines is for your site to be found through other searches as well, such as people searching for the general subject of your site, or the geographical location in which it is most relevant.

For example, it's all well and good for me to be found by searches for 'Gez Smith', but it would also be useful to appear in searches for 'digital engagement consultancy' or 'online engagement training' too. That way, I have more chance of people coming to my site who don't know about me yet but would benefit from so doing, rather than those who already know my name, like my mum.

It is not just how wide you spread your ability to be found for searches related to your website though, it's also about how many of those searches are taking place. I may rank number one on every search engine for the term 'saggar makers bottom knocker[121]', but since there were only 260 searches for it on Google across the entire planet in the last month, I'm not likely to get much traffic from doing so. Far better then that I rank highly for a related but more often searched for term, such as 'ceramics and pottery', which was searched for nearly two and a quarter million times on Google globally in the last month.

Unsurprisingly, I'm not some kind of polymath who knows these numbers out of nowhere. Search engines like Google provide a handy free tool for

---

[121] It was a real job title you know - http://www.thepotteries.org/bottle_kiln/saggar.htm

looking up how often different terms have been searched for, as well as suggesting similar terms to any you want to suggest, and showing how often they have been searched for too. Have a play around with it at https://adwords.google.com/select/KeywordToolExternal[122].

For your site to rank highly for search terms like these though, it has to contain those terms in the first place, otherwise the search engine won't know that that's what your site is about. It sounds obvious, but it's sometimes surprising how easy it is to write content for a website that you think is clear, but which is in reality entirely different to how people actually think about and search for that content.

Now of course, there's something obvious on the horizon here. If you can get your site to appear for really popular search terms by putting those terms on your site, then there's a huge temptation to stuff your site full of popular search words, whether they have anything to do with your site or not. After all, generating high web traffic is just a numbers game, right?

Well, no. At the end of the day, search engines remain popular and make money when people use them, and people are more likely to use them when they know they will return the information they're searching for. If a search engine starts returning unrelated sites, just because they've been stuffed with different search terms or 'keywords', then the search engine's customers become annoyed and go elsewhere[123].

So the search engines have made tweaks and alterations to how they index the contents of the Internet, to make it less likely that sites will appear for any given search term unless they actually are to do with that term. The ways they have done this are many, various and often secret,

---

[122] One other useful thing to do is have a look at the 'searches' part of your website usage statistics. This should show you the search terms people are using to arrive at your site, and give you some idea of which terms your site is currently ranking for and for which it is not.
[123] Anyone who's ever tried to use the search engine built into a UK local authority's website will know the feeling well.

but suffice to say you can now even get blacklisted from appearing in a search engine for trying to game them in this way[124].

Beyond these principles, there are many different ways to make sure you maximise your search engine potential without getting blacklisted, and if you're interested in this then there are plenty of blogs and websites out there to teach you more about it. Suffice to say though, the best way to think of it is this.

The search engine's main goal is to provide useful results for people using it to search for things. These useful results will typically be relevant to the subject of the search, simple to read and clearly laid out. They will also often have lots of people linking to them, as they are so useful. As a result, it is websites like this that search engines prioritise when displaying results, and as long as you make your site interesting and relevant to others, search engines will give it some love.

It may take some time mind you. I only managed to get www.worthyfm.com to the top of the search engines for a search for 'Worthy FM' six months after it was launched, as the main Glastonbury Festival website was hogging the top slots with mentions of Worthy FM on their site. It had been around longer, more people had linked to it, and its content was just as relevant, so it was bound to have a head start initially.

Throughout this section, I've been talking about ranking highly in search engines as a well known 'good thing to do', but it's worth stopping a moment to think why.

First of all, there's the simple matter of convention. It has become accepted knowledge amongst most Internet users now that the higher something appears on a page of search results, the more trustworthy,

---

[124] Many people think search engines allow you to search the Internet. They don't, they allow you to search the Internet that they themselves have searched, and even then only those parts of it they want to show you. If your site gets blacklisted, it can be as if it does not exist at all when it comes to people searching for it.

popular and above all relevant it is likely to be. As a result, everyone wants to be number one on the first page of results.

There is also though the matter of human behaviour. Once you've gone to the effort of typing in a search term and clicking submit, you want to click on something as a result, not adjust your search terms further, or read through additional pages of results. Some of the data out there suggests this hypothesis is very likely true, some estimates showing that 96% of clicks on search engine results happen on the first page of results the user is given[125]. So if you're on page two or onwards, you're really going to be missing out.

Reading and clicking on results

That brings us on nicely then to the third and fourth elements of our search engine user journey diagram, which may as well be bundled together for simplicity. These elements are all about what happens once a user has entered and searched for their chosen search terms, and has been presented with a page of results in return.

As with many things online, you don't get long to grab people's attention here. Your site may be competing with nine others on the same page for that person's click, and they're going to be looking at the top two or three results most closely too, so you've got to make what appears for your site engaging and easy to read.

On a search engine like Google, you get two main ways to do this. One is the title, which also doubles as the link people click on. The second is a short excerpt of text beneath this title, which should, in theory, explain to people what the site or page is about. Both of these are often generated automatically from what you put in your website, but any half decent developer should be able to customise them on a site to make sure, no matter what the page or site contains, that these two elements of text are as engaging and appealing to click on as possible. You can even

---

[125] This data, and lots of other interesting data on the same topic available at http://www.agent-seo.com/seo/click-distribution-percentages-by-serp-rank/

download free bits of software to plugin to your website in order to let you edit these manually yourself.

It's worth spending some time thinking about what is displayed when an Internet search returns your site as one of its results, as getting this part right can be the difference between ranking highly in search engines, and actually seeing some increased traffic as a result of that high ranking.

9.8 Build your own search engine

Of course, making sure your content is easily understood and well regarded by search engines is an absolute imperative of the modern Internet. However, there can sometimes be a case to be made for putting in place your own search engine to make your content as easy to use and understand as possible by its more human users.

On the most simple level, this can be done by providing a simple search functionality within your website. Indeed, most website Content Management Systems (CMS's) contain search functionality as standard these days, allowing you to place a built in search box anywhere on your site, which will then search all of your site's content as soon as it is added.

If your CMS doesn't come with a search engine built in, or it comes with a pretty poor search engine as standard, then you can add in external search engines to your site, such as Google. These external engines will then provide a search functionality that returns results from only your site, and in many cases they can be superior to search engines built into CMS's. After all, search engine companies specialise in and are great at building search engines, whilst CMS companies will only ever have that work as one part of their wider technical capabilities[126].

There is though another approach, that is largely being used in shopping, news service and online consultation and engagement contexts oddly

---

[126] Once again, Google are unsurprisingly the leader here, with their 'Google Custom Search' - http://www.google.com/cse/

enough. This approach lies in building and deploying a custom database, with a sophisticated search engine built on the front.

Why would you want to do this? Well, very often it's easier to build a search engine that exactly meets your needs if you've also built the database it is searching. That way, amongst other factors, you decide what sorts of searches people will want to carry out, then structure the data that is being searched in an optimal way for running those searches. For example, you could create a special set of tags for the contents you enter, which allow it to be searched in a very specific way.

In essence, if you want to build a specialised search capability in a specific topic, be it the contents of an online shop or a list of public engagement exercises, then you need to build the database that sits underneath it too.

Before talking about these, I should declare an interest really. For reasons I've never quite understood, I've always found these sorts of online databases really interesting. Back when I worked on the 'National Project for Local e-Democracy', one of my responsibilities lay in the fascinating Work Package 4 of Work Stream 2, 'Consultation in Partnership', which essentially meant piloting[127] a 'Consultation Finder Database' in partnership with other organisations.

Now, I could relate all sorts of amusing anecdotes from this somewhat ill-fated project, but suffice to say it taught me a great deal about the subject of 'Consultation Finder Databases' (CFDB's)[128]. It was the first time anyone tried to put together a national 'taxonomy'[129] for how consultations should be categorised, along lines such as person type, consultation topic and so on. It never caught on sadly, but I've sort of managed to bring it back a bit over the years here and there.

---

[127] Or 'using' as it could have been more accurately termed.

[128] It also introduced me for the first time to the wonderful Anne Tansley Thomas of Norfolk County Council, one of the most under appreciated experts on e-participation in the UK at the moment. @AnneTThomas on Twitter.

[129] http://en.wikipedia.org/wiki/Taxonomy

Eventually, I was lucky enough to get the opportunity to build a completely new online consultation database, with the expertise of a large and very highly skilled development team behind me[130]. This database, initially for Bristol City Council, then got a huge amount of additional investment from central government to develop it further[131], so it's fair to say I have come to know a good deal about this quirky niche area of digital engagement over the years.

It's part of the reason I'm including it in this book really, and given this book is about digital engagement, you'll forgive me if I talk about these custom databases with custom search engines in the context of the CFDB.

If you're interested in running an online shop instead, or any other sort of database component to your website, then you can probably skip past this section straight to the section below called 'Using your CFDB'.

9.9 Consultation Finder Databases

It's tempting here to tell you how to go about building one of these, but there's little point really, as many of the processes are the same as for any other website, using user stories and so forth. Besides, I think it's probably far more useful to know what a good one looks like, and some of the pitfalls to avoid.

Probably the most fundamental aspect of a good CFDB is the ability to search, filter, sort and display the data as simply as possible in as many ways as possible. Now these two points can often come into conflict when you think about it, as the more options you provide, the less simple it becomes. There are ways of squaring this circle, but we don't need to worry about them here.

---

[130] Seriously, if anyone wants to know what makes a good software company, it's good software developers. Although mixing good developers with bad other team members does take to make developers perform less well. Or leave.

[131] Adding in online survey tools, data analysis software and all sorts.

As long as a user can do these things to the data contained in the CFDB, everything else largely becomes window dressing really[132]. So how should this searching and sorting work?

Well, one of the fundamental principles here is the same as one we saw before, in that you need to provide different levels of detail to different people. Indeed, it's the same approach as covered in Chapter 5 on structured consultation, in that the contents of your CFDB should be searchable on three different levels.

The first level is the most simple, and contains mechanisms as simple as someone looking at your homepage and finding the information they want. Slightly more sophisticated, but still just one click of a button, are things like clicking on the heading of a column on a page to re-sort it alphabetically or numerically.

It's good to try and cover the most common reasons why people will be coming to your CFDB at this level, for example by having a 'featured consultation' section on your homepage, displaying information on the consultation most people are likely to be looking for at that particular time. Once again of course, clear and comprehensible content are imperative in making this sort of work a reality as well.

The second level is the search functionality, where you should only have to type in a small amount of information and submit it before seeing the results you were after. The better the database is built, and the more clearly the content is set out, the more likely this is to work. You could also do what we did and set this search to work on information such as the postcodes affected by the consultation too, so people can easily find what's going on in their area.

The third level is the advanced search, where users can search for information by a wide range of different parameters, some of them set in taxonomies of fields from which the user can select one or many. We'll come to these in a minute, but it's worth pausing to note here a trick for spotting a bad search engine built along this approach.

---

[132] Especially your logo, which does not need to be bigger.

On a good search engine, merely typing words related to your search into a second level search box should return the information you require nine times out of ten. I've seen many such search engines where this doesn't really work[133,] so in an attempt to compensate for this, a large set of advanced search options are presented on the second or even the first level of information. Options such as dropdown menus presenting data ranges, geographical areas and so forth.

This unfortunately also has the unintended consequence of discouraging the public user from searching, as it turns what should be a simple process into one which looks like it's extremely complicated. On a good CFDB, you should only occasionally need to use the advanced search options, so they should be on an appropriately out of the way level of your website.

But advanced search undoubtedly has its place, and very often the taxonomies it contains can be used to improve the higher level searching and filtering as well. But what do you want to include as options in this search when it comes to creating your advanced search? Well, the easiest way to use it is probably in a table, so here you are;

Search category	Type	Detail
Keywords	Free text	This should be a free text box into which users can type anything. In return, the search engine will provide the most relevant results from every piece of free text information in each consultation record, as well as from the contents of the taxonomies.

---

[133] II's the perennial complaint made about UK Local Authority websites, although decreasingly so these days.

Search category	Type	Detail
Postcode	Free text	Where a CFDB is being used to record consultation and public engagement exercises in a specific area, it can be useful to mark the postcodes which will be affected by the results of the consultation on the consultation record itself. A user should then be able to enter their postcode into the search box, and see displayed the consultations about their local area. They should also be able to search for the postcode in a variety of formats, for example 'BS1 1AA' and 'BS11AA' Don't forget that this postcode field will be irrelevant to the CFDBs of some organisations, such as national government departments, for whom all consultations tend to happen in just one area.
Status	Dropdown menu	This should be a simple dropdown menu allowing the user to search for consultations by three different variables; whether the consultation is open to be taken part in, soon to open on a forthcoming date, or closed for participation, ideally now containing a report on the consultation's results and future actions.
Audience	Dropdown menu	This should be a range of audiences at whom the consultation is aimed, for example 'young people', 'older people', 'stakeholders' and other such governmental categorisations of people. Hopefully you might be able to think of and use some more interesting and engaging ones.

Search category	Type	Detail
Interest	Dropdown menu	This should be the topics or interest categories that the consultation relates to, such as 'environment', 'recycling', 'education' and so forth. Again, these should be able to be selected from a dropdown menu in order to filter the search results.
Department	Dropdown menu	If you're a big organisation, it may be that people relate best to the departments your organisation has been divided into, so you should give them the option to search for results just from one department. Having this field can also help you when it comes to building the administration side of your database.
Area	Dropdown menu	Whilst users can search for their postcode, it may be that they find it more useful to be able to search for consultations about a specific area, such as 'city centre'. You can often use the tags here to allocate sets of postcodes that a consultation will be affecting. Indeed many UK local authorities call this field 'wards' so it relates to the electoral wards by which the authority is divided. The only problem with this is that the average user doesn't generally think of where they live in terms of their electoral ward. Don't forget that, like the postcode search, this field will be irrelevant on some CFDBs, such as those for national governments.

Content Field Content

So those are the search options needed for an advanced search section of a CFDB, and I really wouldn't add any more if I were you. You start to lose simplicity and gain little in return if you have more than this amount. But what should those fields contain? What content should you be providing about an individual consultation activity on each of their individual records? Well, a table probably works best again, doesn't it?

I think so, but this time we should start looking at some of the content in terms of it being useful for the organisation that manages the database too. After all, one of the biggest hidden benefits of this sort of database is the way it allows the organisation itself to co-ordinate and not duplicate consultation activities over time.

Content type	Benefit to public user	Benefit to admin user
Title	Gives a clear idea of the nature and contents of the consultation, ideally engaging the reader and encouraging them to take part.	Management and tracking of consultations by title. Note that this usage can often conflict with the benefit to the public user, in that a title used for tracking purposes often contains numbers, keywords and other non-engaging elements.
Overview	Gives an overview of the consultation, hopefully engaging the reader further, or at least allowing them to decide quickly and simply if the consultation is relevant to their interests.	Little, other than increasing public engagement. However, sometimes being made to write out a simple and precise overview of the consultation helps the consultation owner get issues and priorities clear in their own mind.

Content type	Benefit to public user	Benefit to admin user
Why we are consulting	Demonstrates openness and gives context to the consultation, ideally setting it within the wider process of which it forms a part, and informing the reader of what influence the consultation may have within that process.	Little, other than it can help compliance with data protection, providing an opportunity to set out the purposes for which the data collected will be used.
Owner	None, indeed it is often best that this field is not publicly visible.	Assists other admin users in seeing who is responsible for which consultation. This field is also often built into the very architecture of the CFDB software, giving the owner of a consultation things like additional administration privileges over any consultations that they are set as owning.

Content type	Benefit to public user	Benefit to admin user
Contact information	This could contain a number of individual fields, such as name, email address and telephone number, and should be the contact details for channels that are going to be checked and answered on a regular basis. It need not be the details of a real person, and could just be your generic switchboard number or email address, and should be editable separately from the 'Owner' field above, not generated automatically by it.	Helps promote openness and allows you to address queries and concerns that may arise during the consultation process.
Dates	Gives clear dates for the process, such as when it starts, when it ends, when the results and the feedback on the results will be published. These should be editable at any time, in case of project time slippage.	Helps build visibility on consultation activities going on across an organisation, and helps to ensure that the same audiences won't be being targeted by different people at the same time. Also helps when searching for consultations in order to report on them or find previous results.
Related links	Provides channels for the consultation viewer to access information related to the consultation that may be being stored elsewhere on line.	Removes the need to re-upload related information held elsewhere on the web, by linking to it directly.

Content type	Benefit to public user	Benefit to admin user
Related consultations	Provides access to other consultations in which the viewer may be interested in participating, or perhaps access to the consultations that have led up to this one, for example previous years' consultations where a survey is held annually.	Gives a chance to provide additional context information to the consultation, as well as increasing traffic to, and so increasing the response rates for, other consultations you are running.
Related documents	Although called 'related documents', this is generally a catch all field where viewers can download files of any type to access additional background information to inform their consultation response.	Gives you another way to provide information in different layers for different types of audiences, and can also act as a handy repository for consultation documents as well. Having the ability to upload these files directly into the CFDB system also saves you having to contact your IT department to have files uploaded onto the web.
What happens next	This field is often only visible when the consultation has closed, but before the results of it have been published, bridging the information gap that might otherwise arise during that time. It should explain clearly what will happen now that the consultation has closed.	Demonstrates further openness and reduces the number of enquiries you may receive about the consultation once it has closed.

Content type	Benefit to public user	Benefit to admin user
Areas	Enables the viewer to see and search for consultations affecting a location of interest to them, such as where they live or where they work.	Allows consultations to be tracked, managed and reported on.
Audience	Allows viewers to find consultation related to the sort of audience group they form, such as business stakeholders, local residents or members of minority communities.	Again, allows tracking, management and reporting on consultations by these categories, facilitating some legal requirements such as equalities impact assessments and so forth.
Interests	Allows viewers to find consultations relevant to their interests. Also allows potential stakeholder groups to identify the consultations they wish to take part in, for example environmental campaign groups may use this field to search for consultations about the environment.	As above really, it allows you to track and report on these interest categories, although it can also be useful for engaging potential audiences in consultations they might otherwise not have considered taking part in, if they had not realised it was relevant to their interests.

Good front end and backend

Once you start looking at the fields that a CFDB can contain which are of use to an administrator, you start to develop an appreciation of the needs of these administrative users, and the importance of keeping their work nice and simple.

One problem I've seen before with these sorts of databases, and to be honest it's a problem common to many websites, is that whilst the public side of the system, known as the 'front end', may be perfectly well laid out and usable, the part of the system used by logged in administrators to put content into the database, known as the 'backend'[134,] can be a nightmare to use.

Often this is because the database, search engine and other software wrapped up in the CFDB haven't originally been designed for this purpose, leading to confusing functionality or layout for administrators. Sometimes it's because time has been spent by sales people worrying about how the front-end looks, but the backend has been left to software developers to design and build, leading to it making sense to them and nobody else.

Once you start building complex databases, you really do need to think about how content is put into them as much as about how content is searched for and got out of them at the other end. Otherwise, and I've seen it happen, you can have databases that no-one really wants to put anything into, leading to less public information being provided than if the information had just been typed manually into a web page as plain text.

As a general rule, because it's the last thing people focus on, the presence of a well thought out admin system is a sign of attention to detail and attests to the quality of the system more generally.

---

[134] It's always amusing to see which clients stifle a giggle as I explain these terms.

Using your CFDB

Once you've got your ideal CFDB, or indeed any sort of database on your website, what do you do with it? Well, it's up to you at the end of the day. It's got to be something you take ownership of and give love to after all. But there are a few tips I've picked up along the way which I hope will be of use. I use the example of a Consultation Finder Database in keeping with this section, but many of these approaches work well when applied to any other database, indeed they often apply to websites as a whole.

- **Store everything**

   People sometimes ask what sort of information they should be recording on their CFDB, and the answer is everything. If it's a public engagement, formal consultation or other sort of conversational exercise between your organisation and other people, record it on your CFDB. Now it might be that you only want a certain group of people to respond to your consultation, such as restricting an employee survey to members of your staff, or holding a focus group for just ten people, but still, put it in there.

   There are two main reasons for this. One is transparency, which should be high on everyone's agenda if they're looking to be successful at their online engagement work. The other though is for internal purposes. The more visibility people inside your organisation have about what's gone on, what's going on and what's going to go on, the more efficiencies you will start to find in the work everyone does.

   For example, if I want a copy of the final report of a consultation for a meeting I'm going to, a CFDB means I can just go online and download it, rather than having to ask around to find someone with a copy of it stored locally on their computer.

- **Don't archive**

  Following on from this, is an appeal for people to forget the notion of archiving when it comes to CFDBs. Time and again I've seen people state that they require the ability to be able to archive consultations using their CFDB, but as long as the database is well built and the search functionality equally suitable, then there really is no need.

  After all, every record on a CFDB is of potential interest to somebody, even if it concerns a consultation ten years ago. Storing records in the system shouldn't take up too much space, and the cost of such hard drive storage is negligible these days anyway, so why not just leave them as they are once they have closed? Moving them to an 'archive' is a meaningless activity that will only serve to confuse people. Deleting them after a certain time is too.

  Speaking more broadly, the only custom databases that can really get away with archiving or deleting old records are huge ones like eBay. In their cases, storing every record the database had ever contained would become prohibitively expensive. Even then, with computer memory getting cheaper every year as per Moore's Law[135], who knows if this will continue to be the case in the longer term.

- **Take backups**

  If you're doing any sort of work online, or just on computers, then backing up your data should become second nature. Hard discs get corrupted, break or otherwise risk getting destroyed by fire, flood and other acts of god. You should always hold important data in at least two locations on two different physical devices, and the data you're storing in a CFDB or any other database on your website should be no different.

---

[135] http://en.wikipedia.org/wiki/Moores_law

Ideally, your system should allow you to export all of the data it contains quickly and simply, ideally in a .csv format. You can also take this one step further, and tailor this backup system to generate reports on your consultation activity over time. For example, to backup, you might export all of the data held in the system, whilst to report on the consultations run on a particular topic over a particular time period, you might first filter your data before exporting it in exactly the same way as a backup.

Amusingly enough, the Citizen Space system I worked on had the ability to export any data in the system by any applicable search parameters, which was then flagged up as a 'security loophole' when the system was independently security tested. We'd given public users the ability to run many of the same exports as admin users, on the grounds that it would reduce queries for information coming in to the organisation, and UK users could get the information anyway by using the Freedom of Information Act. The mindset still seemed to be that allowing people to take data from government sites and use it as they wished was a curse, not a blessing. We'll look at this more in Chapter 11.

Finally, remember your obligations under any applicable data protection legislation too, as covered in Chapter 10 of this book, and destroy any backups when you destroy the data on the main system, for example if you only have consent to hold the data for a set period of time.

- **Train everybody**

If there are benefits to be had from your CFDB, or indeed any database, containing as much information as possible, then it makes sense to maximise the amount of information that can be put on the system, by giving as many people as possible the ability to do so.

Often it only takes a relatively simple training session to get them up to speed, and the more people that can use it, the less work each person has to do to keep it up to date. Some people worry here about the content that is published, and want to have final sight and sign off of it before it goes live. That's all well and good, but I've yet to see a process like this on a large scale that works well, or isn't just ignored anyway, so I tend to feel that it does more harm than good overall. If you worry about what information users may put on the system, don't block them, train them! If you really can't trust your staff, perhaps you have an HR issue that needs looking into.

- **Publish results and demonstrate action**

This comes up time and again in public engagement and consultation work, but it's worth looking at how the CFDB can help you do this more specifically.

One of the great aspects of a CFDB is its ability to store and manage multiple documents in a simple and intuitive manner. If every consultation has a record in the database when it is open for participation, then it should be a trivial matter to upload a copy of the final report to that same record once the consultation has closed and been analysed.

By doing this, not only do you start to create a research library of your consultation findings over time, which can be of great use for many different purposes, you also demonstrate openness towards your consultation participants, making them more likely to participate in future exercises.

One great thing you can do with CFDBs is go one step further than this, and incorporate a field on each record that displays not just the findings of the consultation, but the action taken as a result of them as well.

We did this with Bristol City Council, by incorporating a 'We Asked, You Said, We Did' section on each record, where three short sentences can be displayed, each limited to 140 characters and each relating to one of those three sections.

Very often, going this far with consultation information will take a change in organisational culture itself. After all, how many organisations routinely record what information led them to do things, let alone publish it? As a result, this section of a CFDB is often not used for about the first 6 months that an organisation has their system, whilst it gathers together enough information to be able to demonstrate actions taken as a result of consultation. No organisation should find this a long term challenge though, as if you can't demonstrate what you are doing as a result of consultation, what on earth are you consulting for?

- **Link it up with the rest of the web**

Finally, as with any system storing and providing information, you should link your CFDB system up with the rest of the web. On the system I worked on, we added a 'social media toolbar' to each consultation record, which meant that someone just had to click on a button marked 'Facebook' in order to share a link to that consultation with others through their Facebook profile. A similar button was provided for Twitter as well.

Another method you can use in this area is to let people take information from your system in the form of RSS or XML technology. We'll look at this more specifically in the next section, but suffice to say you could link up your advanced search section with an RSS feed, to allow people to generate automatic feeds of content relevant to their search terms and use them elsewhere on the web, perhaps through their RSS reader, or by embedding the feed on their own website.

9.10 RSS and XML explained

Apart from search engines, there is one other excellent set of tools available for helping people find you passively, and it again comes down to content and how you make it available. Nowadays, rather than having to visit a website to see new content published on it, you can have the content come to you, using a piece of functionality called RSS.

RSS stands for 'Really Simple Syndication', and is essentially a way of sharing content from one site with another site or piece of software automatically. Using RSS, when you publish a new piece of content on your website, anyone subscribed to an RSS feed of your site will automatically have that content published wherever they have placed their subscription.

For example, when I worked at Delib, we put RSS ability into the consultation finder database we built. As a result, someone could use a piece of desktop software like an RSS reader to subscribe to the contents of that database, and as soon as a new consultation was published on it, the consultation appeared in the reader on their desktop. This way, the person with the reader didn't have to go around checking to see if all of the sites they are most interested in had been updated. Instead, they could just look at one page on their desktop and have all of the content from across the web appear there as soon as it was published.

As you can use RSS to publish content into one website from many others as well, aggregator websites have sprung up. These sites pull together content from many different places, often those vetted and approved by the owners of the aggregator site, and again give people a central point to visit for content they're interested in, just as a blogger might do as we saw before. Unlike a blogger aggregating and publishing links to content though, the wholly automated nature of RSS aggregation can mean that the quality of the information presented can be a little more hit and miss at times.

Extending this idea a bit further, you could use RSS yourself to pull content from one of your sites into another of your sites. Not only does this help link your sites up as we've looked at before, but it can also save you money. Very often, I found clients used to want sites that that looked consistent all the way through, even if they were actually composed of different pieces of software to cover different purposes.

Reskinning a piece of software like this is expensive, and automated methods for reskinning it are generally false economy, but RSS provides a third option. You can have one site that contains all of your information in one place under one colour scheme and brand, but have the information on that site be pulled in from other pieces of software automatically using RSS, removing any need to reskin anything.

We'll look at the concept of open data some more later in the book, but for now just be aware that providing the ability for people to take content from your website using RSS technology is another excellent means of building ongoing passive engagement with the content you publish, either for individuals on their desktops or through other sites pulling in and displaying your content for you.

It is worth mentioning as well that RSS is not the only means of doing this sort of work. Atom is another well used set of standards for doing this sort of work, and you may also hear the term XML used in this regard too. They're all for pretty much the same purpose though, taking content from somewhere, and putting it somewhere else.

9.11 How to tell if what you're doing is working

If you're putting all of this work in, you want to know that it's having some effect don't you? Of course you do, but before you can know whether you're being successful, you have to know what success looks like.

Now this is a fairly obvious point in any evaluation process, but you'd be surprised how many people seem to ignore it. Your site may have lots of people looking at it, but if none of those people are in your target audience, then you'd be hard pushed to claim to be having success. Similarly, if your site is only aimed at a small number of people, there's little point in engaging in 'stat porn', as the often boastful obsession with a website's usage statistics is commonly known.

To my mind, there are four different ways you can evaluate the success of your work online, each with their own positives and negatives. It's up to you to decide which are most useful and of most relevance to your specific website or project.

The four elements are;

- **Site promotion statistics**

  How many people are seeing and reading your promotional activity? What are they doing when they do?

- **Site analytics**

  How many people are visiting your site, how often and who are they? What are they doing when they get there?

- **Site participation**

  Are people posting content to your site? How many people are doing this?

- **Quality of participation content**

  Is the content people are posting any good?

The first thing you may notice is that these four elements flow naturally from one to the other, and indeed this is so much the case that the first three elements in that list, and quite possibly the fourth one too at times, can have a rule of thumb applied to them, known as the '10% rule'.

This rule states that 10% of people at one stage in this process will move on to the next stage. So out of 100 people who look at a link to your site, perhaps contained in an advert or being shared on social media, 10 of those people will click on the link and go through to your site. Of those ten people, 10% of them, or one person, will then go on to take part in your site in one manner or another.

The 10% rule of website user conversion

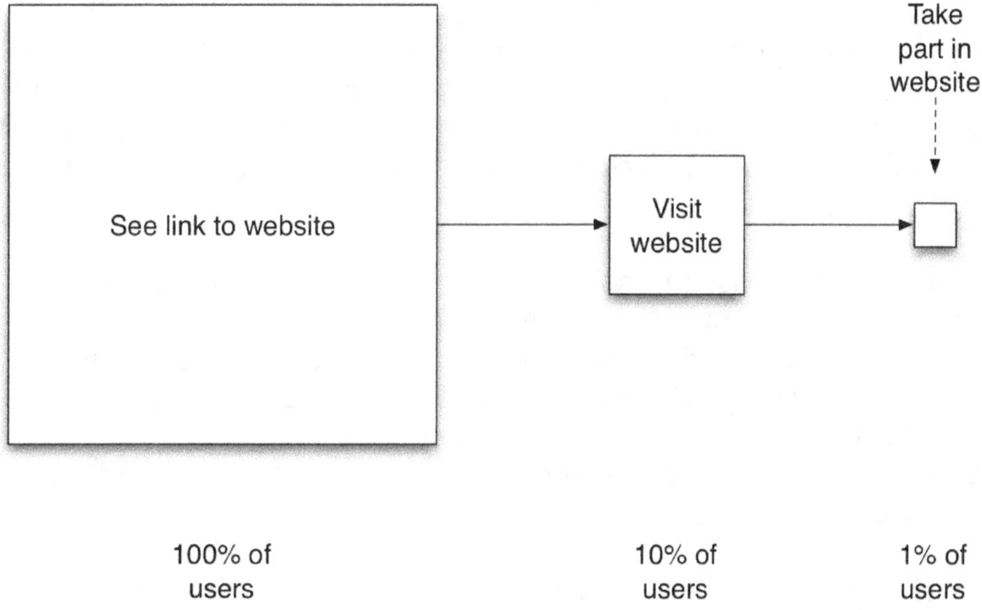

As can be seen from the image above, the drop off rate is quite significant between each stage, giving you some indication of the number of people you need to get to see a link to your site in order to create significant levels of user participation with it.

For the fourth element of the list above, the quality of the participation, it is possible that only 10% of the content that is submitted will be of a high quality, however I have yet to see this proven. It does no harm to think of this as a basic rule though, and work towards optimising the quality of the content submitted by your site users as well, however you may want to judge that.

Element 1 - Site promotion statistics

Measuring the statistics for the promotional activity you put into your website is always tricky. After all, if someone sees your promotional activity somewhere, but doesn't act on it, then you have very little way of telling that they have ever come across any reference to your site at all.

This isn't a barrier to working in this area though, as offline media has been dealing with the problem for years. As Lord Leverhulme is said to have remarked "I know half of my advertising is wasted, but I do not know which half", which pretty much sums it up really.

Offline marketing work will see results, so people do it, and often you can see better results coming through with one tactic compared with another, but there's next to no way to know for certain just how many people see your advert, or how many actually read it having seen it, let alone how many then act on it.

However, even though this sort of thing cannot be known for certain, thanks to this problem arising in offline media, there is one way of measuring some statistics around the activities you do to promote your site online. This is by extrapolating them from the results you can measure, for example the number of visitors your site gets. The more visitors your site gets, the more likely it is that at least one strand of your marketing activity is working.

This also points to a methodology for measuring the reach and impact of your promotional activity, in that, if you run each activity individually and leave a time gap between each one, you can see which activity resulted in the most new visitors. This sort of work can be really revealing, and throw up some unexpected results. It was working with this sort of data that initially flagged up to me the inefficacy of offline advertising compared with online for website promotion. Regardless of the theory, you can just see this to be the case time and again when you do the numbers.

Of course, if you only ran one promotional activity at a time, then you'd pretty quickly start to trail behind those running them simultaneously. There is very often a cumulative benefit to be found in promotional activities, and saturating every available channel with your message can be extremely effective[136]. Very much a case of the whole being greater than the sum of the parts.

---

[136] People often think that too much advertising or repeating of the same message will put people off. However, wiser and more experienced minds than mine from the world of politics have assured me time and again that whilst you may put some people off by saturation marketing, the additional numbers you engage by doing so far and away offset this problem. Whether or not you've got the self confidence to do it is another matter.

However, as we saw with 'split testing' in Chapter 7 for example, there are a number of ways of measuring which promotional activity has the greater impact in comparison with another, without having to run them one at a time. For example, have you ever noticed that an advert for a website might have the name of the publication the advert appears in contained within the URL on the advert? This is so that the advertisers can count how many times each different URL is visited, and be pretty certain that those visits will have all come from the relevant advert. Take the number of people who visit the link, divide it by the number of people who are meant to read the publication the advert is in, multiply the result by 100 and you have some idea of the percentage efficacy of your advert in each publication.

If the advertising is being done online, this task becomes even easier and more covert. With site analytics packages such as Google Analytics (see below), you can view a list of all the sites that have sent traffic to your site, even down to the number of visitors coming from each site. Knowing this, you can focus your marketing and engagement efforts on the sites that will give you the biggest reward, for example the sites with the highest number of dally visitors.

The examples above are just some of the ways you can start to evaluate the efficacy of your marketing and online engagement work, in relation to it drawing traffic to the end goal you have set, be that your website or somewhere else, such as Facebook. There is of course another way of doing this, by coming at it from a different angle.

A lot of this book looks at ways of consulting people online, in order to gain and act on their views and opinions. So, if you want to know which parts of your marketing work and which do not, why not take this approach and just ask people?

If you're getting people to give you their details anyway, whether they're filling in a large consultation document or just signing up to an email newsletter, you could include a quick question in that process that asks 'How did you hear about us?'. To make answering this question as quick and simple as possible, give a list of your main marketing channels as responses from which they can pick one, for example 'Word of mouth', 'Facebook advertising', 'On Twitter' and so forth. Also give an option to select 'other - please state' and a free text box for them to write in their answer.

Of course, this question adds another piece of information to a process you're already trying to keep as short and simple as possible, but if you get your initial list from which people can choose right, then for the vast majority of people, adding this question should only add mere seconds to the overall process.

As we've seen elsewhere though, you should only collect data from your participants if you are actually going to do something with it, and, in my experience, it's this sort of marketing evaluation data that is some of the easiest to forget you're collecting or do nothing with. As with any data you collect on an ongoing basis, you can come to see collecting it as the end goal, and forget that you actually have to do something with it on a regular basis.

So set yourself a monthly task in your diary to review this sort of information, and write it up briefly before circulating it to anyone to whom it may be of use. Good habits across an organisation often start with one person, and often that person has to be you.

Element 2 - Site analytics

Measuring your site analytics is the next step on from measuring your marketing. Site analytics is the generic term for all of the information collected about how people use your website, from how many people visit it, to which pages they look at, even how long they spend looking at each page. Generally a website will have analytics incorporated in it as standard, and even if it does, I'd personally recommend adding the free Google Analytics program to your site to ensure you get the most of out the data you are collecting here[137].

There's something I've just got to get off my chest before we look at this area any more though. Despite it being a word used time and again to

---

[137] www.google.com/analytics/

describe how often something is looked at online, there's actually no such thing as 'hits'.

Well, there is, but the vast majority of people don't know what 'hits' on a website or video actually are.

So often, you hear people say 'my YouTube video got 500 hits' or 'our website's getting a lot of hits'[138] to refer to the number of times a video was viewed or a website has been visited. The thing is, a hit is something different.

So what, geek boy? Why does it matter? Isn't it fine as long as most people use it to mean the same thing, which by and large they do? Well, perhaps, but if everyone used the term 'hits' correctly, then we'd get rid of an occasional scam I've seen done.

A hit, then, "*is a request to a web server for a file*"[139.] Web pages could in theory be made of just one file, and in the early days of the Internet they often were, so possibly this is where the usage of hits in this sense comes from. However, nowadays, most pages usually have a few different files on them. A file could be something like an image on the page for example, so when a page loads, each image on it is loaded as well, and each of those loadings counts as a hit.

The trick I've seen played before now is to tell people the number of hits a website has received, and trust that will people assume you mean the number of people who have visited it. One that sticks in the mind in particular is a trial a local authority did of a piece of software they were thinking of buying. They used it for an engagement exercise alongside a public meeting that was running at the time, and were told by the company that they'd got 114 hits. They said they were happy with this figure, and were telling the press that 114 local people had been engaged.

---

[138] Journalists, especially local ones, are particularly bad at using 'hits' to refer to any count of anything traffic wise online. If you are one, please stop!
[139] http://en.wikipedia.org/wiki/Hit_(web_request)

But when I looked at the webpage for the project, I counted 19 files loading when I opened it. So, dividing the number of hits by the number of files on the page, it turned out the actual number of times that page had been loaded was 6. Apparently they had no way of telling which hits were caused by them looking at the site before it went live as well, so it's entirely possible that not a single local resident ever actually looked at the page at any point, let alone during the actual meeting itself.

So please, when you're talking about the number of people that visit a website, call it by its correct term, don't call it a hit.

But what is the correct term? Well, it depends what you're looking at really, but there are a two very common ones that will help you sound like you know what you're doing; unique visitors and page views.

A unique visitor is one person who has visited at least one page on a website. So, if your site's had 5,000 unique visitors in the last three months, that's 5000 people that have looked at your site. Well, it might not be, as each visit is actually recording that a computer has visited that page. So, to say 5000 people have visited the page, you would have to have had each person use a different computer or computer network, which sometimes doesn't happen. Still though, the unique visitor is as good a benchmark as any for keeping a basic overview on how many people are visiting your site.

A page view, on the other hand, is a single time a page has been looked at. So if a website has more than one page, then a single unique visitor may register more than one page view whilst looking at a site.

Already from this, you can see a performance target emerging. After all, if you want as many people as possible looking at as much of your site as possible, then you want to see a high number of unique visits with a high average number of page views between them.

Even better, this sort of data can be mixed up in other ways, for example you can look at how many unique views each page has had in order to start seeing which of your pages are the most popular. Alternatively, compare unique views for each page with the total views for each page, to see which pages people are most coming back to, and which are only getting looked at once.

Also contained within most analytics data is information related to the people who are looking at your site, such as what Internet Browser they are using, what operating system they are using (i.e. Windows vs. Mac vs. Mobile Phone), even which country they're in. This can be really useful for all sorts of purposes, such as making sure that your site has been tested in all of the different browsers your visitors are using, or getting an overview of whether your site is just popular in your home country or whether it has global reach.

Some analytics packages even have functionality built in, to enable you to analyse and report on the data they collect in extremely sophisticated ways. For example, on Google Analytics, you can set 'goals' on your website, objectives which you think users should complete whilst visiting. You can even specify the pages you'd like them to go through to complete that goal, and so track whether people are using your site as you intended, or whether one particular page is blocking them from going any further.

Imagine building that into every online survey you ever launched, and getting a real idea of how people are using your surveys, and what sort of questions or steps In the process are blocking them from going any further.

It can be really interesting to look at this sort of work, and indeed, doing this is one of the reasons why I first became so opposed to requiring users to register before they can take part in a consultation. You can just see the registration process killing off a huge percentage of potential participants when they reach that stage.

Ultimately, site analytics form such an important hub for each element of the evaluation process, that listing all of the possibilities they provide would require a book in itself. Other aspects of using site analytics are covered in other elements in this section, showing how they fit into lots of other ways of evaluating your online project.

However, no matter what analytics data I've ended up using and how, the one rule I've always applied to it is that the data has to be interesting. If it's interesting to me, then I'm more likely to look at it and make use of it. If it's interesting to others, then they're more likely to make use of it too.

When it comes to heavily numerical and statistical data like this as well, then simplicity can often help to keep it interesting. You can do all sorts of clever things with site analytics packages, and over time you may want to learn to. But for now, just have a play around with them, see what seems interesting, start noticing patterns in the numbers, and above all enjoy them. There's no bigger boost to your self-esteem than to see a sudden influx of people coming to look at your work, even if you'll never know who most of them are.

Element 3 - Site participation

When it comes to measuring participation on your website, you could measure any number of things, depending on the ways you've provided for people to participate. As such, this section can only really cover just some of the possibilities in order to give you inspiration for your own, as an exhaustive list would be impossible.

One thing it is worth being clear on first though, is what participation on your site actually is. In essence, it is someone being more than a passive viewer of your site's content, and actually providing content of their own in some form, be it clicking a button to indicate a preference, or posting page after page of diatribe on your discussion forum.

So, the key metrics you use around this area have to be very much led by the sort of engagement or participation project you are running. However, here are some ideas to get you started, along with some of their pros and cons.

Amount of content submitted

Reminiscent perhaps of the somewhat scathing comment about the number of votes for the winning candidate in a safe seat, that they are weighed rather than counted, you could choose to measure the sheer volume of participation content submitted by users.

Certainly this can look good, and for some projects it's an important point to flag up. When I was lead consultant on the UK Government's Spending Challenge and Your Freedom National Dialogue websites, there was something oddly compelling and relevant about measuring the projects in terms of the millions of pieces of content they generated. Not least in setting a benchmark for the sort of scale of participation people can and should be aiming for in some circumstances[140].

However, whilst this can all sound very impressive, it says nothing of the quality of the participation content submitted through the two sites, and indeed some would argue that not very much of use came out of them at all. I know these people to be wrong, and I've seen the laws that have been amended and abolished as a direct result of public input through these projects, but their point is still important. After all, a site with poor security could receive hundreds and thousands of comments all from spambots, without doing anything or engaging anyone.

So, enjoy simple measures of site participation, and use them to add value to your evaluation process, but don't see them as the be all and end all, and be suspicious of those who do. On the other hand, I'd want to see a pretty good case made for a site seeing very little participation, probably in terms of the quality of content received, before thinking it a success. The Internet's a busy place these days, and you don't usually have to do a lot to get at least a few people taking part.

Following on from this metric, and related to it, is the notion of trying to compare simple participation data with the financial costs of your website, in order to measure the return on investment, or otherwise.

Here, you see people saying things like 'the site cost us £5,000, and 100 people took part through it, so that's a cost of £50 per participant'. These numbers are sometimes then used to justify ceasing web work and going back to methods such as paper surveys, which can cost as little as a couple of pounds per response. I've never been a fan of this approach and justification though, and not just because it loses people like me business.

---

[140] I had hoped that it might move at least some people away from the idea of celebrating 'innovation' and towards celebrating actual results. Sadly, I'm not sure that it has.

Rather, I tend to think that if you're focusing on this approach, and looking to derive the 'value' of the site through such a simple calculation, you miss two important points.

First is that you should be focusing on maximising your participation rate, and doing everything you can to get that cost per response figure down, rather than lamenting it being high. Once everything's set up, it's largely as cheap to receive one piece of content online as it is to receive one million pieces. Sure, there may be some additional data storage and bandwidth costs with higher levels of participation, but spread over time and properly planned for, these needn't actually be that significant. I've seen projects that have had costs of well below one penny per participant, something I've never seen an offline method achieve.

Second though, you also then start to focus too much on participation as a measure of volume or quantity, ignoring the true value of the participation data you are receiving. It's a unique example perhaps, but I'm almost certain the UK Government has saved money overall as a result of the Spending Challenge dialogue. For the costs of the site, which were pretty minimal anyway, will have been far outweighed by the savings government has been able to make as a result of the ideas people submitted for saving money. Sometimes just one good idea can make a huge difference to an organisation, and the more work you do online, the more likely you are to come across it.

If you get your process right from start to finish, and you make sure that the responses you're inviting are of real value to you as an organisation, then it's often hard not to see greater value returned from your site than the investment you put in. Potentially, one idea could save you the cost of the entire website or more, and this is not a possibility that should be overlooked through crude calculations of value that are based on mere numbers.

Number of registered users

Aside from the content itself, there is another element to consider when it comes to site participation, and this is the number of registered users the site gathers during its lifetime. Now, whilst it may be that your site gives participants the opportunity to register a full profile for themselves containing all of their personal details, it could be that being a 'registered user' in this sense could mean something as simple as them providing their email address. This is because the main benefit you are looking to get out of 'registered users' is the ability to contact them again over time.

Of course, having a full profile on a website may be of value to the user themselves in terms of how they participate and how they manage that participation. However, the value you're looking to maximise here is the ability to turn these users from one off participants into regular participants by contacting them on a regular basis. One of the most significant costs of any engagement or participation project can lie in the recruitment of participants in the first place, whether that's through advertising online or standing in the street with a clip board.

As a result, every person you get to give you their contact details is one less person you've got to go and engage from scratch. If you've got their personal email address, then when it comes to your next project, all you need to do is send a bulk email and you will have instantly re-engaged a significant number of people. Indeed, re-engaged people who have already expressed an interest in your work by registering their details with you.

It seem a touch cynical perhaps, but there really is an immense amount of value and cost saving to be found in gathering people's contact details through your online project, and so I'd say the number of 'registered users' your site has, no matter what form that registration takes, is a metric it is well worth keeping an eye on and looking to maximise.

Number of regular participants

Similar to the idea of registered users above, is the number of regular participants your site has. I say similar, as again, the more regular participants your site has, the less time and money you will have to invest in engaging new participants and marketing your site generally. As mentioned elsewhere in this book, very often the only way to build a high traffic website is to build your repeat visitors, and there's not a huge amount of difference between building regular site visitors and regular site participants. However, it is likely that the number of repeat participants will always be lower than the number of repeat visitors, due to some of those repeat visitors being lurkers[141].

Of course, it may be that your site doesn't really have much scope for building regular participation. An online discussion forum for example will have far more scope for building a community of regular participants than will a one-off online survey, but I still think this is a metric that is worth looking at for any website you may wish to run. After all, you may want to run another online survey at some point in the future, and if you have managed to keep people returning to your site in the intervening time, then you should see at least some of those people taking part in your next survey.

How you measure repeat participation is up to you of course, and largely dependent on the sort of participation you're encouraging or allowing. To be honest, I tend not to see this metric in terms of data or statistics, and see it more as something you just develop a sense of over time. If your site allows lots of participation, then you should be on there fairly regularly anyway, keeping things in order and generally being a good host. Through doing this sort of work, a good host can soon get a sense of whether things are as they should be, or whether they're changing in any particular manner.

In terms of how it should fit into your evaluation processes, levels of repeat participation aren't really worth worrying about too much, at least as long as they are staying static or increasing. However, if they start to drop, especially if they drop suddenly or dramatically, then you should start paying attention to them.

Occasional drops are sometimes unavoidable, and even expected, for example you'd have to worry about the happiness of your site's participants if they're on there on Christmas Day rather than pursuing more traditional activities. A drop in July and August is normally temporary and caused by summer holidays as well. If you're seeing a drop in participation though, and there's no immediately obvious reason as to why, then you really should investigate and resolve the cause of the

---

[141] For more on lurkers see Chapter 7.

drop as soon as you can. The Internet is a fickle place, and once a site starts to fall out of favour with its users, then its demise can be rapid and permanent. Just look at the fall of the once ubiquitous Myspace website in recent years if you want proof of this.

If your site doesn't have much in the way of mechanisms to build regular participation, and there's no reason why it should if it doesn't need them, then you can do similar monitoring work by using your analytics program, which should, if it's any good, tell you how much of your site traffic is coming from new visitors and how much is from people who have visited your site already.

Once a site has been live for a while, you will generally see a higher percentage of traffic coming from repeat visitors than for new visitors, and a switch in this ratio, especially if sudden or dramatic, should give you equal cause for alarm.

It may be of course that your number of repeat visitors is suddenly being dwarfed by an influx of new traffic, causing the normal ratio to reverse. However, unless you've just done a huge amount of marketing work, you should be equally alarmed as to where these new visitors are suddenly coming from.

Suddenly becoming the centre of attention on the Internet is rarely a good thing I've found. It usually means you've done something wrong[142].

Element 4 - Quality of participation content

This is perhaps one of the most important elements of any web project that allows participation. Any site that allows a user to enter content, even as simple as sending a message through a contact form, should have some targets put in place for the quality of the content that comes from the site users.

---

[142] What capitvates the interest of the Internet seems largely the same as what captivates those who read tabloids; sex, scandal, crime or funny pictures, especially of cats.

After all, even with just a contact form, you want to minimise the need for people to contact you to find information, so perhaps you could measure the types of emails you get through, to see if your site is filtering out the common questions early on. Alternatively, are you checking whether the email addresses people are giving you are real ones or just 'anything@example.com'[143]?

Of course with a more fully fledged digital engagement project, the quality of the content users enter into the site can be of paramount importance, and targets should definitely be set in a number of places here. Often the most important target you can set is the quality of the information being submitted by site users about themselves and their ideas or responses. Generally, it's that that you want to get out of your web project, and that with which you can make decisions.

You can get some pretty odd results if you get this part wrong, the best one I've seen of which was a genuine comment left on a government backed youth engagement website, which just said 'Poo poo poo I live in a big dog condom'. You can just imagine the submitter's delight when they saw that comment sitting on the website for others to see, which of course then encouraged others to do similar. It all got sorted out, but it just goes to show how important it is not only to moderate your public content, but to write questions that encourage a more constructive response.

Question writing is an art in itself in a way, and I'm not even going to attempt to teach it here for one simple reason. It's the phrasing of the questions being asked in any public engagement or consultation process that can cause the biggest headache. Often even people within the same organisation argue vehemently about the phrasing of questions, and legal challenges have even emerged against consultation processes on the basis of question writing.

---

[143] The domain name 'example.com' is reserved for people to use for testing purposes, and as such any email address that contains '@example.com' is guaranteed to be false. http://en.wikipedia.org/wiki/Example.com

This is because even the tiniest change in nuance in a question can lead to differences in the answers you receive. You can even use questions to predetermine the outcome of the answer the person will be giving, like in my personal favourite example, 'Have you stopped beating your wife yet?'. It doesn't matter whether you say yes or no to that, you'll still look bad.

This is not to say you should be afraid of this area and not try to get to grips with it, you just need to be careful and be seen to be being careful as you do this sort of work. Share questions and invitations for comment widely with people you know for their feedback, and see how they would answer the questions you are asking.

Be aware though, that if you go too far down this road, you can end up with a perfectly worded question that no-one wants to answer. In the process of being as accurate and neutral as possible, a question runs a real risk of becoming overly wordy, technical or generally otherwise boring. Again, many times simplicity will be your friend for squaring this circle, and a really simple question will often lead to the most interesting answers. Just look at some of the famous interviews by Jeremy Paxman, the UK news broadcaster for examples of this approach[144].

Also, don't forget the context in which your invitations to participate sit as well. Even if your questions or prompts are friendly and inclusive, you can still put people off with the quality of the rest of your site. How comfortable would you feel about sharing your personal information and opinions with a website that looked like it was put together in a hurry by someone typing with drum sticks? You get the best content when people feel comfortable and at home using your site.

Often, the content you receive will also have a great deal to do with the sort of people you attract to your site. If you market yourself towards children and young people, you'll generally receive different content than

---

[144] Especially his interview with Conservative Home Secretary Michael Howard in the Mid 90's - http://www.youtube.com/watch?v=1KHMO14KuJk

if your promotion activities were aimed at PhD students. That's not to say one is necessarily better than the other by the way[145].

Often it can be useful to review the content being submitted as it comes in, even if you won't be formally analysing it until the process has ended. This way you can make sure not only that the content is usable, but that it is representative of all of your target audiences. Whilst you shouldn't alter the questions once people have started answering them, you can carry out more engagement work towards specific audiences if you notice you're not getting much response from one or more of them.

Don't be afraid to go even further in this area and provide different questions to different audiences too. For example, you could allow people to state whether they are a member of the public or a member of staff at the start of a survey, and then use that information to present them with different questions as they go through the process. If you allow people to speak about their specialisms, then you make it easier for them to provide you with their knowledge, improving the quality of the content you receive.

In terms of how to monitor whether or not you're receiving quality content through your site, that really is something only you can judge, as only you know what you're hoping to receive. I certainly wouldn't try to automate this process, or reduce it down to just numbers, so take an interest in what people are saying right from the start, and get stuck into looking at it as soon as you can.

9.12 Stopping the traffic

There is one important aspect of getting people to visit your website that is very often forgotten, which is surprising really given its importance. That aspect lies in reversing all of your hard work, and stopping people from looking at your website.

First of all, why would you want to do this? Well, it may be that you were only running a short project that has now ended, and so the website

---

[145] Personally I've often found young people to speak the greatest sense, at least in the most comprehensible way.

needs to come down as well. Very often public engagement and consultation projects in the UK run for 3 months, as a result of government guidelines advising that length of time, so once that time is up, the site may need to come down too. Alternatively, your organisation may have been renamed, rebranded or otherwise rejigged, and it's cheaper to take one site down and put a new one up than it is to alter the existing site.

However, before you decide to take a website down, have a think about whether there really is no need for it anymore, or whether, with a bit of repurposing, you could still gain value from it. If the site's for a three month engagement project, how about taking down the public participation parts of it, and replacing them with the results, reports and actions that have arisen from the project? That way you can provide feedback on the project, enhancing your reputation amongst participants, and you also create a handy backup location for the project files in case your computer crashes or someone else takes over your job.

Bear in mind though that if you're going to leave a website up in this manner, and are not going to be checking back on it regularly, then you really do need to disable any ability it may have contained for users to post content to it. Here's a cautionary tale of the one time I neglected to do this which has taught me never to do it again.

A few years ago, I was called in to provide some online public engagement elements for a very large, very high profile consultation project that an organisation was running across the whole of a city in the UK. The project was pretty rushed, the client in essence throwing the last of their budget at boosting the number of participants in the last four weeks the consultation was open, but it went well. Amongst other things, we provided them with a website where people could post ideas, and others could rate them and comment on them.

Of course, with only being live for two weeks, the website didn't rank very highly in search engines during the project itself, but that was no matter, as I was doing lots of other work around it to get people to visit it. Once the project was over, the client didn't have the time to do a proper close down process, but that was no big issue, as the site still looked good, and so we decided, with the client's permission, to leave it online just as it was, to act as a bit of a case study for prospective future clients.

Then one morning, a year or so later, I received a phone call out of the blue from a member of the public. They had searched for this organisation's name on Google, and come across our site as one of the first results. Presumably over time Google had given the site more and more weighting from the links to it and the residual traffic it was receiving too[146].

The only problem was that over the year, spambot programs had evolved to become even smarter, as they are doing the whole time. As a result, the security elements we'd put in place to prevent spam comments being published on the site had become ineffective, and spambots were now merrily posting links on the site to some of the most eye watering pornography I've ever seen.

This is what the concerned member of public had come across in an innocent search for this organisation's name, and needless to say they were none too impressed. Of course, we immediately removed the ability to add any more content to the site, and deleted the spam comments, but it was a close shave.

There are two lessons from this experience really. The first is, of course, that if you're going to leave a site live but stop looking at it, make sure no new content can go live on it without your knowledge. The second is that if you want to leave a site live over time, you really do need to keep spending money on it, either in the form of your own time, or through paying your supplier for ongoing support.

Some people seem to think that if a site works when delivered, then it should work forever more and so no ongoing support costs should apply. However this is to ignore the fact that whilst the site works with the Internet as it is at the time of delivery, it may not continue to work as the Internet evolves and changes over time, which it most certainly will. In this case spambots evolved to get around the original security features, but there are many other ways in which a constantly evolving Internet can

---

[146] I do suspect Google uses a site's traffic as part of its weighting calculation if that site is using Google Analytics, which this one was.

create threats to older websites, and it pays to have someone keeping an eye on this for you at all times.

Website archiving

There is a problem though with taking websites down, and it lies in the way that certain parts of the Internet operate. When a search engine like Google finds your site and indexes its content in its database, it keeps a copy of what it has indexed, and this copy very often remains stored by Google even if the original is altered or deleted. This copy is viewable by clicking the 'cached' link next to a result in a search engine, and allows people to see what sites used to contain even if they have since changed. Of course, the same effect can be achieved by someone saving a copy of your site content themselves, either through copy and paste or by taking a screenshot of your site at a certain point. Indeed, there is even a whole website dedicated to indexing the Internet for archive purposes, known as the 'Wayback Machine'[147].

All of this means that content you put on the web will very likely be accessible in one way or another for the foreseeable future, whether you delete it from your site or not.

Now, this is a slightly different situation to closing down a website from public participation, as these archive processes can't bring back to life ways of posting new content, only the content that was posted. However, it does mean that any attempts you may be tempted to make to 'rewrite history' and pretend that you never said something online will likely be futile. Indeed, the public relations damage you will suffer from such an attempt will very often do you more harm than just leaving the content online would have done.

There's not a lot you can do about this really, other than be aware of it, and treat every piece of content you publish or allow others to publish on your site as if it will be visible forever more. In a way, I find this situation quite useful, as it forces one to apply a high degree of quality control and rigour to one's online content at all times. It also removes any bad habits

---

[147] http://www.archive.org/web/web.php

people may have around putting content online and thinking that they will come back to improve it later, as invariably you never do.

Custom 404

One final thing to say about taking content down from the Internet is to make sure you do it in a careful and considered manner. As a result of the various archiving capabilities working across the web, not to mention links from other sites to your own, if you take a piece of content down, you are running the risk of creating a dissatisfied and annoyed website user. There is little more annoying than searching for a piece of content online, finding a link to it from a search engine or another website, then clicking on the link, only to find that the page that was being linked to has been altered or removed.

The best way to deal with this situation, if you are planning on removing content from your site, is to do two things.

The first is to make sure any page you remove is replaced with a page of information on why the page has been taken down, and who the user can contact if they wish to get hold of the content that used to be there. Second, you can create a 'custom 404' page, 404 being the error number for when a page is not found on a website[148]. This page will be displayed automatically every time someone tries to visit a part of your site that is no longer there, saving you from creating a new page each time.

If you create a nice 'custom 404' page, apologizing that the user has not found what they were looking for, and suggesting what they can do to find what they were after, then you create a much more pleasant user experience, and more satisfied users of your site.

---

[148] http://en.wikipedia.org/wiki/HTTP_404

Chapter 10. Security, data handling and data protection

I would say there's a real crisis in terms of data protection and security when it comes to public engagement and consultation in the UK, but the word 'crisis' implies many people are aware of it and are trying to do something about it. Perhaps it's more accurate to say there's a whole lot of risk stored up in lots of places, and not enough people seem concerned.

I've worked on some projects where data security has been treated as being beyond important, each piece of information collected or response received treated like the crown jewels. I've also come across, although thankfully seen more than worked on, some projects that have had all kinds of data protection risks and nothing seeming to be done about fixing them.

First of all, what should you be trying to protect, and why should you be trying to protect it? This falls into two categories, protecting your content, and protecting the content submitted by site users.

10.1 Protecting your content online

First of all, don't worry about hacking. Whilst I've had lots of clients phone up and say "my site's been hacked!" when something's gone wrong with their site, never have I actually seen a site that has actually been hacked. Instead, generally what has happened is something has happened to the site that its owner didn't expect or want. Spambots leaving comments on blogs and discussion forums are common culprits for such 'hacking', as is user error breaking pieces of functionality.

For the most part, hackers are the stuff of Hollywood movies and over excitable journalists. That said, if you've built a website, or even just an online survey, you need to make sure that the content you have put into it stays secure and unchanged, unless you or someone you've approved goes in to change it.

A lot of the security needed for this lies at a very technical level, and outside of the remit of this book really. But if your website's security requirements were implemented correctly from a technical viewpoint when it was built, then the weakest link in your site's security becomes real people. If someone does want to hack your site, they are naturally going to start by trying the easiest ways to do it first. If someone wants to log in to your site to access the data it contains or make changes to it, then the easiest way to do this is to use exactly the same login screen that you would.

Most login screens for the administration side of websites are easily guessable to someone with a little bit of knowledge. For example, if you use a site built in Wordpress, you can usually put '/wp-admin' on the end of the site's URL to get the login screen. For other platforms, very often adding '/admin' or '/login' on the end of the URL will do the same thing.

So, it may sound obvious, but the easiest way to 'hack' a website is to go to the login screen and enter the username and password needed to log in, just as you would.

Unless the 'hacker' has found a login username and password in some other way, the easiest way to gain access to a site through the login screen is to try to guess the username and password. Often, it's not the password of any individual site administrator that's guessable either, it's the 'backdoor entry code' as it were, set up during the site's construction.

You see, when a site's being built, people somehow think security is of lesser importance, and so are more relaxed about it. For example, you may want to send the site to a few people to look at before it goes live, so rather than faffing about creating each person a username and password to log in to the site to test it, you create a generic set of login details to send to everyone. Something like;

username: admin
password: 12345

All well and good, but once the site goes live, do you remember to delete that login? I'd say, from what I've seen, you probably don't. So, there it sits, an easily guessable set of login details for your site forever more, or at least until something goes wrong and their existence gets noticed[149].

Broadcasting has a good rule here that's worth applying to websites. Just as you should always treat a microphone as if it's live, always treat a website in the same way. If you create a username and password for logging in to it, make sure both of them are as secure as they can be, right from the start.

So how do you make a username and password secure? Well, it's usually not the end of the world if one of them is reasonably guessable, ideally the username. People often like to maintain a common username across their different logins for different systems, and allowing them to do this on your site does make them more likely to login and use it. I know I've given up using sites more than once now after forgetting the username I used to access it.

However, the password should always be kept secure. Password security can be a whole field in and of itself, but here are some good guidelines for ensuring password security.

Make it random

'Password', 'admin' and '12345' are all very predictable passwords and should never be used. In addition, if you use the name of something or someone associated with you, then you make it easier for people who know you well to guess that password too. You can even get computer programs that will run through things like the dictionary submitting each word in turn as the password to the site until it finds the right one.

For this reason, it is important to make the password a 'non word', for example a word with some numbers or symbols inserted in it. You could

---

[149] Incidentally, a similar thing often happens with content. For some reason, when people are asked to create test content for a site, they all suddenly become comedians and write stupid things. This content again gets left in the site when it is launched, and is generally forgotten about until someone important notices. I've seen it happen more times than I wish I had, often whilst showing that very site to important clients, which is always an awkward experience.

use '1' or '!' to replace the letter I for example, or the number '3' instead of an E.

Never tell anyone else your password

It may sound obvious, but telling someone else your password is a great way to compromise your security. In addition, this will often not just cause a security risk for the site you're giving someone your password to, but for other sites as well, as many people tend to use the same password for accessing different sites. To prevent having to think which password you use where, it's easiest just to make it a rule never to share any of your passwords with anyone ever.

Avoiding telling people your password is made doubly important by another trick 'hackers' can play. If they want to access a site, they send an email or make a phone call to someone in the website's organisation, pretending to be an employee who has lost their login. Wanting to be helpful, the recipient then gives them the password or creates them a new one, essentially doing the hacking for them.

If someone asks you for a password or login to a site, find out who they work for, look up that organisation on the web, find the switchboard number, call it and ask to be put through to them. That way you should, in theory at least, be able to verify that the person is who they say they are. Unless the entire website and switchboard are part of the scam too of course. I generally find you can rarely be too paranoid when it comes to data security.

Never write your password down anywhere

This includes any notebooks you may have as well as your email. Most emails are sent in an unencrypted form, and so could be intercepted by anyone with half a mind to do so, and once sent they often sit around on servers or backups of those servers for a long time, waiting for someone to stumble upon them. When I worked at Delib, we only ever used to give clients passwords to their websites by telephone.

However, there is a problem with password security, in that putting too much security in place can actually make sites less secure.

This happens when website designers try to be helpful, by making sure that you can only ever create a secure password, typically requiring you to use one which contains a combination of letters, numbers and/or symbols, or one which is over a certain character length. The thing is, if you don't normally use a password in that format, then the password you create for this sort of site will be far more easily forgotten. If a password is more easily forgettable, you're more likely to write it down, adding to the insecurity.

Another security risk can come from what you do when you forget a password, when you click on the 'forgotten your password?' link on the login screen. Whilst these links can provide a secure way of resetting your password, I've seen some absolutely terrible examples of them before now. For example, one asked you to verify who you were by entering a large amount of other personal information about yourself, your mother's maiden name and so on.

Now if you're connecting to that site using an insecure connection, then in effect the site is making you transmit all of your security information in a format that others could intercept and use to impersonate you elsewhere, making you far less secure than you would have been if you'd not requested the password reset in the first place.

I even once saw a website respond to a forgotten password request by just sending it to my email address in plain text. Needless to say I sent the site owner an email pointing out this epic security failure and never used the site again.

So, I have to say I'm much more of a fan of ensuring that everyone knows how to create a secure password and does so for every site they use, rather than trying to force them to create a secure one and introduce more security risks in the process.

(D)DOS attacks

If someone doesn't like you, your organisation or your website, there is an alternative to 'hacking' into it and damaging it, and that is to knock it offline so no-one can use it.

The most common way of doing this is through what is called a 'Denial of Service' or 'Distributed Denial of Service' attack, commonly shortened to DoS attack or DDoS attack. There are lots of different ways of carrying out this sort of attack, but in general it involves sending a large number of requests for information to the server hosting the website.

When a server hosting websites is set up, expectations are generally set as to how many people are likely to visit that site over any given period of time, and resources put in place to handle this amount of traffic accordingly. Obviously, for major global sites like Google, the resources made available to handle its traffic are immense, but most other sites will have much more modest expectations and correspondingly lower resources available.

So, if someone decides to flood that website with requests for information, effectively mimicking the effect of huge amounts of people all visiting the site at the same time, the website or even the server it is on will not be able to cope, and will generally go offline to protect itself.

I've only ever seen one real DDoS attack happen to a digital engagement website, and I've still no idea who did it or why, other than that they were based in Russia. I have though seen the same results as a DDoS attack happen to digital engagement websites when they have got too popular. After all, if a DDoS attack mimics lots of people visiting a site at once, then lots of people visiting a site at once will mimic a DDoS attack.

For this reason, it is important when setting up any new digital engagement website to give some consideration to the amount of users it is likely to have and making resources available accordingly. When I worked on the UK Government's 'Spending Challenge' and 'Your Freedom' national dialogues, the vast majority of the budgets for the two sites was consumed by making resources available to handle the huge amount of traffic expected, and the sites were still taken offline by the sheer volume of visitors at certain peak times[150].

---

[150] At its peak, the Your Freedom website was receiving 1600 visits per second.

Given the widespread usage of the Internet and the speed with which messages can spread across it, you can never know for certain when your site traffic might balloon unexpectedly. When I worked with the BBC Trust on their consultation on the future of the BBC 6 Music radio station, the first I or the Trust knew about the strength of interest in it was when the server the site was on fell over due to the huge amount of traffic it suddenly received. There was no way we could have anticipated that, we just had to deal with it.

Now, I'm not saying that every digital engagement site should have massive amounts of resources allocated to its hosting just in case, but you should be aware of how quickly site traffic can spike, and at least have a contingency plan in place in case it does. For as participating online gains ever greater popularity, I suspect issues like this are going to arise more and more frequently.

10.2 Protecting content submitted by your site's users

Whilst ensuring the security of your content is important, protecting the content submitted to your site by others is the most important aspect of data security, both from a moral point of view and a legal perspective as well. In this section I will look at the security of respondent or participant data from the point of view of the law in the UK, but from what I've seen of other jurisdictions, there are sufficient similarities to make the below at least of interest to those living elsewhere. Incidentally, I am not a lawyer or giving you any legal advice here, so always be sure to check up on the specifics of any given situation if you're unsure.

In the UK, the primary piece of legislation governing the electronic storage of data submitted by others is the Data Protection Act 1998[151]. To my mind it's a very clear and well written piece of legislation, designed to be used on an everyday basis, but all too often people don't take the time to understand its requirements. I'm always amused when people bandy round the term 'Data Protection Act' when they want to stop something happening, or have got annoyed that something can't happen, but only rarely are they right in referring to this piece of legislation.

---

[151] http://www.ico.gov.uk/for_organisations/data_protection.aspx

Accepting that most people won't read the act, the government even published a brief set of principles to follow, which if you do, you'll most likely stay on the right side of the act. These are;

---

1. Personal data shall be processed fairly and lawfully and, in particular, shall not be processed unless –

(a) at least one of the conditions in Schedule 2 is met, and

(b) in the case of sensitive personal data, at least one of the conditions in Schedule 3 is also met.

2. Personal data shall be obtained only for one or more specified and lawful purposes, and shall not be further processed in any manner incompatible with that purpose or those purposes.

3. Personal data shall be adequate, relevant and not excessive in relation to the purpose or purposes for which they are processed.

4. Personal data shall be accurate and, where necessary, kept up to date.

5. Personal data processed for any purpose or purposes shall not be kept for longer than is necessary for that purpose or those purposes.

6. Personal data shall be processed in accordance with the rights of data subjects under this Act.

7. Appropriate technical and organisational measures shall be taken against unauthorised or unlawful processing of personal data and against accidental loss or destruction of, or damage to, personal data.

8. Personal data shall not be transferred to a country or territory outside the European Economic Area unless that country or territory ensures an adequate level of protection for the rights and freedoms of data subjects in relation to the processing of personal data.

Now, as I say, I am not a lawyer, but there are a few interesting real life situations that arise when you're following that act that people often seem to miss.

First of all, how often do you see, clearly stated, the purposes that the data collected will be used for? When consulting or engaging people, you ought to have a purpose clear in your mind as to what you're going to do with the data you collect, so it shouldn't be too difficult to state to participants. This part of the act is a reason why it's good to have a section of your consultation information titled 'Why we are consulting'[152].

Second, as part 3 above points out, data collected shall be adequate, relevant and not excessive. Whilst those are all debatable terms, this is one I personally feel lots of organisations get wrong, especially when asking participants to say a few things about themselves.

If you're looking to engage people in a digital engagement exercise of any kind, then it's obviously useful to know a bit about them, so you can see if where people live or who they are affects what they think about an issue. However, so often I see consultations where people have presented their equal opportunities monitoring form in its entirety as their page of demographic questions, asking people about their ethnicity, sexuality, income and all sorts. I'd argue that unless you're actually going to use this data in the analyses you run, collecting it is excessive and not relevant, meaning you're breaching the Data Protection Act by doing so[153].

'But our equalities team/corporate policy tell us to collect this information' I often hear in reply to me mentioning the above. Well, if that is the case, then feel free to raise an urgent concern with someone that they're asking you to break the Data Protection Act 1998 in so doing, unless of course you know that the data will actually be used.

---

[152] See the section in Chapter 9 on Consultation Finder Databases for more.

[153] I once got told I knew nothing about how UK local authorities worked when I told someone this, which amused me really. I think the truth was that I did know how they worked, I just disagreed with it.

Part 5 of the above, on the length of time you should hold the data you collect is a really tricky one for online consultation and engagement, on three different levels really;

1. If you download a data file onto your computer and analyse it, do you then always delete it after you have carried out the analysis and produced the final report? If not, you could be in breach of the act. Incidentally, you should ideally always let people know how long you're going to keep the data for too.

2. Do you back up your computers anywhere? If so, are you deleting the data files from the backups too? Is the company that is hosting the website, and so all of the data files it contains, backing up the site regularly as well? If so, are the data files getting deleted from the backups.

3. Has the data been backed up anywhere else? If you run an open discussion style consultation on a topic, it may be that Google indexes the discussions that take place. In which case, the contents of the discussion may well appear in Google's searchable cache for evermore.

Ultimately, whilst this part of the Act seems to be breached as regularly as it is unwittingly, I do suspect it may have to be rewritten sometime soon to take into account the realities of how data storage now works on the Internet.

Finally, part 8 is a fun one. If you're storing personal data, you're not meant to transfer it out of the 'European Economic Area'[154] unless the country you're transferring it to 'ensures an adequate level of rights and freedoms of data subjects'. Now, I've been working in this field for nigh on 10 years, and I'm still not sure how rights differ from country to country, and which countries are ok to transfer data to. But time and again, I see people using third party software for collecting data online without the slightest regard to where the data is ultimately stored.

---

[154] Different from the European Union, see http://en.wikipedia.org/wiki/European_Economic_Area

www.surveymonkey.com is the current leader for this, used by lots of public bodies in the UK for building online surveys and collecting people's personal data, but do these people check where Survey Monkey stores the data collected?

Personally, being based in the USA, I suspect Survey Monkey is fine to use in this regard, but the points remains. If people go on using random third party software without checking, they're running a real risk of being challenged for breaking the Data Protection Act, however unwittingly.

10.3 When you can use data submitted

Under the terms of the Data Protection Act, you can only use someone's data when they have consented for it to be used. So, you could try saying that by using your website, someone has consented for their data to be used, and indeed write this into the site's terms and conditions. However, this isn't really enough from a moral perspective, and I doubt it would be enough if challenged legally either.

So, for each instance where you ask someone to submit data to you through a website, you should make sure the following three conditions are met;

1. It is clear to the submitter what will be done with the data they have submitted.

2. It is clear to the submitter that the data will be handled under the terms of the Data Protection Act 1998 or the equivalent legislation in your jurisdiction.

3. The submitter has given active consent to their data being used in that way, either by clicking a button marked 'submit' or, for double security, ticking a box agreeing to the terms of usage for the data before clicking submit.

This last point may seem obvious to some, but I was once involved in a bit of a philosophical debate about it. When I was managing the development of the Citizen Space e-consultation platform with UK Central Government, we initially had the option of setting the survey part of the system to store the data a user entered on one page as soon as they moved on to the next page. This initially seemed appealing, as it meant that the organisation using the system would be collecting as much data as possible, even if the respondent dropped out halfway through the survey and never came back.

The thing was though, using the system this way, we would have been collecting and using data without anyone actively giving their consent for us to do so. So, we changed it so that any data not submitted wasn't stored in a way that was accessible by anyone but the original creator (so they could come back and complete their response later), and all such data was automatically deleted once the consultation closed, unless it had been actively submitted in the meantime.

What was useful in coming to this conclusion was, once again, thinking of the comparable offline analogy. Someone filling in a response online is like someone filling in a paper survey, and someone submitting their response online is the same as them putting the survey in a stamped addressed envelope and putting it in a postbox. If they never post back their paper survey, even though they've filled it in, you wouldn't be able to use the data. So if they never actively submit their online response, then you shouldn't be able to use that data either.

Many systems will by default store information without asking for active consent, so do be aware of this and make sure yours is not doing, or at least not doing it in a way in which you can access that information without it being submitted.

The problem of opinion tracking

Of course, one thing we haven't looked at in this book so far is the idea of searching the web to find out what people are saying on various different websites, collating that information together and reporting on it. Sometimes called 'Opinion Tracking', this practice is certainly a tempting proposition, not just because people are talking with each other online the whole time, but also because no matter how lovely you make your website, people still have an annoying habit of talking about you on someone else's site.

If you could develop a piece of software that would automatically collate conversations going on on thousands of different websites and enable you to report on them, the insight you could gain into any given topic could be immense.

However, there is a good reason this idea has not been expanded upon in this book, and that's that doing so may well be illegal. In essence, if you carry out such 'Opinion Tracking', you risk collecting and using people's personal data in an electronic format without their active consent. Indeed, not only may it be illegal, but most reputable market research bodies and membership organisations actively prohibit their members from doing this as part of their codes of conduct.

So, it's a nice idea, and being the Internet I'm sure some disreputable types will start making money out of it soon, if they are not already doing so. However, it's not one I'm interesting in pursuing any further myself, and I'd recommend you didn't either.

Of course, this doesn't stop you reading what people are saying online and acting upon it, it would be ridiculous if it did. But once you start gathering that data together and running analyses on it, you're rapidly getting into some pretty dodgy territory. A shame in some ways, but there you go.

10.4 Protecting your reputation online

In some ways, this section could fit into Chapter 7 on Online Engagement, but in many ways protecting your reputation online is closely tied up with protecting your security. For one of the best ways to encourage people to attack your site or threaten your data security is to have them dislike you. Often attacks like this are used to pull people down from their pedestals, or get information out of them that people reasonably feel should be made freely available. So, the fewer people dislike you, the fewer problems you are likely to encounter.

Of course, one other reason to attack someone or something online is for the lulz. I shan't say too much about it, as I can't pretend to speak for the people who attack sites for this reason, other than to say that lulz is a corruption of the Internet term 'lol', and doing something for them generally means something akin to doing something because it's funny to the person doing it, or just for the sake of it. There's a whole world out there around these principles, and it's a world to be aware of, and to be aware that it often does good as well as bad. Groups of people generally tend to develop some social consciences after all.

Protecting your reputation online isn't as big a field as protecting it offline at the moment, although it is growing the whole time. We have already seen some spectacular car crashes with reputations being ruined through the Internet though, and I suspect it will take a few to happen in each different sector before each sector wakes up to the risks of it.

I've dealt with situations like these before[155], and the one thing I've found is that the speed of the Internet really hits you when things are going wrong. You have to be ready to react to something almost immediately on a 24/7 basis, and expect the unexpected.

Over time though, I've developed a few rules to follow to get you through the worst of any situation like this.

- **Involve more people.**

   Get all of the people who are relevant to dealing with the situation together in one room, close the door, and get them involved in finding solutions.

- **Be ready for it at any time**

   Alistair Campbell, former 10 Downing Street Director of Communications and Strategy, is said to have commented that being a teetotaler made his job handling the media much easier, as he was never drunk or hungover when a problem arose. If you think something could go wrong, get a rota together and make sure there's always one person alert and 'on call' at any given time.

- **Watch the Internet**

   Forewarned is forearmed, so if people are having a go at you

---

[155] I shan't say which, as it would kind of defeat the point of handling them successfully in the first place.

online, read everything they say and take it on board. If they're complaining about something you could easily fix, then fix it!

- **Be nice to everybody**

  Nothing defuses angry people like being nice to them.

- **Never delete bad comments whilst the situation is going on**

  People online will accuse you of censorship at the drop of a hat, there's even a well-known 'Internet law' that relates to this. If you delete a comment because you don't want others to read it, then you will look far worse than if you had just left it there in the first place. After everything has settled down again, it may be appropriate to go back and remove some of the more heated arguments, to stop them accidentally kicking off again, but even then don't delete them all.

- **Be open and honest**

  Sometimes, you may have ended up in trouble because people think you are being less than straight with them. If that is the case, then be as straight with them as you can from now on, even if being straight with them means explaining why you don't want to do what they want you to.

Of course, if you want to stop anything getting to a crisis point with your website or online reputation, you generally want to be being open, fair and honest with people all along. There are thought to be possibly one billion websites in existence, a figure that is growing all the time, so if you don't give people a reason to make yours a target, they probably won't.

At the end of the day, managing crisis communications online is something you have to learn for yourself, by living online and immersing yourself in it every day. In the meantime, be careful out there. To go back to the participation party analogy, I don't know about you, but every time I threw a big and raucous enough party, I always got something nicked or broken by persons unknown.

10.5 Procedures for handling data

Handling data safely and securely is not a difficult task once you get the hang of it, and again it is worth having a distinct policy document for your organisation, one that is as easy to understand and follow as it is widely promoted.

In addition, you should always have a copy of your data handling and protection policy on any website you use to collect data from others. It is worth looking at the elements of such a policy in more detail here in order to understand how they work and the implications they hold.

Details of your nominated data handler

Being a nominated data handler is not a responsibility to take lightly, as in many cases this person can be liable for any breaches in data protection that may occur. However, you do need one, as you cannot avoid liability by not doing.

It is in your interest to make this position one of importance within your organisation as well, as the role should be combined with responsibility for making sure the policy is consistently and accurately applied by all, even combined with the responsibility of delivering the training that all staff who handle data should undergo.

Data will only be used with consent

You must make it clear that you will only use data that people submit with their active consent, and so the policy must state that any data collection process must have an opportunity for individuals to give that consent built into it.

Data will only be used for the purposes you have set out

You must make it clear the purposes you will use data for, and state clearly that you will not use data for purposes other than those you have stated.

How data is to be stored

This should include information on how you store data both electronically and in hard copy or other formats. Give consideration to the security factors around data storage here. Do you need a lockable safe for storing hard copy data securely? Does that safe need to be fireproof? What electronic devices will you use for storing data? Will it be individual employee computers or shared virtual hard drives? Will any of the data be stored in such a way as to be accessed remotely from outside of your offices? What backup regime will you have for preventing data loss in the event that the original storage system fails?

How data will be accessed

What processes will you use for accessing data? If you store data in a password or lock and key protected environment, who holds those passwords or keys? What procedures have to be followed in order for others to gain access to this data? On what grounds will access be given? How will you record who has been given access and when? What procedures will you use for removing access from people if they leave your organisation?

Who data will be shared with

Ideally, you should as a rule not be sharing data you collect with others in order to reduce the risk of errors. However, there are always circumstances in which you may gain additional value from the data by sharing it, so set out how and when this may be done. Would you anonymise all of the data before sharing it perhaps?

There are also sometimes legal situations that require you to share data, or conversely limit how it can be shared. For example Principle 8 of the UK Data Protection Act sets out rules around this area, and there may be other legal bodies who may have the right to access data you hold, such as a police force or legal system.

How long data will be stored for

You must set out how long the data will be stored for. Of course, this could be indefinite, but typically you do not want to be storing data any longer than you have to, as the longer you hold it, the more risk there is of something going wrong. Of course, there are often additional costs associate with storing data over the long term, especially if it is in hard copy format.

Typically for a public engagement or consultation exercise, it is reasonable to store data from it for three months from the end of the exercise. If you are setting any sort of time limit on the storage of data, you should set out how it is to be destroyed securely once its time limit has expired. You should also have an audit process in place, ideally run quarterly, to check for any data that is being held over its time limit.

How to object to your data being held

Even after they have given you their data, individuals can often still have the right to know what data of theirs you hold, as well as the right to ask you to destroy that data, especially if it is held in an electronic format. You should set out how individuals can find out what data you hold on them and how they can object to you holding it. Often this procedure is best handled through the nominated data handler mentioned above.

The consequences of breaking any section of the data handling policy

Data security is a serious matter with serious consequences for organisations that break it. Accordingly, whilst I don't tend to encourage this in policy documents as a rule, you should set out what disciplinary measures will be taken in the event of an individual breaking any section of this policy.

How the relevant people will be trained in this policy

Finally, a policy is no use as a written document filed away somewhere, it has to be read and understood by all employees. Often the best way to do this is to include training in your data protection policy as part of your induction program for new members of staff, as well as promoting refresher courses in data protection and handling to all staff on a regular basis. The more people who understand your policy, and the better they understand it, the less likely you are to encounter breaches of it. Whilst you can discipline staff for breaking it, unless you have actively offered them regular opportunities to understand what it means and how to use it, you can't just blame your staff if anything goes wrong.

Chapter 11. An overview of open data

Open data, the concept of making as much of the data and statistics held by an organisation[156] available for free online, could almost sit within the chapter of this book on unstructured consultation. However, it has its own unique character to such a degree, being almost completely unstructured, and holds such importance that it merits a chapter of its own. In this chapter I shall be referring primarily to experiences of open data in the UK, although the open data movement is naturally worldwide.

One thing government bodies in the UK have got quite good at, from the mid 1990's onwards especially, is collecting data on what goes on around them. Measurements of performance, incidents, activity, behaviour, travel, it's all getting logged on a daily basis. Whilst all this data has a primary purpose for the people that collect it, there are of course potentially myriad secondary uses for it, beyond the original purpose.

Of course, history's probably going to benefit from it, although future historians will probably have to take on a more statistical role than they already do in order to cope with the sheer volume of it that computers have now allowed us to collect. After all, let's not forget the huge impact computing has had on how much data we all can store, and how little it now costs to do so. Where previously any information we wanted to store had to be written, printed or typed with a typewriter, now it can be typed straight into a computer to be edited, backed up, searched and a whole lot more, all at the touch of a button.

Two other big barriers to data storage used to be the workload of creating the data, and the physical space to put it in once collected. On the latter, computer memory is now so small and cheap that physical space has become comparatively meaningless, and on the former, computers can now create the data for us too. Air quality monitoring stations, cash points, ANPRs[157], and all manner of other computer based contraptions can collect data 24 hours a day, every day of the year.

---

[156] Typically a government or public sector organisation.
[157] http://en.wikipedia.org/wiki/Automatic_number_plate_recognition

Of course, let's not get carried away here. Whilst the fact that there's seemingly limitless data and combinations of data available out there leads technically to a limitless range of potential uses for the data, some data is more equal than others. After all, just look at which facts get studied most in history; interesting things like wars, royalty and the exercise of power, not the data that exists on the plight of Victorian cotton workers in and around Manchester[158].

So just as it is in the study of history, so it is in the study of the present day, carried out by and large by journalists, lawyers, campaigners and very intelligent but slightly odd Internet people. Of all the data public sector organisations hold, it's generally the data that's the most useful, controversial or just generally interesting that gets the attention.

So then, there's lots you can do with public sector data, and there's lots of it about, so what's open data got to do with it? Well, as mentioned at the start of this chapter, open data is about getting organisations to release the data they hold for anyone to look at, analyse and interpret however they want. I say 'getting organisations to', because traditionally there has been a massive reticence on the part of public sector organisations to release the data they hold. Perhaps unlike others though, I don't think there has necessarily been this reticence because of dark politics and conspiracy. Instead, I think, in the UK at least, that there are three significant reasons behind it.

The first is the Data Protection Act, and the Government being so effective in getting everyone scared of it. As a result, I've sometimes seen even relatively innocuous open data work get blocked by organisational policies or 'security concerns'.

After all, no-one wants to be the person that accidentally releases some data that should have been kept private, such as an individual's personal information. Thankfully, when these problems arise, they tend to create a situation that looks so absurd that it's laughable, but this still stops it getting released sometimes.

---

[158] Unless you were Engels, and who *actually* studies him?

Second, very often the people collecting the data haven't seen it as very interesting. After all, I've had enough data entry jobs in my time to know that it's not a job I'm looking to do again soon. Large amounts of data can easily become boring when you work with them day in and day out. This doesn't mean they're not of interest to someone else.

Third, and this is where some conspiracy may lie, if there is any in this at all, the data isn't often kept in that good a format. For when the data is collected, it's collected to fit one, often very specific, purpose. If it's only used by one person, they may write it or store it in a bit of an idiosyncratic way. This means that the data is very often next to impossible to do anything else with even if it is released[159].

But that's not to say that open data isn't useful, very far from it. Already we have seen some excellent uses of public data. For examples, 'Ernest Marples' is an excellent project to make UK postcode data freely available, so that it can be used to facilitate a wide range of other public engagement websites for free. Ironically, for a short time the UK Government shut it down, but it has since seen the error of its ways and allowed the data, collected and administered using public money, to be made freely available to the public who pay for it[160].

In addition, some of the best applications for different data sets, bringing the biggest benefits to civic society, are doubtless still to be discovered. So, all organisations can do in the meantime is free up and release this data for public use, allowing people to explore, experiment and reuse it in a variety of different ways, until the greatest benefits are found.

How then do you go about getting the most out of the data you hold? Well, it's pretty simple really, and should be kept pretty simple, because when you're handling that amount of data, the more complexity you create, the more likely you are to do something wrong.

---

[159] If I seem a bit oddly informed in this area, it's because one of my first jobs was in the statistics department of a local authority. My seminal work, 'The reasons behind school attendance in Bristol', remains a classic of its genre. Probably.
[160] For more on the Ernest Marples project, and the story behind its somewhat difficult birth, see http://ernestmarples.com/

First of all, find out what data you hold. You may already know, in which case all well and good, but I'd still encourage you to type out a comprehensive list of it, along with the path name for the file and some other relevant information. The mere act of doing an exercise like that will both make the data easier to find when you come to publish it, and will also doubtless flush out a few bits of data that you might not have previously considered as relevant to anyone but yourself. There's a template you can download and use for this on my website, and in the appendices to this book too.

Once you know where all of the data is, copy and paste[161] each file into a new folder on your computer. Then open each file one by one and go through them, asking the question 'Is there anything in here that identifies any individuals, or gives away their personal or private information?' If there is, delete the copy of the data from the folder you copied it to. Eliminating any data that should not be released for good reason at this stage can save you a lot of work further down the line, and helps to make sure nothing gets out that actually shouldn't. You could always come back and see if you can anonymise the data later on if you have the time.

Once you're satisfied that all the copies of the files you have could be released to the public, go through each of them again and ask the question 'If I gave this data to someone else, would they be able to make any sense of it at all?'. If the answer is no, amend it until you think it is. For example, use the 'find and replace' function of the software that the data is held in to replace abbreviations with their full words, or save the file with a filename that makes it clear what the data contained in it is, and when it dates from and to.

I deliberately say go through them again, rather than combining the two questions in one task, as if you try to answer two different questions about information in one go, you're more likely to make mistakes.

Once you've got all the data in one place, are happy that its content can be released and that it's in a presentable state, go and speak to your manager and ask them about releasing it. I feel sort of bad having to say

---

[161] Don't cut and paste, you want to keep the original file where it is.

this in a way, as if it were me, having got to this stage, I would now just bung it on the web and go about the rest of my day. However, we're still a long way from the concept of open data being that widely known about, let alone encouraged. There are a few excellent local authorities here in the UK when it comes to their willingness to provide open data, but even they always have more they could do. As for private sector organisations making use of it, I've yet to see any examples at all.

So, for the sake of your job, go and speak to someone more senior than yourself about the idea of releasing it. You never know, they may know how beneficial releasing open data can be to both an organisation and the public good more widely, so you can bang on. If they do not, why not offer to write a brief report for them on what benefits open data would bring, and see if they can raise it with their management, and so on upwards?

If you get approval to publish it, don't stress too much about where you put it online. What people want at first is the data to have a general look through. It may be some of them get back to you and ask for clarification on some of it[162], or let you know which bits they find interesting. As long as it's all in one place on a website somewhere, ideally your organisational one so you can claim the credit for it, then just let the local media know about it and get on with your day job.

---

[162] You are of course free to say no at this point, you've opened up the data and probably shouldn't invest too much more time or energy in it at this initial stage.

For those visual types amongst you, here's a flow chart of the above process;

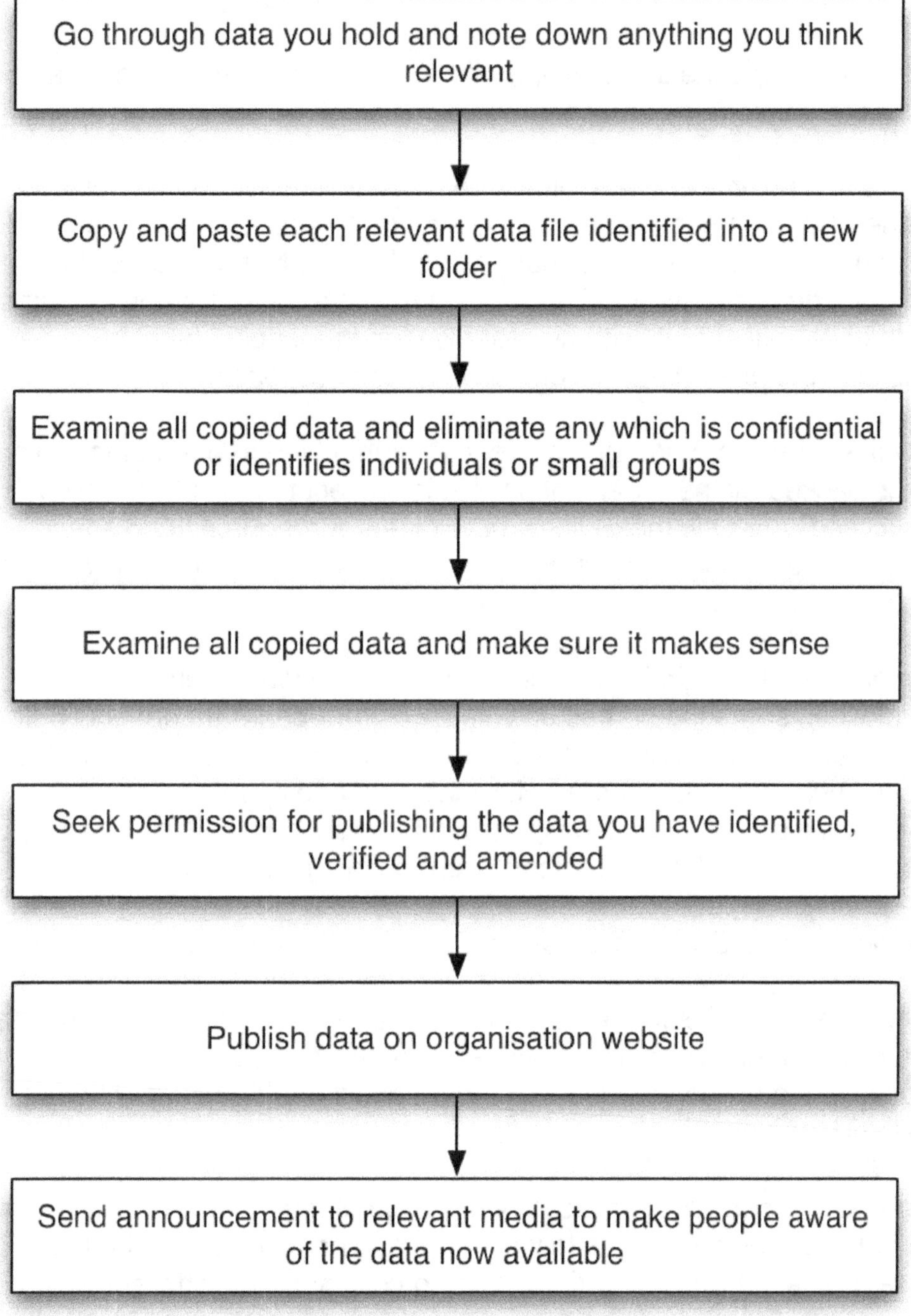

As for the time it should take to do the above, well, unless you've got a particularly data intensive job, or are actually a professional archivist, all of the above shouldn't take any more than half a day of your time at first, so no-one can say you've been wasting time on a pet project.

As for what happens then, well, that's up to whoever reads the data and decides to make use of it somehow.

It's this last point that's sometimes so crucial when it comes to open data; the idea that it's up to anyone and everyone to decide what should happen to the open data that has been released. Not only does this approach generally lead to better outcomes in a shorter amount of time, but the alternative to it, with an organisation prescribing what must be done with the open data, is generally far less successful.

Now this may seem odd at first, as you might think an open data project that is backed by the organisation that is subject to it would be more likely to succeed. After all, they'll likely put in greater resources and spend more time removing barriers. However, there is often one fatal flaw in how these projects work.

This flaw can be entirely unexpected and unintentional, but it comes about when someone comes up with ideas for open data projects before looking at the data itself. Generally, organisations like to know what is happening to their open data before they release it, so an open data process will sometimes start with a call for proposals on how open data could be used, and those projects are then given resources.

The problem here though is that you've put the cart before the horse. How can you know what you can do with open data until you've checked what is capable of being done with the data? I've seen many open data pilot projects now which have started with great ideas, only to come to nothing when it's been found that the data just can't be made to work in the intended manner.

There are all sorts of reasons why data sometimes doesn't work. Perhaps the data your project needs to work is not being collected in the first place, or maybe one set of data is being collected in a different way to another set. Either way, the project usually ends up grinding to a halt with problems like these, unless the participating organisation is so keen on open data that it starts funding the collection of new data. Sadly, this seems unsurprisingly uncommon.

So, the safest approach to take really is just to put the data out there and let people play around with it to see what interesting things can be done. The more you try to proscribe what people can do with the data, the less likely it is your project will work. This is not to say you can't do anything at all though, as you can give the process a nudge at certain points.

One great way of ensuring that best use is made of your open data is to help people to use it. Making sure it's clearly labelled and easy to find online is of course one part of this process, but there's still something more proactive you could be doing as well.

This thing is called an Open Data Hack Day, there have been a fair few of these events taking place over the last few years, and the idea behind them is simple. Someone, perhaps an organisation or perhaps just a someone, decides to call together anyone in their local area who is interested in working with open data to spend a day working with it together. Apart from getting together and working on open data, there are no other rules necessary for a successful day really.

The idea is that these people working together, sometimes whilst being fed beer and pizza, can make a large amount of progress in a single day, enough to kickstart some of the ideas into successful projects. What they have produced at the end of the day will be very unlikely to be anything like finished websites, tools or processes, but that's fine as long as you've got some good solid proof of concepts that show the projects that are worth continuing further.

We organised one of these once here in Bristol, and it was a really good day. We gave people who came along a venue to use with some different private meeting rooms, some data to play with if they wanted (in this case, all of the response data from the Your Freedom National Dialogue, anonymised of course), and possibly some cake or something too. In terms of who we invited, we just sent emails around the local web development community, which happens to be quite large in Bristol. However, it doesn't just have to be developers who can come along to these, anyone who might have a good idea on how to use data could very usefully be invited too.

The outputs of this Open Data Hack Day were varied at the end of the day. Some people did work using some of the local travel information that the council held, to improve travel information for Bristol, others tested concepts more generally. One that particularly stuck in the mind was the guy who built a simple piece of software that attempted to turn each of the responses to Your Freedom into a traditional Japanese Haiku poem. Most responses wouldn't bend to this form, but some that did, or at least nearly did, had me in stitches. Gems such as;

"Simply repeal IR35
IR35 was introduced to stop
By all means make sure"

or;

"When we are abroad
We pay vehicle tax to
Foreign vehicles"

or indeed;

"The New World Order
Children should remain with their
Supervision"

Now you may say this software was entirely silly, and on the face of it you'd appear to be correct. However, silly as the Haikus were, they proved that it was possible to run automated analysis and reporting on a significant percentage of public submissions, something that could be extremely interesting to explore further. I never have yet. I don't have the time and I'm not much of a coder, but I'm now more sure that there are some genuinely useful possibilities available in this area if I ever want to come back to it.

So then, you may see open data as a threat, but you really will get more out of it if you encourage people to work with it without trying to control what they can do. What people come up with when working with open data doesn't just have to be handy little websites that simplify information either. Who knows, people may look at the data and have an idea for something your organisation could change to improve what it did, save money or anything else you may not have spotted before.

If you're open to change and improvement, and you should be if you're serious about engaging people anyway, then people will be more likely to work with you using the data, rather than against you.

Above all, open data is meant to be surprising, interesting and fun. Treat it in that way, and I'm sure you'll be rewarded by it.

Chapter 12. How to buy digital engagement software and services

There is a school of thought out there that you needn't pay anything for digital engagement. After all, there's so much free software out there now, so many online help files and user guides, that if you pay money for anything then you're being ripped off.

It's a school of thought that I fully support, but also one which I wish would realise its own limitations. I came across it most clearly when I was running the development of Citizen Space, an open source online consultation and engagement platform into which the UK Government invested a great deal of money. A huge amount of work was required to build the software to meet the needs of the many and varied consulting organisations who were to use it, as well as to meet the needs of the Government's myriad Internet guidelines, and still remain simple and usable whilst it did so.

All throughout the project, there were murmurings here and there that the money we were being paid to develop it was just another example of the private sector ripping government off, and that the same results could be achieved if a bunch of technical types were gathered together for a weekend and stocked up with laptops and pizza. Such thoughts were of course nonsense, but it does worry me how little people understand about how building digital engagement software works, meaning some organisations refuse to part with any cash and fail as a result, whilst others pay fortunes and still find they achieve very little.

As well as providing training and consultancy, I've been working in the technical development of digital engagement systems for many years now, so it seems to make sense to dedicate a chapter of this book to what I've learned about software development processes, and the procurement process that often precede them.

12.1 Free vs. Open source vs. proprietary

First of all, it's worth understanding some of the terms you might encounter when buying or using software.

Ultimately, like any words, pictures, music or video on the Internet, all software belongs to someone or some organisation, usually the one that originally developed it. What is actually owned is not particularly exciting, comprising mostly of lines and lines of computer code which, when put together and put online correctly, make the software that you actually see and interact with.

As all software is owned, it is up to the owner who they let use it and how, normally covered by some manner of licence. In order to use the software yourself, you have to agree to the terms and conditions of the licence. However, just because there is a licence in place, it doesn't necessarily mean that money has to change hands.

Some software is given away free for people to use. Free forms of software are generally more limited than versions that are paid for, the idea being that people can try software for free, and if they like it, they can pay to enjoy the additional functionality provided by the more comprehensive paid for version. Alternatively, the owners of the software rely on goodwill and karma, and invite people to make donations to them if they have liked using the software.

Free software doesn't have to work along this model though. After all, Facebook and Twitter are two pieces of software than anyone can use for free, and don't really provide more functionality if you pay for them. Indeed, unless you count buying advertising on these platforms, you can't really pay for them anyway. You still have to agree to the terms and conditions of these free sites in order to use them though, effectively taking out a licence on using the software, albeit no money changes hands.

In a similar vein to free software is open source software. The idea behind open source software is that the source code, the lines and lines of code that go to make up the software, can be provided for free to anyone on request. In addition to this often allowing the software to be used for free, because the actual source code can be inspected, individuals using the software can write their own code to add functionality to it, and share it with others in return. In this way, open source software can in theory grow and develop extremely quickly, as many different people contribute to it, and in some cases this does indeed happen.

This is not to say that open source software is necessarily free however. There are various different forms of open source software licence under which a software owner can release their code, and some allow people to charge for work as part of this. Other forms of open source licence have a particularly clever clause in them which require any changes anyone makes to the open source code to be released for others to use under the same terms as the original software. In this way no-one can take open source software, amend it and claim it as their own that they sell for money[163].

Finally, there is proprietary software. This is software that someone has built and allows others to use under licence, generally paying money to do so on a per licence basis. Software such as Microsoft Word is proprietary in this manner, requiring a licence fee to be paid for each computer on which it is used.

To understand these licences, it helps to understand how people make money out of them. As after all, unless people get paid for the work that they do, they tend not to be able to carry on doing it.

Proprietary software is simple. You invest a sum of money in building the software in the first place, and then hope to receive more money back than you invested by selling licences to use it.

Free software is less straight forward, but generally, having invested in building it, you hope that you will get paid money as a result of doing so, either by people making donations, or by using the free software as part of your portfolio of work when pitching for new work. After all, if you've built a piece of free software that is used by millions of people, you're going to have a pretty strong and widely known reputation as a result, leading to more work coming your way.

Open source sits in the middle of the two really, as you can sell it for money, and you can also sell work around it, for example additional customisation and development, ongoing support and training, hosting,

---

[163] For more information on the different forms of open source licence available, see http://www.opensource.org/licenses

and everything else that can go on around software. However, due to the fact that you are in practice unlikely to recoup the original development cost of the software in this manner, the more successful open source pieces of software generally have their initial development funded by an external source.

For example, when building Citizen Space, the UK Government paid for the initial development of the software. This was a large initial outlay, but as the software could then be used for minimal cost by any Government body that wished to, the Government as a whole would make a net overall saving, in comparison with each government body paying licence fees for similar software on an ongoing basis.

No matter under what form of licence software is released, the most important point to remember is that somebody somewhere will always be looking to make money from it, either directly or indirectly.

So, which form of software should you choose to use?

Well, it really is up to you, and often depends on what it is you're looking to do and what software is currently available for that purpose. Personally, I think open source software is the way people should go. Partly due to the money you save from using it, but also because by using it you're not tied in to any one software supplier over time. If your original supplier goes bust, you still own the source code, which you can take to another supplier for them to continue to support and maintain. Similarly, if you find your original supplier is charging you too much money for ongoing support, maintenance or hosting, then with open source you're free to terminate your agreement with them and shop around for a better deal.

In addition, as others can add to and amend the software's original code, you can also benefit greatly from new functionality that they develop, and often receive it for free, rather than having to pay for upgrades.

However, there is one thing to be aware of with open source software, and there's no better name for it than the following title.

12.2 Avoid platform fetishism

Nearly all open source software is built using an open source platform. This platform provides the base on which the software can be built, and often requires a specific sort of programming language to be used in adding to or amending it[164]. There are a number of different open source platforms available, the most well known of which are Drupal, Plone, Wordpress and Ruby on Rails.

The problem you get with them though, is that each software developer or software development company generally only works with one type of platform. Each will have arrived at their decision on which to use in their own way, but a problem arises when their choice of platform turns into a fervent evangelism for that platform at the expense of all others.

After watching many arguments go on between different developers about how the platform they have chosen is clearly superior to all others, I have come to realise that, in reality, none of them are better than any other. They all have their strengths and weaknesses, and very often the only reason people insist the one they have chosen is the best is because it's the only one they know how to work with, so they have to insist it is the best, or else they might lose work to someone else using a different platform.

The fact that there is no 'best' open source platform to work with is one thing, but what really turns this sort of behaviour from a belief into a fetish is the fact that nowadays, it doesn't really matter which platform you use. As discussed elsewhere in this book, protocols such as RSS and XML mean data can easily be shared between different software and different platforms, so if you use one platform for one purpose, you can just as well use a different platform for a different purpose and not have your website's users be any the wiser.

Regardless as to why people get so fervent about their chosen platform, I have seen this fervour cause very real problems for organisations before

---

[164] Despite starting from scratch not that long ago, the world of software development is sadly as prone to the curse of the Tower of Babel as the real world.

now. Whilst working at Delib, I once wrote a proposal for an e-consultation website based on the open source Plone platform. The person running the project liked the proposal and was on the point of commissioning it, when their IT department suddenly stepped in and insisted that a different proposal be chosen because it would be built using Drupal, a platform they already used for their main website. As a result, they said it would mean that they could 'integrate' the new proposal into their site in a way they could not using Plone.

Unfortunately, no amount of pointing out that in reality they could integrate Plone in exactly the same way as they would Drupal cut any ice, and they used a Drupal site. Three months after the site was launched, rather than being integrated into their main site as they thought, it instead disappeared from the web, never to be seen again, just as I thought it would. Unsurprisingly, the fact that the two sites were built in the same platform hadn't made integration any easier, as they were still essentially two different sites doing different things.

So, please don't get caught up in the odd fetishes of IT people when it comes to which platform to choose. Unless you're doing something really specialist, the chances are that you can integrate sites built in two different platforms just as easily (or with as much difficulty) as you can two sites built in the same platform. Indeed, it may well be that by using different platforms for different purposes, you get to benefit from their different strengths whilst avoiding their weaknesses.

12.3 Buying software through competitive tendering

Very often, web projects come with considerable budgets attached, or organisations want to make sure they get the best value for money. In either case, a formal tendering process can be the resultant method of deciding which software to buy.

As will become apparent, I'm not a massive fan of buying software through tendering, a fact which is quite probably influenced by the amount of times I've had to fill in tenders in order to make sales. There are various reasons why I think the tender process is very often bad for all concerned, but before we consider these, it's only right to have a look at the alternatives to spending money, as there certainly are a lot of them out there at the moment.

Free software

I'm a big fan of free software. It's hard not to be really. Partly because it's free, obviously, but also because in IT, it's always the future. There is a very real trend in software for anything that costs money today to be free tomorrow.

A lot of this can be put down to the continual development of software, combined with the fact that software can be replicated thousands of times for little additional cost. As software develops, older versions of it become less desirable, but copying it and giving it to somebody only takes a few clicks of a button. So the inherent value of the old software decreases, whilst the production costs remain minimal, leading to a constant decline in price.

Of course, you may be the sort of person who always wants to have the latest version of any software going, but if you're not, and the older software does what you need it to, then an older free version may well be just what you need.

This need not necessarily be the whole story, as you can of course get software that is both free and up to date. Google provides a huge range of free software for you to use through the web, including mapping, spreadsheets, word processing, calendars and more. So much so, that if you're looking for some sort of group management and collaboration system, you probably couldn't do much better than use what Google has to offer.

The only argument I've ever heard against taking this approach is that 'you don't know what these companies are doing with your data'; the implication being that somehow any information you put into these free platforms will be at risk. I've never been entirely sure of the specific risks one is meant to fear here, but I imagine they range from the data being used for marketing purposes, to it being stolen and used for nefarious purpose.

Whatever the case, this argument is pretty much nonsense. From a security point of view, huge corporations such as Google will have had the time and budget to conduct far more rigorous security testing than a relatively small digital engagement software supplier. In addition, the global reach of their brand ensures that if security breaches do happen, they become global news, thus presenting a real risk to their profits. Since they've got the money to make sure their security is water tight, and so much to lose if it isn't, you can place far more trust in the security of free software provided by a massive global name than you can in any smaller and more niche companies.

As for them using your data for other purposes, well, they might, but this is hardly an issue. They have hundreds of thousands of simultaneous users using their software at any one time, and the likelihood of them looking at your data specifically is beyond minimal. Instead, if they do make use of it, it will be in an automated and aggregated manner, perhaps to assess trends of who is using their software and the sort of things they are using it for.

In many ways, the only risk of using free software is if it is being hosted in another country, in which case your data will be subject to the laws of that country rather than your own. Often this is not a problem, but if you are storing sensitive data identifying individuals, then you might be best looking at alternatives.

Software has advanced so far that there is likely to be a free piece of software for pretty much any purpose you can think of these days, and a good Googling will give you lots to consider. However, here are a few examples of software I have successfully used before, and the purposes to which they can be put.

Group collaboration

Google Groups - http://groups.google.com/

Google Docs - http://docs.google.com/

Google Calendar - http://www.google.com/calendar

Yammer – http://www.yammer.com

Collaborative document writing

Mixed Ink - http://www.mixedink.com

Wikis - http://www.mediawiki.org

Online surveys

Survey monkey - http://www.surveymonkey.com/

Discussion forums

php Bulletin Boards - http://www.phpbb.com/

Blogging / Website CMS

Wordpress - http://wordpress.org/

Blogger - http://www.blogger.com

12.4 Building software yourself

What if you just can't find any free software that does everything you want, but still don't want to spend any money? Well, why not build it yourself? After all, if you've got an in-house IT team, or some IT skills yourself, surely you could just build the software in-house and save a load of money?

Well, in short, no. No you couldn't.

I've heard lots of people over the years say that they're planning to build their own software, are in the process of doing, or have tried to do so. Only very rarely though have I heard of anyone who has built their own software successfully or been happy with the end results.

There are two main issues going on here really. The first is one of specialism. Unless you or your IT team are specialists in the sort of software you intend to build, whatever you end up with will always be inferior to software built by an organisation that does specialise in this area.

The second is one of collaborative gains. In order to build their software, a specialist organisation will have have examined lots of different approaches, different platforms and different experiences from a range of organisations in order to build something that fits the majority of requirements. All of this work will take a substantial investment of both time and money.

Indeed, when I led the development of the Citizen Space online engagement platform, we calculated that, had we been paid for all of the work we did at standard day rates, we would have spent close to one million pounds over the 18 months it took to build. I wouldn't be surprised if other comparable systems out there had seen similar levels of investment. Given this, it's hardly surprising that systems built by organisations for their own use just don't compare in terms of usability, functionality and security.

In short, building your own software is generally a false economy, if indeed it ends up being an economy at all.

Of course, there is another approach. Why not benefit from the time and money others have invested in research, and build some software for yourself that closely copies what others have already done? Well, you could, but in my experience it generally ends up being a bad idea, and one that leads to the detriment of others and ultimately yourself.

I've seen exactly this take place before now, and hopefully the following case study will serve as warning to others. I've anonymised it, as what's done is done and cannot be undone, but it serves as a useful case study on the damage this can do to everyone involved.

Many years ago now, I was responsible for sales of a relatively simple piece of software, designed to engage, inform and consult participants on a particular subject. The idea was that by using the software, organisations could help their customers understand more about their work, as well as influence how it was carried out in the future.

It sold well, and each year, we used some of the profits from sales to invest in improving the software, adding new functionalities and improvements to make it more flexible and useful for organisations who used it. We gave repeat customers a discount too, so each year, if they chose to use it again, they would get more functionality whilst spending less money.

One particular public sector organisation often seemed interested in buying the software, although they never did. We thought that they came close to buying one year though, as they went through a phase of phoning us regularly to ask questions about how the software worked, which is generally what organisations often did when they were keen to buy.

We answered their questions accordingly, but had to say no when they eventually asked if we could send them the code for the software, or if by buying the software they would be entitled to receive a copy of the code. After all, if we gave away the code, there would be no reason for anyone else to buy it, meaning we couldn't keep supporting the clients who already used it, and would have no profits to reinvest in making the software better year on year.

Then, one day, we saw that this organisation had developed their own piece of software, which, apart from a few design differences, worked almost exactly the same way as ours. Even the name was similar. 'Ho hum' we thought, they had seen our system and decided to develop their own version in house. They'd not done a bad job of it, and if they were never going to buy our software anyway, then we'd not lost anything.

Moving on a few months though, we came to learn that the copying organisation had partnered with a national regulatory body, and were offering the copied software for free to any other organisation that wished to use it. Their marketing information around it even contained a term we had specifically trademarked for our software too. Now this left us really stuck. For whenever we tried to sell our software, organisations could rightly point out that there was a piece of software out there that did exactly the same thing, only for free.

We still sold some of our version of the software that year, but not as many as previous years, and so when the year came to an end, we looked at the figures and realised that there was no money spare to make more improvements to our version of the software.

As we were making these annual improvements to the software without adding to its purchase price, it meant that whilst some organisations had benefitted from getting what they previously couldn't afford for free, many more had lost out by not getting free improvements to the software they already had. As none of the users of the copied software were paying for it, there was no money coming in for developing that further either. In essence, all further development in this specific area of engagement software in the UK had been stopped for that year.

At the time of going to press, the latest seems to be that the copied software is indeed now dying, as there's no money coming in through the free model under which it was given away. No money coming in means no support or further development can be provided, and every 'sale' will just generate a further cash loss.

It is hardly a surprise that the free version is dying really, but all the more frustrating in a way. A free model can never be sustainable in the longer term, so all this one has done is set development of the area back a couple of years at a loss to all concerned.

So if you copy someone else's software, then whilst you may gain in the short term, the damage you do to the market in the long term is very real and very risky. It is only by making money that private companies will want to invest in developing software, and if a market is undermined by free versions, then private companies will look elsewhere for future tools to develop, leaving that market stagnant and stuck in the past[165].

12.5 What makes a good tender

As mentioned above, especially in the public sector, when buying software you have to go through a tendering process. This could be as simple as asking for a few different quotes before choosing the one that you like, or it could be as complex as going through a full legal tendering process, with the hundreds of pages of form filling that can often go with it.

---

[165] Before someone points out that this seems to conflict with my advocacy of open source software with no licence fees, I would point out that open source doesn't mean people don't get paid. You can happily charge for work you do in setting it up for someone then hosting and supporting it, or even developing it further. The highest value project I've run to date was in fact one to build open source software, which ran well into six figures.

I've seen hundreds of tenders for digital engagement software now, and whilst I've seen some good ones now and again, I've also seen some real shockers; tenders that will actually leave the purchaser in a worse situation than if they had never gone to tender in the first place.

The first fact to know about tendering is that it will cost you money. Often people are dimly aware of this, but sometimes they seem to be completely oblivious to it. However, I've not yet met any tenderer who fully understands how much tendering costs them.

This is because whilst tendering will cost you money in the form of the time taken to write the initial tender documents, and then to evaluate them before deciding, it will also cost you money as whoever you appoint will charge you for the time it takes them to fill the tender in too.

As far as I know, when I worked at Delib, I was the only person in the private sector who actively admitted this fact, but it's true of every single supplier out there. It's worth repeating once again, that in order to carry on trading, a business has to make sure that all of the work it does is paid for. If you make a business spend literally days filling out complex tender paperwork, they will have to find the money to pay for that time from somewhere, and the only place it can come from is their clients.

They may of course wrap the cost of tendering up in a licence fee, or in higher hosting and support costs, but they will charge you for it one way or another. Of course, not every company can win every tender process it goes through, so they will also have to charge you for the time spent filling in those other tenders that they didn't win, most likely ones you have not had anything to do with.

So, whilst you may be compelled by policy or law to go through a tendering process, it pays all round to keep that tendering process as simple as possible. The more time everyone has to spend on it on both sides, the more it is going to cost you.

There's another reason for keeping tenders simple however, in that the more prescriptive you are in your tender documents, the less the organisations responding to the tender can propose interesting and cost effective ways to meet the goals you ultimately have.

I'll go into this in some more detail in a moment, but first, let's look at a blog post I once wrote about the worst digital engagement tender I had ever seen, one which remains my benchmark for utter awfulness even after all this time.

> *"Whilst we've seen large tender documents before, we've just been sent the largest one we've ever seen - 9 different documents totaling 58 pages and featuring (on a quick count) 298 separate questions to answer. Not just 'yes/no' ones either, but things like writing bespoke architecture diagrams and a project plan. You know, the sort of thing that's best done once you've actually had a kick off meeting with a client.*
>
> *Some similar tenders have seemed silly before, but this one really makes the ridiculousness of this sort of approach become all too apparent. Here's why...*
>
> *1. The project had been designed by committee, clearly. In a 'functionality requirements' specification, running to 135 different requirements, every possible digital engagement tool under the sun had been thrown into the pot, some that even contradicted each other. There was no reference to how any of this will fit with internal process, what the actual user cases are for the functionality. Nothing, in essence, that is needed to have an online engagement project be successful. If the authority does end up with a system that complex, I'd be amazed if in practice even half of it got used in any meaningful way.*
>
> *2. In addition to functionality, it had many and various IT requirements. Fine, you need to check your system's going to meet legal accessibility requirements, and that the data it collects will be secure. Beyond that though, why would you need to ask if the system requires a web server? It's an e-consultation system. It would be very impressive to see it operate without one.*
>
> *The best bit was when it asked how the supplier would integrate with a sort of system that the authority may buy in the future, but they haven't chosen which one to buy yet, or even really investigated what's out there at all.*

> *3. The tender asked a good few questions about licensing and licences. How much is one licence, how much are additional licences, etc.? Standard for some suppliers, but an approach that implicitly rules out an open source approach, where the licence cost is, erm, free. Setting out questions like this implicitly excludes the authority from taking a cheaper licence free option.*
>
> *Similarly it was shot through with references to other proprietary software, including Microsoft. How do you answer these questions when you don't use proprietary software for your system?*
>
> *4. Here's the real kicker though. It would have taken us many, many person days to fill in all of the required information and send it back. But we sell open source software, which is designed to keep the cost as low as possible, largely charging just for the time of setting it up with minimal ongoing costs.*
>
> *So, when we looked at it, we worked out that, quite apart from the project looking like a confused jumble of ideas, we would actually have lost money on it whether we had won the tender or not. The cost of the time involved in completing the tender would have exceeded the cost of the software itself."*

It's the last point of this somewhat frustrated blog post that's the real killer. If we'd filled in that tender, because we would propose to supply open source software in response to it, we would actually have lost money. We would have been the cheapest of all of the options presented to the authority[166,] and we would have provided the same functionality as the other options, but because responding to the tender would have taken longer than the deployment of the software itself, the authority had, through poor tendering, excluded itself from buying the most cost-effective option.

---

[166] The tender was from a UK local authority, but I shan't say which.

With that painful absurdity out of the way, let's look then at what makes a good tender document or general procurement process for buying digital engagement software.

12.6 10 top tips for writing a good digital engagement tender

1. Set out who you are and the problem you have clearly

It should go without saying really, but for any tender, you need to let prospective tenderers know what your organisation does, where it's looking to go and how the tender fits into this. This has to be done clearly though. As a prospective tenderer, your eyes tend to glaze over if you are presented with page after page of jargon based information, doubtless fascinating to the original organisation but of little use to anybody else. Don't forget, if you make yourself look like a good organisation to work with, the tender responses you receive are more likely to be competitively priced, as people become keener to work with you.

2. Don't think you're doing anything new

Having said there can be a benefit in making yourself look like an enticing organisation to work with, you can easily go too far with this. If you write lots of flowery words about how you're a pioneering organisation looking to pilot a groundbreaking new approach, you'll just come across as a somewhat naive organisation who can probably have a few tricks pulled on them without noticing. There's nothing new in the field of digital engagement nowadays, it's all been done before somewhere, and suppliers are far more likely to be aware of this than you are.

In addition, don't try to negotiate discounts on the basis that working with you will bring more work for the supplier from other organisations. Whilst I've seen occasional enquiries come in out of the blue after referrals from existing clients, I've never seen them lead to a sale without having to put in just as much work as I would have done if I'd found the lead myself. No matter how great your reputation, no matter who you are, working with you will not make the supplier more money. Especially if you're proposing paying them less money than the work actually costs.

3. Write user stories, not lists of functionality

At the end of the day, what are you looking for in buying software; a bunch of functionalities on a screen, or a series of ways for real people to do real things? The correct answer should be the latter, so don't presume you know as much as a subject specialist in deciding which functionalities will meet your goals.

Sometimes people seem to think they're protecting themselves by writing a detailed list of things software must do, as they have a checklist to compare against the final outcomes. But if you try to play that slightly legalistic game, then you actually make it easier for people to use semantics to do things the way they want. 'The chosen solution must integrate with x' might sound water tight, but there are so many ways you can interpret the word 'integrate' that it's actually a pretty meaningless question.

Instead, give potential suppliers a list of goals you want people to be able to achieve by using the software, and let them explain how their software will meet these goals in return. You might end up receiving some ideas you'd not even thought of.

4. Give an indicative, not a fixed, timeframe

At the time of tendering, every supplier will have different amounts of work on and different amounts of work booked for the future. If you let them know the rough timeframe you're looking to have the work done by, they can pretty quickly decide whether they have the capacity to tender for the work or not.

Also, by keeping it indicative, you allow suppliers to point out if the timeframe you think is realistic or whether, in their experience, it's actually bonkers. Encouraging open and honest conversations like this from the start will help them to continue throughout the project.

If you allow people to warn you that your timeframe is not realistic, you also protect yourself against a supplier who may claim that they can meet your deadline when they cannot. As in reality, if someone says your timeframe cannot be met once the contract has been signed, there's often not a whole lot you can do about it.

5. Keep the legals simple and clear

Whilst the worst thing you can do is write a big list of functionality for people to respond to, there may be a few elements of the project which you have to specify for legal purposes. These can include things like accessibility requirements, who owns the software once it is built, assuring your ownership of all the data in the system and so on. Again though, make reference to external quality standards rather than trying to specify elements too tightly yourself. If you say the website must meet W3C accessibility requirements to AA standard, then you're covered. If you say the website must contain functionality to increase and decrease the font size, then you'll show yourself up as someone who doesn't know that all major web browsers now allow people to do that as standard.

Another point on this area is to be very careful about the expectations you have of responding companies. I know the UK Government is currently making this point as well, but if you require any responding organisation to present three year's worth of accounts and so forth, then you restrict yourself to only working with suppliers over three years old. In reality, this longevity doesn't necessarily make them any more or less likely to go under, and isn't really of much relevance to their quality of work or otherwise either. There are dreadful companies out there who have been trading for years, and some really good ones who are only just getting going.

6. Write it all in one editable document

There is nothing more difficult when responding to a tender than having to switch between different documents to make sure you've understood and covered each point required. All this additional work will be charged back to you by the winning bidder one way or another anyway, so save yourself money by collating all the information into one document.

Also, if you make the document editable, it means that those responding can easily cut and paste parts out of it for their own reference. If you put it in .pdf format, then you cannot copy and paste from the document, making the response far more difficult to write.

Incidentally, not everyone uses Microsoft Word, so try to send the tender document out in .rtf or .txt formats instead if you can[167].

7. Put one person in charge of writing the call for tenders/proposals, not a committee

It's surprising how often the need for clear leadership, so evident elsewhere, gets forgotten when putting together a tender document. You can usually spot these tenders a mile off, as they contain more text than they need to, and often contain a long list of different functionality requirements too, as if each person in a group had been asked to write a wish list. It will all end up getting reduced down to more simple terms by those responding anyway, so you can either do the work yourself, or have external organisations charge you their standard day rates for doing so. The former is definitely the cheaper option.

8. Allow responding organisations to write responses in their own format

It may seem tempting to set out a format for people to follow when they respond to your tender, as you might think you can then compare responses with each other more easily. However, if you constrain how people respond, you constrain the information they can provide you with, meaning you may not end up making your decision based on all of the facts.

For example, I often used to see tenders where a format was given for how costs should be displayed. This format invariably contained a line for giving the annual licence fee, but as I was selling open source software, there was no licence fee. So whilst there was a cost I needed to charge for the software, there was sometimes nowhere to write it. This didn't make the software free, it just made the tender process more annoying for all concerned.

---

[167] If you've used Microsoft Word to write the tender originally, click 'save as' and then change the format to 'Text File' before saving.

Whilst a tender process necessarily has to follow some legal or quasi legal rules, a good tender process allows the best proposals to shine through their structure and appearance as well as their content. If you're going to work with a company, it's good to know that they can present information clearly and logically from the start, rather than find out later on that they cannot.

9. Let people know the outcome whether they were successful or not

This may sound obvious, but you'd be amazed the amount of times I've seen it not happen. Perhaps it's the exhaustion from evaluating a range of tender responses, perhaps it's just an oversight, but I've frequently had to chase organisations to find out whether I won a tender or not. Once, I only got to find out I'd lost when I saw that organisation's logo appear as a client on a competitor's website.

It's just common courtesy to let everyone who took the trouble to respond to you know whether they were successful. Even if it's relatively brief, giving them feedback on where they fell short if they weren't successful makes you a lovely person too.

10. Turn your tender a living document from then on

So often, I've seen tenders list a huge range of points the successful bidder must meet, only to never hear half of them mentioned again once the tender is won. Indeed, it may sound cynical, but you can sometimes see points in tenders and think 'I'll say yes to that regardless, because I can just tell they're never going to check up on it'.

If you've written your original tender well, you should be able to use the user stories within it as a checklist for progress reports as you go along, as well as for the final project sign off agreement. As both sides will have had input into them by that point, they provide an excellent common point of communication between buyer and supplier.

12.7 How to buy support for your software

Once you've chosen a piece of software to use for a digital engagement activity, you will generally need to buy support for it. The word 'support' here can cover many different things, but generally includes things like;

- Answering questions about the software as you encounter problems, and receiving prompt answers.

- Making amendments to the software as you find you need them.

- Making security updates to the software as soon as problems are discovered.

- Fixing the software when it breaks.

It is this last point that, to be honest, I always found to be the most frustrating when dealing with clients.

From our perspective, software sometimes just breaks as people use it, and so the client needs to put budget aside to pay for the work needed to fix it. However, from the client's point of view, software should carry on working just as it did when it was first delivered, and if it breaks, well, then that's our fault and we should pay to fix it.

I can see the client's point of view here in a way. After all, if you don't really know how software works, and most clients didn't, then as long as you don't do anything stupid to it, it shouldn't break and that's that. Sadly, software just doesn't work like that. Anything that can go wrong with it generally will, whether it's a bug that's missed when the software is being developed[168], the disc on which the software is running wearing out, or any manner of other problems. Going back to the rule we looked at earlier in this chapter, if there's work to be done on software, then someone is going to have to pay for it to be done.

---

[168] Do you ever get that message appearing out of the blue, asking you to update software installed on your computer? That's generally bugs getting fixed that were missed the first, second or hundredth time around.

All software suppliers will look to have the cost of supporting and maintaining their software covered, so all it comes down to in the end is how they end up getting that money out of you. At Delib, we used to charge for it at our standard day rates. So, when a client bought a piece of software, they would generally buy a couple of days of our time at the same time, to be used over the coming year to fix any problems that arose.

This is where we used to run into problems, as, in the competitive market of digital engagement, other suppliers would offer to provide the same support for free. However, when you looked at what the other suppliers were charging, it became pretty clear that the same support costs were just being wrapped up in the cost of the licence fee, often charged annually. The client ends up paying the same money, but because they've been told the support is free, the option where you have to pay for support somehow appears more expensive.

Incidentally, it really is not possible to roll support costs over from one year to the next, or whatever time period you choose to operate the support agreement under. Even if no support time is used, having people on standby during working hours in case support is needed still costs money. If you roll two days support time over for three years, then the company has to pay for someone to be available for 6 days over those three years, whilst only getting paid for two of them. It just doesn't work, and will lead to your supplier going out of business, potentially leaving you without any support whatsoever.

So, the best way to see support and maintenance costs for software is as a kind of insurance. If nothing goes wrong, then all well and good, but if it does, then things are in place to make them right once more.

Incidentally, one final note on support. Feel free to decide how much support you may or may not require, and make sure you're getting the best value for money from what you buy, but do not try to dictate to your supplier what model they should use for their support.

The model they are offering will be one they have worked out in the wider context of their overall business, and if you make them change it, they will incur more cost, which they will then have to pass back on to you. I once saw a tender which said it was mandatory that the supplier provided free support. Unless the organisation then chose a supplier who did work on a 'free' support model, they had just caused any other supplier to rework their business model, adding more cost to the final bill.

12.8 How to work with your supplier

If you've decided to buy some software, and have settled on precisely which software it is you want to buy, then it would be a mistake to think that the process ends there. Of course, with some software and some suppliers, making the final payment pretty much marks the end of the contact you will have with them. However, with most digital engagement suppliers currently out there, you will want to maintain some sort of ongoing relationship, even if it's just for some support from time to time.

What the supplier gets out of this ongoing relationship is of course more money. But it is really foolish to focus on this fact and allow it to colour the communications you have with them. For if approached in the right way, developing a good relationship with your supplier can lead to benefits for both sides, rather than being a one sided money drain from organisation to supplier. I've worked with hundreds of different clients now, so here are some tips on how to build a good relationship with the software suppliers you use.

Don't treat them like salesmen

Whatever field the supplier is working in, it is likely that they have chosen to work in it because they have an interest in it. Of course they want to continue to sell things and make money, who doesn't, but part of the reason they want to do this is so they can carry on working in that field and not have to look elsewhere.

If you treat your supplier as if all they are interested in is money, not only do you make them more likely to act in that way, you risk missing out on the other benefits the supplier may be able to give you for free. To take an extreme example, I once did a really fun little project with a UK local authority around online discussion. It went well, but was seen as a pilot of such work for the authority, and as such the website was only sufficiently funded to be live for a few months.

Sadly, just before the project ended, both of the individuals working on it on the client side left the organisation for jobs elsewhere, without finding anyone willing to continue the work on their side either. However, we still had their site live on the web, and at a dedicated URL as well. So, when the project came to an end, I phoned the organisation to ask what they would like to do with the site, as it was still getting lots of traffic but the content was looking increasingly out of date.

Every time I called them though, I managed to get about 15 seconds of conversation before the person on the other end hung up. Indeed, I was once told in no uncertain terms that they weren't interested in buying anything and to go away. When I tried emailing, the emails went unanswered. In essence, the organisational culture was paranoid of being sold to by the private sector, and the people there wanted nothing to do with what they saw as IT consultants charging them money.

This would have been fine if I had been trying to sell them something, but I wasn't! I was merely trying to find out what they wanted to do with their website now the initial project had come to an end, and see if anyone wanted to update the content on it. In essence, I was trying to prevent the site causing damage to their organisational reputation by looking out of date and neglected.

Eventually I had to give up trying to help them, and after what seemed like a respectable amount of time, we downloaded all the data from the site, sent it one last time to the person who was supposed to be our contact, and took the site off line.

Be honest about your budget

One of the most frustrating things about being a supplier is knowing how much money you may or may not have to work with. Now before you think 'Of course it is, you want to know how much you can earn out of us!', I can promise you this isn't the case.

For every problem online, there is always a range of solutions, from the quick and cheap to the complex and expensive. In addition, there are sometimes problems that just don't cost much to solve and never should, but there are also ones which will always cost lots of money no matter how you try to approach it.

So as a supplier, you can offer clients a range of solutions, but that generally just confuses them, and it's all a lot more simple if you know which option a client can actually afford. The problem is, clients never want to tell you how much they're willing to spend.

I've always found this odd in a way. After all, in many other areas of life it would be a pretty strange situation. Imagine walking into a shop and saying you wanted to buy a suit, but refusing to say how much you had to spend on it. You probably wouldn't get very far.

Knowing a client's rough budget before writing a proposal for them means you can write a proposal that's both feasible within their budget and makes best use of every penny to boot. Sure, you might not want to specify the exact budget at an early stage, indeed you may not know it, but letting people know whether you have £50 or £50,000 will make a huge difference to the quality of the proposals you will receive in return.

If you're worried about suppliers charging you more than they would have done if they didn't know the budget, then include a short question in your call for proposals/tenders, asking the potential supplier to comment on the budget for the project. If they can't justify their costs in a convincing manner, perhaps they are trying to rip you off. If they can though, then you'll have given the project a great grounding on which to base future discussions on cost, especially if the project is a long one.

Incidentally, one final point on the issue of budgets. Always make sure there is 10% contingency included in it, unless it really is just a simple purchase of pre built software. You will end up using some of this contingency, and it removes a huge amount of stress from the client/supplier relationship if both sides know they can be open and honest about slight rises in cost as soon as they are uncovered. Otherwise the supplier can feel like they have to hide any problems that come up, and shift the cost of fixing them onto the client's support agreement once the project has been delivered.

Remember, it's not in any company's interests to be seen as the most expensive in the market[169,] and competition, when working correctly, should help keep prices from becoming extortionate.

---

[169] Admittedly, some companies might think it is, but generally they only sell to clients who are naive enough to confuse price with quality, and thankfully there aren't too many of those about.

Chapter 13. Appendices

Well, with the book at an end, I can only thank you for reading, and, like at any good party, give you something to take home. Not cake and a balloon sadly, but some appendices, containing things like template forms for you to use alongside various parts of this book.

There's a few reasons for including these appendices, which I hope will give you a flavour of their different purposes.

- First of all, I'm forever searching for generic copies of documents like these when I'm working on different projects, so it's handy for me to have them all in one place at last. I hope you'll find the same too.

- I'm giving away some content here, an example of a thing that makes people like you online (they're also online for anyone to use at www.gezsmith.com/resources you see). In a shameless piece of passive aggressive marketing, I hope you like me a little bit more for giving you these for free.

- I hope these appendices will start being linked to and turning up in web searches for certain areas. The more people that find them, the more people may learn, and by teaching others how to do things, I make the industry easier for us all to work in, myself included.

- However, I'm not giving away everything I know here, just common examples, keeping my most advanced work available only to paying customers.

- This means I can do more research into topics like these.

- Then share the findings freely again, allowing everyone to be able to benefit.

Appendix 1: Example Information Architecture Diagrams

Writing an Information Architecture (IA) document for a website or online engagement project can help you to understand all of the components your site will require, and allow you to communicate this to others for their input.

Below are two information architecture diagrams for generic websites, one designed to provide information, another to facilitate discussion and consultation.

Generic Information Website IA

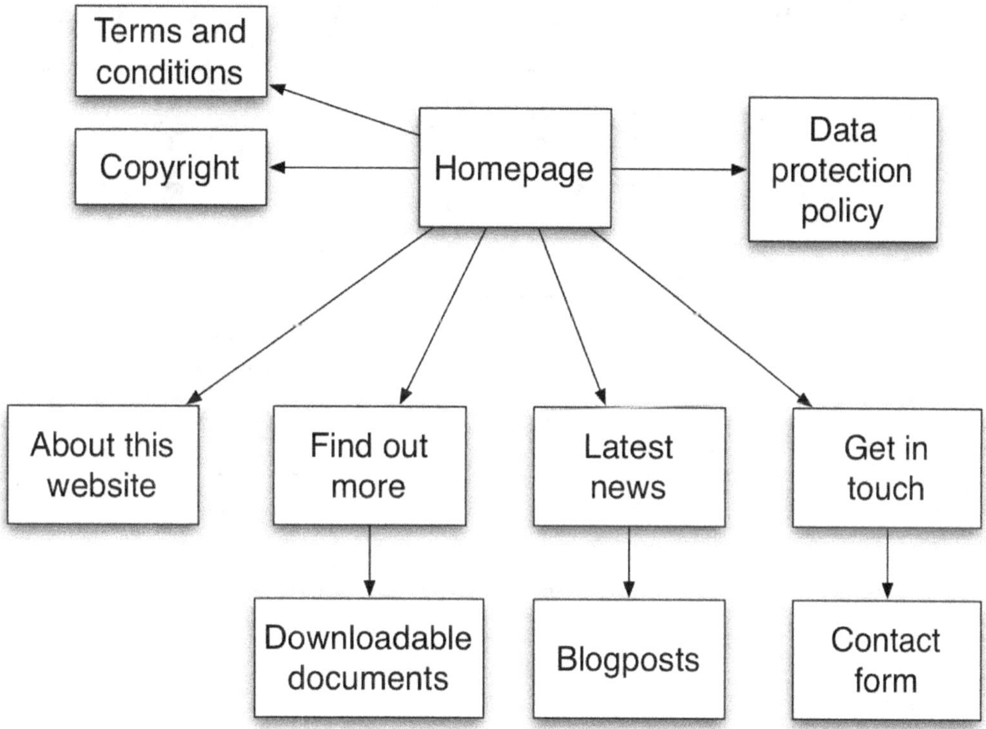

Discussion And Consultation Website IA

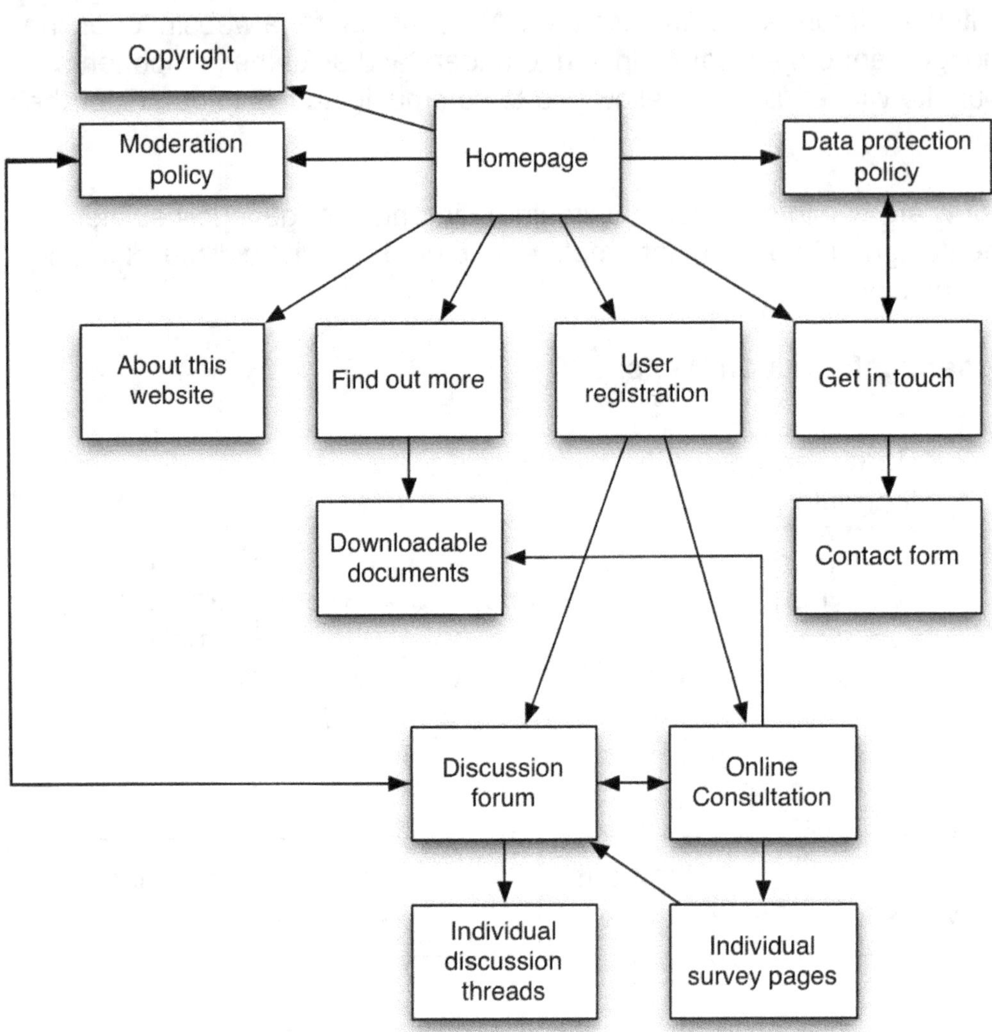

Appendix 2: Example User Stories

As a............member of the public
I want to.....be able to find contact information
So I can.....ask a question about the website

As a...........member of staff
I want to....be able to read the latest news
So I can.....keep up to date with my organisation's activities

As a...........stakeholder organisation
I want to....be able to register my details
So I can.....be notified when consultation is published

As a..

I want to...

So I can..

———————

As a..

I want to...

So I can..

———————

As a..

I want to...

So I can..

———————

Appendix 3: Example User Journeys

User journeys can be an excellent way of planning out the steps your typical site users will have to take in order to achieve the tasks on your website that you want them to.

Below are two example user journeys for a website, the one on the left mapping out the steps a user might need to take to get in touch with you through your website, and the one on the right covering the steps a user might need to take to take part in a consultation on your site.

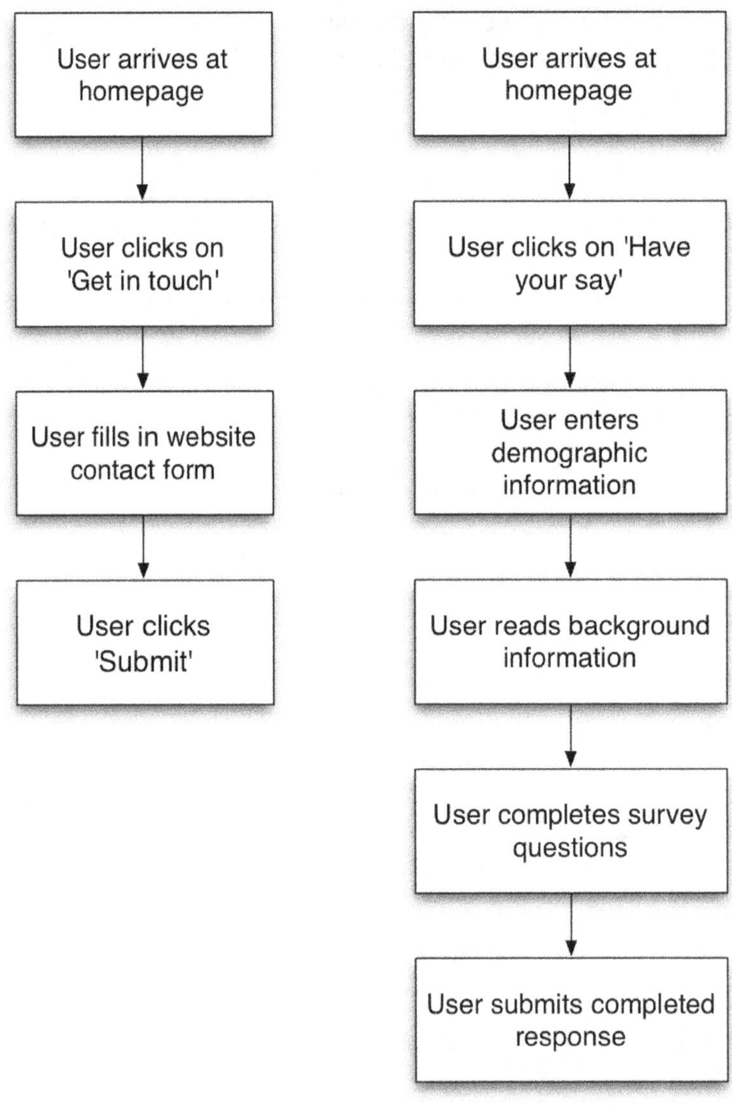

Appendix 4: Generic Moderation Policy

On this website you can post comments which will remain publicly viewable by others using the site. These comments are governed by a moderation policy, to ensure they remain within the law and appropriate to this site. As a result, all comments posted to this site may be moderated by <ORGANISATION NAME> in order to ensure these rules are followed.

As a rule, we want to encourage you to discuss and comment freely using this site, however any content submitted by site users may be edited, moved, merged or deleted at any time entirely at the discretion of the moderators. Content likely to have this happen to it includes;

- Personal or confidential information relating to yourself or others, especially information which is personally identifying such as name, address, etc.

- Threats or incitement to violence.

- Duplicate or similar content to that already existing on the site.

- Spam or content advertising commercial products, services or events without permission.

- Obscene content such as pornography, gore or content otherwise likely to alarm or offend.

- Any other content liable to violate the law, such as libel or copyright infringement.

In addition to moderating content, moderators reserve the unrestricted right to temporarily or permanently ban any user from using the site, including banning by IP address or range. Such bans will normally only ever take place for severe or repeated breaches of this moderation policy.

This moderation policy may be subject to alteration at any time by the website owners, who will make reasonable efforts to ensure that all site users are aware of these changes as soon as they occur.

If you have any queries, comments or concerns about this policy, how it is being implemented or content which may be in breach of it, please contact us at <CONTACT DETAILS>.

Appendix 5: Open Data Recording And Check List Form

Filename	Contents	Confidential?	Publish?	Location

Appendix 6: Template Email Sign Up Forms For Public Events

Name	Email address

By adding your details to this list, you confirm that you are happy for .... to hold and process this data in accordance with their data handling policy, available on request, and to use it to contact you in the future.

You are free to stop receiving information from us at any point by contacting our nominated data handler.

Data handler name...

Email address...

Name	Email address	Age	Postcode

By adding your details to this list, you confirm that you are happy for
.... to hold and process this data in accordance with
their data handling policy, available on request, and to use it to contact
you in the future.

You are free to stop receiving information from us at any point by
contacting our nominated data handler.

Data handler name..

Email address..